Changing Gears

A Family Odyssey
to the End of the World

Nancy Sathre-Vogel

Published in the United States by: Old Stone Publishing

ISBN 978-0-9837187-3-4

Cover and book design by Mark D'Antoni, eBook Designworks

To all the people who made our journey magical.
I thank you, from the bottom of my heart.

-NSV

Other titles by Nancy Sathre-Vogel

Bicycle Touring with Children:
A Guide to Getting Started

What Were We Thinking?
Bicycling the Back Roads of Asia

Twenty Miles Per Cookie:
9000 Miles of Kid-Powered Adventures

Table of Contents

Prudhoe Bay
Fairbanks
Whitehorse
Dawson Creek
Missoula
Green River
Moab
Albuquerque
El Paso
Del Rio
McAllen/Reynosa
Poza Rica
Veracruz
Chetumal
Villahermosa
Spanish Lookout
Tegucigalpa
Managua
Panama City
Jaco
Cartagena
Manizales
Pimampiro
Baños
Piura
Trujillo
Lima
Puno
La Paz
Santa Cruz
Cafayate
Mendoza
San Martin de los Andes
El Bolson
Rio Gallegos
Ushuaia

When Bears Don't Read the Guide Books

"Go, Davy, go!" I screamed in terror. "He's chasing you! Pedal fast!"

Only moments ago, the 400 pound black bear had been standing a mere four feet from my side. Now I stood, rooted in place, and watched it chase my ten-year-old son down the road.

"Go, baby!" I shouted. "Pedal!"

Davy pumped with all he had, knowing full well his very life depended on it.

It had been a long day on the road in northern British Columbia. After cycling sixty miles, we were tired and looking for a suitable spot for our tent. My husband and other son, on a tandem bike, were a mile or two ahead of Davy and me as we pedaled wearily on our heavily-laden bikes.

"Look!" I cried. "A bear! Up ahead! See him grazing in the ditch?"

"Wow!" Davy murmured in wonder. "He's huge."

Bears, in general, are afraid of humans and do their best to stay away. As we traveled through the Yukon and British Columbia we had grown accustomed to seeing bears grazing quietly in the ditch on the side of the road.

Motorists frequently left the safety of their vehicles to get better photos of the bears. I often marveled at how close people got to the animals, and yet the bears seemed uninterested in them. Motorists, however, had the safety of their vehicles to retreat to. As bicyclists, we had no cover at all. I vowed to stay well away from any wild animal I encountered.

Davy and I pulled to the opposite side of the road and stopped a respectable distance away — I had a good telephoto lens and had no need to get close. I had just pulled the camera out of my handlebar bag when the bear came up to the road and lumbered toward us. We froze.

"Holy Mother of God!" I exclaimed quietly. "He's coming this way. Bears aren't supposed to come toward people." Davy and I stood quietly, not quite sure what our reaction should be to the fact that a massive bear was drawing near.

A few minutes later, the bear turned and headed back down into the ditch thirty feet away, apparently unconcerned with our presence. Our hearts resumed beating and we began breathing once again. I stashed my camera and we readied ourselves to take off.

Suddenly, out of the blue, the bear leapt onto the road right beside us. My heart skipped a beat or two as I struggled to maintain my composure.

"It's okay, Mr. Bear," I said calmly and quietly as the massive beast plodded to within four feet of my side. "We're just leaving. It's okay."

I gazed into his cold, black, glassy eyes. Blades of grass stuck out on either side of his grizzled face. I panicked as my mind replayed all I had read. "Stay calm and talk quietly to the bear as you slowly back away," the books had said. The problem was that I was straddled on my bike and couldn't back away.

The bear ambled toward the trailer I hauled behind my bicycle, where I carried all our food, and sniffed. I had no way of knowing how hungry he might be. He came back to stand by my side.

Mr. Bear and I stood staring at each other for nearly a full minute while my mind played through every book and pamphlet I had ever read about what to do during a close encounter with a bear.

The first thing they all mentioned was to remain calm, which was much easier said than done.

The second recommendation was to talk to the bear. That I could do. "It's okay, Mr. Bear," I said. "We're just leaving. We mean you no harm — no harm at all. We're just passing through and are more than happy to give your territory back…"

Thirdly, they said to back away slowly. Never run as that will provoke a chase; never turn your back as that will provoke an attack. The trouble was that I couldn't back away. If I backed up, I would jackknife my trailer. If I moved forward, I would put my back to the bear. I couldn't go sideways because… well, bikes don't go sideways.

I was stuck. With each passing second, I became more and more certain I would soon meet my maker. It wouldn't be long before the bits of grass hanging from the bear's mouth would be replaced with bits of Nancy.

I was doomed, but Davy was far enough away to have a chance. He stood, twenty feet away, straddling his bike and looking back at me.

"Davy," I said quietly. "Ride away slowly, honey. Just start pedaling very slowly and ride away. Please, sweetie."

Davy stood his ground, unwilling to leave me.

"Honey, go!" I pleaded. "Please!" It was bad enough that he was about to lose his mother. He didn't need to watch me being mauled as well.

My son hesitantly turned around, put his feet on his pedals, and began pedaling slowly. The bear followed.

"Go, Davy, go!" I shouted. "Fast!"

Davy quickly gained speed as he pedaled furiously.

For a split second, I pondered my options. On the one hand, I was relieved; I no longer had a bear standing by my side. On the other hand, that very same bear was now chasing my ten-year-old son down the road.

With every motherly instinct within me, I jumped onto my pedals and shifted into my highest gear and my adrenaline-fueled legs quickly brought my bike up to heretofore unknown speeds. I blasted past the bear and caught up to Davy.

"Keep going!" I urged as the bear chased us. "Pedal, sweetie! Keep going!"

I can't say how fast we traveled, but I do know that bears can run up to thirty-five miles per hour. Our legs pumped, our hearts pounded, and our breath came in raw, jagged gasps. We watched in our rear-view mirrors as the bear fell farther and farther behind.

"Mom, I think we're safe now," Davy said when it had become obvious the bear would not be able to catch us.

"Not yet, sweetie," I panted. "Not yet. Keep going."

The bear was a tiny black speck in the distance before I could bring myself to hit my brakes. Davy and I ground to a stop in the middle of the Alaska Highway and reached out to cling to one another.

As we trembled and shook, and our heart rates slowly returned to normal, the only thing I could think of to say was, "We did it, baby. We did it."

Chapter 1

Crazy is Not Necessarily a Bad Thing

"You're crazy," one of my high school students told me one day shortly before we set off. "I call you my crazy teacher."

"Why's that?" I asked.

"Because nobody actually does what you're doing!" she replied. "I mean — people talk about riding a bike around the world, but nobody actually does it!"

I supposed she was right — we weren't exactly choosing a well-worn path through life. Most people chose to live in a house with a yard and a bunch of cars in the driveway, but we decided to go our own way. We sold or stored nearly every physical possession we owned and reduced our belongings down to what would fit on three bicycles. Three bicycles' worth of stuff for the next three years. I wondered if maybe we were crazy after all.

But as I stood there on the shores of the Arctic Ocean and looked ahead at the road that would take us southward, I couldn't help but feel *they* were the crazy ones. The journey ahead could only be magical — how could it not be when the four of us were together exploring our planet? Yes, we would struggle over passes and collapse into bed at the end of many long days on the road, but we would be *living*. Truly living. Was that really crazy?

Yet I still had to consider the fact that my husband, John, and I were about to attempt a feat that had never been done — bike the Alaskan Dalton Highway with ten-year-old twins. Originally built in the 1970s as a supply road for the oil fields on the shores of the Arctic Ocean, the Dalton Highway had long been known as one of the most challenging bicycle routes in the nation due to its rough conditions and sheer remoteness. It would be many miles of nothing more than dirt track meandering through pristine Alaskan territory. Maybe there was a reason it had never been tackled with kids. Maybe we should get back on the plane and leave it that way.

My mind went back to that look in my sons' faces — that look of sheer determination and excitement when they talked about the journey. They were determined — resolute in their desire to cycle from Prudhoe Bay, Alaska, to Ushuaia, Argentina. I owed it to them to at least allow them to try. If we failed, we would fail trying.

My mind wandered to the day our journey began two years earlier. That beautiful spring day, John slumped into our house after a particularly rough day in the classroom and collapsed into his favorite chair by the window.

"Nancy," he said, "I don't want this anymore. I can't do it. I need to get away. Let's quit our jobs and take off on bikes."

My response was your stereotypical mom response. "Are you crazy? Have you lost your bloody mind? We are parents, dear husband! We have children! Parents — with children — don't just quit their jobs and take off on bikes."

We were living the American Dream. We had a big house in the suburbs and two cars in the driveway. We had stable teaching jobs and paychecks coming in every month. And he wanted to throw it all away for *bicycles*?

As time marched on, John kept talking about that dream of his and I realized I needed to take him seriously. An amazing thing happened: I started to think that maybe, just maybe, I was the crazy one, not John.

I woke up early and dropped the kids off at before-school daycare before spending all day with other people's kids. After school I picked up my sons, fixed a quick dinner, took them to soccer practice, washed the dishes, threw the clothes in the washing machine, and collapsed into bed exhausted. I never questioned that because… well, I was a parent, and that was what parents did. And I thought *he* was the crazy one?

Two months later, once school was out for the year, we hit the road. John and the boys rode a bicycle built for three; I was on a single bike. Everything we needed — tent, sleeping bags, stove and cooking pot, clothes, and homeschooling supplies were lashed, strapped, or buckled to the bikes. We spent the next twelve months cycling around the USA and Mexico, and our sons spent their third grade year in the school of life.

While cycling the Pacific Coast, we had met other cyclists on their way to Argentina. "Let's go, Nancy!" John begged. "Let's just keep pedaling south!"

As tempting as it was at the time, we simply weren't prepared for a journey of that magnitude. We had abandoned our house — we could do that for a year but not for three. We hadn't organized our finances. And our triple bike was an awesome machine for North America, but it wasn't the bike for the Andes. We continued on with our North American tour and set our sights on the Pan American Highway in the future.

Now we were there.

That year on the road had been twelve months of magic. As a family, all four of us learned more than we previously thought humanly possible. By the time we headed back home we had pedaled 9300 miles and knew we wanted more. Much more.

As a family we made the decision to cycle from Alaska to Argentina during the boys' fifth, sixth, and seventh grade years, and set about preparing for a much longer tour than any of us had ever attempted. It would be more than twice as long as the thirteen months John and I spent cycling in Asia before we were married. We knew it would be three years through extreme conditions, but the background preparation threatened to overtake us and derail the project before we even got on the road.

John and I became single-mindedly focused on making the Pan American journey happen, and spent every day working out tiny details. Our to-do list grew longer by the day — could we pull this off in a year? Remodel the house for renters, dismantle the boys' treehouse, create a website and look for sponsors, and research how to manage and access our money from remote corners of the world. Figure out how to ship the bikes and gear to the northern end of the world. Get everything we owned sorted into three piles — "sell," "store," or "take with."

It was a whirlwind of activity, but each piece of the puzzle was critical. We couldn't — simply couldn't — take our boys up to Alaska and not be prepared. No detail was too small; nothing could be overlooked. Every piece of gear we would carry was essential.

One evening we took a break. All four of us sat in the living room just to be together. The chaos of the preceding months had taken a toll on us all and we needed to stop — even if only for a few hours. "You guys will probably be the youngest people ever to cycle all the way from Alaska to Argentina," I mentioned. "You're pretty special!"

"Maybe we'll get in the Guinness Book of World Records!" Daryl said hopefully as he held up the record book he had been reading.

"I'm sure you could," John confirmed.

"What do you think?" I asked. "Do you want me to contact Guinness and see what would need to be done?"

Grins broke out simultaneously on both boys' faces. "Yeah!" they cried.

12

A few weeks later we had our answer: the record started in Prudhoe Bay on the Arctic Ocean rather than Fairbanks, where we had intended to begin our journey. If our sons wanted to break the record, they would have to cycle the Dalton Highway. Davy and Daryl would be the first children to attempt it — if they did. I wasn't convinced it was worth it. We held another family meeting.

"Here's the deal, guys," I explained. "The record starts way up north in Prudhoe Bay. We're planning to start in Fairbanks five hundred miles south of there. If you really, really want to go for the record, we'll go to Prudhoe Bay, but you need to understand how hard it is."

"Five hundred miles? We can do that, Mom," Davy interrupted.

"You need to know that it's 350 miles of dirt road, and when it rains the road turns to soup. It'll be much, much tougher than anything else you've ever done. And you need to know we most likely won't make it through — lots of cyclists way stronger than us have been beaten by the Dalton."

"Let's do it!" they both agreed. "We can make it!"

That night as I lay in bed trying to sleep, my mind went wild. All along I had figured the trip wouldn't be all that arduous — we could simply hitch through the difficult parts. But now, if the boys were to make a serious attempt at the world record, that would not be an option. No matter how hard, no matter what kind of obstacles lay in our way, we would be committed to pedal over them.

I wasn't worried about John — he was as strong as a bear. I didn't worry about the kids — they had an unending supply of energy and could do whatever they put their minds to.

But me? I didn't trust my own abilities. Could I really cycle all the way from the Arctic Ocean to Tierra del Fuego? Did I *want* to? I had always been the weak link in our family. I was the one who tended to give up when things got tough. Rather than having legs of rock-solid muscle like John and the boys, my legs resembled jelly. The extra forty pounds I was carrying around wouldn't help matters either.

I played back our conversation of earlier that day in my mind. I saw the fierce determination in my sons' faces; I heard the excitement in their voices. How could I take that dream away from them? I was Mom — I was supposed to be the one who encouraged and supported her children as they reached for their dreams. And here I was considering taking the dream away before it even started. Could I do that to them?

"What would you do if you were not afraid?" I asked myself as I lay in bed that night. "If you weren't afraid of what people would say about you, or of the unknown, or of failure, what would you do?"

If I answered myself honestly, I had to say I would ride my bike from

Alaska to Argentina.

The trouble was that I *was* afraid. Very afraid. Terrified, in fact. I was terrified of the 15,000-foot passes. I was afraid of battling headwinds for thousands of miles along the Peruvian coast. I was afraid the cold would be too cold and the hot would be too hot.

In short, I was afraid of failure. I didn't want to face the agony of defeat or the humiliation of having to say I had failed in what I set out to accomplish.

It was about four in the morning when that EUREKA moment happened. At that moment I realized that we had a 50/50 chance of failure. The way I figured it, a 50% chance of failure also meant a 50% chance of success.

If we never set out in the first place, we were looking at a 100% chance of failing.

By morning I had made my decision — I would do it. The four of us would pedal every mile between Prudhoe Bay and Ushuaia together. I had no idea if it was physically possible for me, but I was determined I would give it everything I had. If we failed, we would fail trying.

A few months later our lives had been reduced to eight boxes consisting of three bikes, two trailers, and three bins filled with everything we would need for the next three years. We were excited. We were determined. We were unstoppable — until we got to the airport.

"You want to take all this with you?" the agent said as her eyes widened in surprise. "All of it?"

"Yep," John replied. "We do."

"We're going to break the world record," Davy explained. "All this stuff is everything we'll need to ride our bikes from Alaska to Argentina."

The ticket agent began to calculate the excess baggage charges.

"I'm sorry," she said a few minutes later. "You will be flying three different airlines, so I have to charge you for each of them. The total comes to $1800."

Eighteen hundred dollars?

"We can't do it, Nancy," John said. "There's no way. We can't afford $1800. Let's just start from here. Let's throw away the plane tickets and ride south from Boise."

"Please," Daryl pleaded. "Please Daddy, let's go to Alaska." Tears slowly rolled down his cheeks.

"I want to go to Alaska," Davy added. "Can't we? Please? Our goal is to ride from Alaska to Argentina — not Boise to Argentina."

John and I looked at each other and knew we couldn't kill their dreams before we even started. I pulled out the credit card.

We were on our way — on our way to the adventure of a lifetime.

Chapter Two

A Little Bike Ride Down the Dalton

Dalton Highway, Alaska

One year nearly to the day after our journey around the US and Mexico finished, I surveyed the enormous pile of gear strewn about our feet in the warehouse of the Arctic Caribou Inn in Prudhoe Bay. I wondered, once again, if we had planned well enough. Adequate rain gear? Check. Appropriate warm clothing? Check. Tent, sleeping bags, and stove? Check, check, check. Sufficient food? Maybe check. We had planned the best we could. Now, only time would tell if we had done it well enough.

"For the record," an oil worker said as he picked his way through our piles, "I drive this road on a regular basis, and I think you're nuts."

"I think you may be right," I retorted as I glanced out the window at the road we were about to tackle.

The four of us had arrived in Prudhoe Bay the day before. Now, the boys were out throwing rocks at icebergs floating in the nearby lake while John and I attempted to sort our massive piles of gear.

In the next few hours we piled our gear and more than fifty pounds of food on our bikes. We were about to pedal from the northernmost terminus of the Pan-American Highway on the shores of the Arctic Ocean to Fairbanks, five hundred miles away. And beyond that? We would keep our bike tires pointed south until we could go no farther at the southern tip

of South America. At least that was the plan.

Even after so many months of planning, preparing, stewing, fretting, and organizing, I wondered if we would actually make it. *Could* we actually make it? The odds were against us. How many ten-year-old kids had ever cycled the Dalton? None. The Alaska Highway? None. The Pan American? None. We were drawing blanks as far as examples to lean on. We would have to be our own example.

At long last, all three bikes were put together, racks and panniers (saddle bags for a bicycle) mounted, trailers attached, and gear stashed. John and Daryl had the tent, sleeping bags, and tools packed on their bicycle built for two. Davy had pillows and sleeping mats on his tiny single bike. I carried food for the four of us on mine. The time had come.

"You'd better take off now," the manager of our hotel urged. "Take advantage of this weather; there's no way it'll hold up here."

"You ready, kids? Ready to start riding the longest road in the world?"

"You bet!" Davy exclaimed.

"Sure!" Daryl added. "Let's go!"

The sun shone brightly and a clear blue sky stretched forever. The temperatures hovered around the 60's. In short, it was perfect; we couldn't ask for better. John and Daryl hopped aboard their tandem bike, Davy and I straddled our singles, and we were off — off to the other end of the world!

Spirits were high as we pulled out of the parking lot and headed toward the Dalton Highway. We were doing it! Finally! Daryl was thrilled to be on the bike with Daddy. Davy was filled with pride at being entrusted with his own bike, but that all came crashing down the moment he hit the gravel. Davy's bike, unwieldy and unfamiliar with panniers and dry bags lashed on, had slipped out from under him the minute he hit the loose gravel of the Dalton. I jumped off my bike and scurried over to help him.

"It just... just... went!" Davy exclaimed on the verge of tears. "It's like it's not even my bike. It just feels too weird and I can't control it."

And we still had 17,000 miles to go.

In time, Davy got used to the feel of his loaded bike, and we continued cautiously on our way. We reached the gate to the oil fields — as far north as we were allowed to go. We snapped a photo to document the moment for Guinness World Records and asked the guard to sign our witness book before pushing on.

A mile later we passed a road sign informing us we had 240 miles to go before we would reach Coldfoot, which was nothing more than a gas station and restaurant on the side of the road, and 494 miles to Fairbanks. Many miles of nothing. No grocery store. No convenience store. No houses. Just mile after mile of caribou, musk ox, bears, and moose. Mile

On the North Slope of Alaska, our first day on the road. The sign wasn't kidding - until Coldfoot there wasn't even a house, never mind a store or restaurant. It was the most remote stretch of our entire trip.

after mile of rough arctic grasses swaying in the wind.

In the land of the midnight sun, we pedaled until we tired. The sun was still high in the sky when we pitched our tent on the side of the road — the sun wouldn't set for another month or so. We were well north of the Arctic Circle, that imaginary line around the globe marking the place where the sun would at least dip beneath the horizon every single day of the year. Here, three hundred miles north of that line, there was no difference between 2:00 in the afternoon and 2:00 in the morning.

Using water from a nearby stream, we cooked pasta over our tiny camp stove, and then filtered water to fill our bottles. We were totally self-sufficient out there. We *had* to be self-sufficient. There was absolutely no one to rely on but ourselves.

While I cooked and John filtered water, our sons pulled out their tiny stash of toys — a handful of plastic Star War figures — from Davy's handlebar bag, and sat next to the stream playing. Those few toys were their only connection to the life we had just abandoned.

As I lay in the tent that was just barely big enough for the four of us, snuggled into my sleeping bag under the bright light of the sun, I thought about our journey. Daryl rolled over and slung his arm over my chest and I gazed into his sleeping face. My baby — but he wasn't much of a baby anymore. Were we really doing the best thing for the boys? Would they be better off in a classroom in their local school? Was a journey to the ends of the earth a better education? Yes, this life was different from the life of their peers, but was it better? Worse?

17

Over the next two years, those doubts plagued me repeatedly as we slowly made our way southward. In time I came to the conclusion that our sons' lives were different from the norm — not better or worse. But at the time, so new to the road and in one of the most remote areas on our planet, I wasn't quite there yet. I spent the night wondering what might happen. All the good, and all the bad. So much could happen, but all unknown.

We allowed our own natural body rhythms to wake us in the morning. With twenty-four hours of daylight, we could ride when we wanted and sleep when we wanted. John and I arose early and set upon cooking a big pot of porridge for breakfast, then dragged the kids out of the tent. We stuffed sleeping bags into stuff sacks, rolled up the tent, cleaned and packed the stove, washed the dishes, and headed out once again.

It was another bright, glorious day, and we needed to take advantage of the good weather. We had been warned time and time again that weather in the arctic was unpredictable and nasty. We weren't looking forward to rain and headwinds, but for now we flew along the flat tundra with a strong wind pushing us forward. Davy was in his element, thrilled with the independence his own bike afforded. We rode side by side along the rough gravel road chatting about the caribou grazing beside us or the lack of trees in the tundra or the tiny wildflowers dotting the ground. I could hear Daryl and John chatting up ahead.

"Davy, look!" I shouted as I pointed ahead of us. "One of Santa's reindeer!"

Just ahead a caribou leapt nimbly onto the road and stopped to stare at us. His enormous antlers jutted out on either side of his face like branches on a tree. A few seconds later, he was off, loping through the marshy swamplands the tundra had become in the quick spring thaw.

"Wow!" Davy murmured in awe. "Did you see that Mom? Did you see how he just stood there watching us? He was beautiful."

"This is where Santa keeps his reindeer when they're not pulling his sleigh," I told him. "Santa himself lives farther south — down in North Pole."

"Aw, Mom! These aren't reindeer — they're caribou!"

It took a bit of convincing for him to believe they were both.

A while later we reached a pull-off and climbed off our bikes for a break. As the entire area was a swampy mess, finding solid ground other than the road was a challenge. In the winter months, the tundra was frozen solid, but now, in the spring thaw, the top layer had melted and grasses were growing rapidly in the mud due to the extended daylight hours.

I pulled out a baggie full of snacks — granola bars, trail mix, gummies, dried fruit, and other assorted goodies. Four hands vied for space inside the bag as each of us searched for our favorite, and then we sat back and munched. A few seconds later, another hand was in the bag. Then another. And another.

"Did you know those chunks of grass out in the swamp are called tussocks?" I asked as we munched on our snacks. "They start out with one little grass seed taking hold and sprouting in the swampy water. The next spring, the old blades of grass die and new ones grow — but the old blades don't decompose like they normally would. Any idea why?"

"It's too cold?" Daryl mumbled as he chewed gummies.

"Kinda. In the winter, it's too cold for the organisms that would normally eat the leaves and break them down. And in the summer, there just isn't enough time for them to do it. So the old leaves never decay and new leaves grow every summer. In time, they build up into these tussocks you see."

"They're hard to walk on," Davy told me. "When we were playing tag, they kept wobbling around and I almost fell off."

When I finally dragged myself off the ground and went to stash the remaining snacks in my pannier, I panicked. The baggie was nearly empty. A few granola bars lay in the bottom of the bag, but that was it. I had diligently packed one baggie per day for the fifteen days I figured it would take us to reach Fairbanks. One baggie with what I thought at the time was plenty of snacks to get us through the day. And now, today's baggie was nearly empty and we had only barely begun.

I started to think about the food I had packed. More than fifty pounds of food was stashed in my trailer, but I knew now that it wouldn't be enough. I had carefully planned snacks and meals for four hungry cyclists for fifteen days but, if the boys continued as they were eating now, it wouldn't be anywhere near sufficient. All four of us, unaccustomed to the demands of the bike, were eating way more than I had budgeted. Davy, a growing boy powering his own bike, had so far eaten nearly three times as much as I had calculated. If this pace kept up, we would run out of food with many miles still to go. And there was no way to resupply.

As I pedaled, I considered our food. We had been fortunate to run into a couple of motorcyclists in Prudhoe Bay. "We packed a whole bunch of freeze dried meals before we left home," they said, "but we haven't used hardly any of it. Can we leave it in Coldfoot for you?" At the time, I didn't think we would need it, but I told them we would appreciate their help. Now, I hoped they really had left it — it was apparent that what I had packed was nowhere near sufficient.

The Brooks Range. We were headed up to our first pass at 4,643 feet.

Twice that day we stopped at a stream to filter water and cook. Pasta and porridge filled us up for a few hours before we dove into our rapidly dwindling supply of snacks. How much food can four people eat? I started contemplating how I could stretch our food supply to make it last.

Davy thrilled at the independence of his own bike and quickly outpaced John and me. He raced ahead, then sat patiently for us to catch up. "This is great!" he told us as we took a break at the top of a hill. "I love having my own bike!"

"It's better on the tandem," Daryl challenged. "I get to talk with Daddy all the time!"

"Maybe we should load Davy down?" John mumbled as he lay exhausted on the ground. "That would slow him down."

John and I had made the decision to put Davy on a nearly empty bike. He had four panniers and a big waterproof dry bag lashed on his rear rack, but there was very little weight in those bags. He carried our light, bulky pillows and sleeping mats. We would load him down later, but for now he had a free ride.

When we got tired and were ready to call it a day, we found a dry spot for our tent and got organized for the night. The sun was shining brightly and warmed the tent while the four of us played cards and wrote in our journals inside.

Each of the three days we had been on the road, we had asked Daryl to ride Davy's bike for a few miles. Every time, he claimed he hated it, he secretly enjoyed it - a bit anyway.

"Tomorrow I'm going to ride Davy's bike for one hour," Daryl wrote. "I know I said I hated it but it's actually pretty easy to ride that thing once you get used to it. All you have to carry is three mats and some clothes.

"It's not without disadvantages though — I have to be much more wary. On the tandem, all I'm wary of is the Alaskan pipeline, caribou, and that river we might have lunch at. I'll have to be wary of cars and deep gravel. I hope I don't fall down."

"Let me guess," we heard a voice from outside. "The homeschooling family on their way to South America, right?"

John and I scrambled out of the tent. We were in the middle of absolutely nowhere but, with no trees to hide our tent, we were very visible from the road. Even so, we knew nobody on the north slope — or so we thought.

"Hi! I'm Tom," the man said as he extended his hand. "We exchanged emails a couple months ago."

One of the many things we had had to do to prepare for our journey was figure out how to transport three bikes, two trailers, and a massive amount of gear up to the Arctic Ocean. Leaving our hometown of Boise, most planes were small commuter planes with no space for all our gear, let alone a tandem bike. In the end, we had flown south to Phoenix before turning north in order to be on large planes that could handle all our gear.

But before we decided to fly, I had researched every option I could think of. We toyed with strapping the bikes on top of our van and driving to Prudhoe Bay. A friend would drive the van back to Fairbanks and sell it. That option was problematic in that it wasted a full week, and we were pushing our narrow window of opportunity to get south by winter as it was.

Another option was to somehow ship the bikes and gear up to Prudhoe Bay, then we could fly empty-handed. But where to ship them? I contacted all the geocachers who had planted caches on the north slope to ask for help. Tom was one of them. "I work in Prudhoe Bay," he had told me. "I'll ask around." In the end, that option didn't pan out, but we planned to meet Tom when we arrived in Fairbanks.

And now — here he was, standing before us in blue jeans and green polo shirt with a massive smile gracing his face. "I saw those bikes and the tent and figured it couldn't be anybody else. We see a fair number of cyclists up here, but not with a tandem and a bunch of trailers. Is there anything I can do for you?"

Jackpot! An engineer from the Alaska pipeline left us a huge bag of goodies: raisins, granola bars, M&M's, trail mix, and more. We were fortunate to be the recipients of this gift as it had become painfully obvious that I hadn't packed enough food to get us to Fairbanks.

"Since you asked," John said, "we've realized we don't have nearly as many snacks as we're going to need. You don't happen to have any granola bars or anything, do you?"

"No, I don't have anything with me," Tom replied. Our hearts fell as we heard those words. "But I tell you what — I'll leave you a bag of food at the gate to the pipeline pump station tomorrow morning. I have a meeting in the morning, so I won't be able to meet you there, but look behind the gate and I'll leave some goodies."

We awoke to clear blue skies again — unheard-of in the tundra, or so we had been told. I thanked my lucky stars as I packed my bike — good weather four days in a row, and a bag of goodies awaiting us twelve miles away. We climbed aboard and set off down the rough dirt road.

"Jackpot!" Daryl exclaimed as his eyes widened to the size of the boulders we had just been bouncing over. He gazed upon the booty in wonder. "Wow!" The four of us pawed through the massive bag of snacks Tom had left us.

"I want Oreos!"

"Gimme trail mix!"

"I want the gummies!"

That's it for the day. Here, I'm getting ready to set up camp. Notice the Brooks Range in the background. In a few days we would cross them.

It was massive. Absolutely enormous. More snacks than I ever could have dreamed of. Tom had loaded us up with every kind of snack known to mankind. We ate three each, then I stashed the rest in my trailer. I knew we still had a long way to go.

Up ahead I could see the mountains looming before us. The Brooks Range was our first major obstacle, and one I feared more than ever. Weather in the far north was a major concern, and I had read more stories than I cared to recall about bad weather on the pass crossing the continental divide. Other cyclists had reported rain or hail or a full-on blizzard as they crossed at this time of year. We had packed the boys' winter jackets just in case, and were prepared with full rain gear. But still — if bad weather hit up there, we were in trouble.

Mile by mile, we drew closer to the mountains. The tundra was abuzz with activity in the short summer season. There was a very narrow window of time for plants and animals in the tundra to proliferate, and bees were busy pollinating the flowers that had sprung up in the tundra. Herds of caribou and musk ox grazed on grasses that had just transformed the tundra from a vast ice field to a giant lush green carpet. Many species of fish could be seen through the clear waters of the rivers and ponds we passed.

The boys were thrilled to be on the road again. They were in their element, outside where they belonged. They loved playing with sticks and stones, running through fields covered with wild flowers, and jumping from boulder to boulder. Even though our lives were anything but easy, the boys were thriving on the challenges and loving being in Mother Nature's handiwork.

DAY 5 Day five dawned with sunny skies and tailwinds — unheard-of luck. We thanked the man upstairs for holding off bad weather and headed into the narrow valley winding up to the pass. The road climbed gradually and we bounced over the rough rocky surface. Going was slow, but we managed to keep moving. The wind shifted into a headwind and we slowed even more. But still — it wasn't rain, so all was well. We would choose a headwind over cold rain any day.

We were nine miles from the top when we noticed dark clouds amassing over the mountains. Patches of sunshine broke through here and there, and we hoped it wouldn't be too bad on top. We would know soon enough.

Six miles later all hell broke loose. Rain poured from the skies and then wind drove hail into our faces like BBs. We scrambled to cram all our gear into plastic bags and get our raingear on. It was a mad frantic dash as the heavens unleashed their fury.

The fury was short-lived, however, and by the time we got ourselves and our gear protected, the rain had passed. We continued up. John, a much stronger cyclist than I, managed to pedal up the pass. Davy and I didn't. We pushed our heavy bikes up the climb, leaning into the handlebars in order to use our whole body to push. Step by painful step we crept up the mountainside past massive piles of snow left over from winter.

Minutes passed, then hours, and still we pushed. The top remained somewhere up there, unseen beyond the next switchback. Or the one after that. "Keep it up, Davy," I tried to encourage him. "You're doing great." He smiled back at me and kept plodding up the mountain.

"This is it!" John shouted down to us. "We're at the top!" Up ahead I could see John and Daryl silhouetted against a massive wall of snow.

"We made it, Mommy!" Daryl called. "We did it!"

The top! We had made it up our first pass! We were standing 4643 feet higher than where we started at the Arctic Ocean! We thanked the weather gods for holding off on the rain, even though it was cloudy and dreary, and headed down.

We awoke the following morning to the pitter-patter of rain on the tent. Steady drizzle. Black skies. Mucky roads. Stay? Or go? We had learned on our previous bike tour that we hated riding in the rain. A warm rain was tolerable, but a cold rain was downright miserable. Although we had rain gear, riding in rain was still awful. We could keep our legs and torso dry, but there is no good way to keep feet and hands dry and warm while cycling. And the mud — rain would turn the road into a deep, mucky mess that swallowed bike tires and refused to let them spin.

As much as we hated the idea of riding in the rain, we hated the idea of no food even more. We only had a certain amount of food and no way of getting more. If we hung out in the tent for the day — and ate food — there would be even less to get us to Fairbanks. And besides, what if it was raining really hard tomorrow? At least now it was just a drizzle. My boys stood before me like baby birds as I shoveled a few spoonfuls of peanut butter into their mouths, then we packed up our bikes, and took off.

Water dripped off my helmet onto my nose as I pedaled through the quickly worsening mess in the road. Rain had fallen steadily all day, and all four of us were tired and cranky. Bickering between us had risen to astronomical proportions as we fought hunger and cold. Our stove got wet and wouldn't light. Attempts to sit by a stream to pump water were futile in the mud and we ended up having to haul up pot after pot of water so John could filter on the side of the road. We were miserable.

Finally we called it a day. Slipping and sliding in the muck, we set up our tent on a grassy patch and quickly threw sleeping bags and pads inside. I managed to get the stove dried out and John held a tarp over me and the stove as I cooked Rice-a-Roni.

Rather than sitting in the mud, we stood in a huddle holding our steaming bowls of rice. We were wet and cold and muddy and hungry. Maybe, just maybe, the Dalton Highway would win the battle after all.

By the time we woke up the next morning, we had an entirely different problem. We lay in our tent snuggled up in our sleeping bags and stared at the mesh screen above us, listening to the ferocious buzzing surrounding the tent. Overnight, the mosquitoes had hatched and were desperate for food. We were prime sources.

Although we had heard stories of the mosquitoes in Alaska, we had yet to see even one. But that morning, hordes of the critters slathered our tent like peanut butter on bread. Humming, buzzing, swarming our tent waiting for the moment we emerged.

"Okay — here's the plan," John directed. "We'll get everything packed up as much as we can before we open the tent. All sleeping bags stuffed, all pillows packed. Everything waiting right by the door. As soon as I open that door, the mosquitoes will swarm in, so we need to move fast."

As mosquitoes feasted on every bit of exposed flesh, we dashed and scurried around the campsite packing up. John and the boys took down the tent while I prepared breakfast. We ate walking in circles to minimize the number of bites we ended up with. The good news was that it wasn't raining.

We had crossed the tree line while battling rain the day before, and now the road was nothing more than a narrow ribbon etched through thick, dense forest. Trees rely on photosynthesis to create their food, and photosynthesis requires energy from the sun. With so few days of sunlight up north, trees simply couldn't sustain themselves. Now, we had reached that magical line where there were enough days of sunlight for trees to grow.

The trees were small, but plentiful, and were more beautiful than I could have imagined after not having seen any for so many miles. If not for the mosquitoes, life would have been perfect. With chocolate, even more perfect.

"Hey guys! Want some Coke and chocolate?"

We looked up in surprise at the white van passing by, and at the smiling face hanging out of the driver's door. "We're on our way back into town tomorrow and have some extra food. You want it?" Who was this angel anyway?

We quickly made friends with Hugh, a tour guide in the area, and the people who were on his tour to the arctic tundra. They were all more than happy to part with a bit of their stash, and we were more than happy to take it. Hugh handed us a big bag of trail mix, a bunch of chocolate, and a package of peanut-butter-filled, chocolate-covered pretzels. Our eyes bugged out at the manna from heaven, and we thanked them all profusely. The four of us stood there on the side of the road with bags of chocolate and cans of Coke in our hands and thanked the gods for sending such a wonderful gift.

The next day life got even better: we reached Coldfoot. We piled off our bikes and headed into the restaurant. Inside! In a building! A real live building made of wood and metal with glass windows! It had been eight days since we left the shelter and protection of the Arctic Caribou Inn. Eight days of life in the outdoors. We were ready to be pampered with tables and chairs and a real toilet — for a little while anyway. We ordered a few enormous breakfasts and ate until we couldn't eat any more. I even convinced the cook to refill my empty peanut butter jar.

But even better than a meal at the restaurant was the enormous bag of freeze-dried meals the motorcyclists we had met in Prudhoe Bay had left for us. We pored over them, checking each one out. Macaroni and cheese… beef stroganoff… chicken fried rice… blueberry crumble… We were in heaven. We had food.

Our lives improved even more when we headed outside to pack away all the bags of freeze-dried food. Hugh and his tour group showed up again and handed over all their left-over food before they returned to Fairbanks; cheese and turkey and bread and tomatoes and potato chips and cookies. For John and me, he had beers; for the kids, Sprite and Coke. Food! Our chances of making it to Fairbanks just got a whole lot better.

Life became a perfectly choreographed dance as we learned to deal with the mosquitoes and rain. We figured out how to put up the tent and get organized in record time. Everyone had their job and executed it perfectly — our blood supply depended on it. All the while, mosquitoes ravaged any part of our bodies they could find exposed. The hordes saw us as an open all-you-can-eat buffet.

We had discovered the mosquitoes weren't quite as bad in the middle of bridges, so we took full advantage of that fact. When it was time to cook, we waited until we crossed over a major river with a nice, long bridge. I grabbed the stove and headed out to the very middle of the bridge before setting up the stove. We ate pacing back and forth across the bridge. Fortunately, there wasn't much traffic on the Dalton Highway.

But the worst part of the mosquitoes was what I dubbed Itchy Bum Syndrome or IBS. I discovered the mosquitoes couldn't bite through my rain gear, so I wore that most of the time and put DEET on my hands and face. But when nature called and I had to drop my drawers, it was sheer torture. After each time I headed behind a tree to do my business, I returned to my bike scratching my bum like a monkey scratches his armpits.

As we continued southward, we left behind the relatively flat northern areas and entered into hills. Monstrous hills. Steep, 15% grade, knee-busting, bike-walking hills. As we slowly crawled up the hills, mosquitoes attacked. We slopped bug juice on top of sun screen and sweat. We were a mess.

One day we came across a large, crystal clear river and looked forward to a nice bath — until we felt the icy water. Daryl and I braved the nearly-freezing temps and plunged in. John and Davy splashed a bit of water on their faces and called it good.

Days blended together, becoming a blurred tapestry of hills, mosquitoes, heat, freezing water, and hunger. The longer we were on the road, the more the boys were eating. Even with our gifts of food, I feared we would not have enough to get us to Fairbanks. I carefully rationed our snacks and doled out spoonfuls of peanut butter to the boys to keep their caloric intake up. Even so, food was rarely far from our minds.

John and I cut back on our intake in order to save food for the boys. Rather than eating one whole bag of freeze-dried food each, we shared one. We gave our snacks to the kids. We were perpetually hungry, but figured we had enough body fat to get us through. The boys didn't.

We celebrated when we reached the Arctic Circle — now the sun would set at last! Even though the sun barely dipped below the horizon, it was a sign that life would eventually return to normal and we would sleep in darkness again. What we didn't relish, however, were the hills the Arctic Circle brought.

For some reason, south of the Arctic Circle, the hills on the Dalton Highway become massive. Ozarks on steroids. Huge, steep climbs, followed by equally huge, steep descents. Up and down. Up and down. Many of the climbs we walked, pushing our heavy bikes. Others we ground up slowly, inch by painful inch. And all the while, mosquitoes swarmed around our heads.

And then came the flashing blue lights.

"May I see your ID please?" asked the security officer who had pulled up behind us. The blue lights pulsed ominously. "I hear you folks camped by the pipeline last night. Some workers called me this morning."

"We did," John responded. "It was a great spot — a bit buggy perhaps, but otherwise it was comfortable."

"You are aware it's illegal to camp in the pipeline corridor, aren't you?"

Oops.

For days we had been camping next to the oil pipeline. With the dense vegetation south of the treeline, the only two places we could find a spot big enough to set the tent up were in the middle of the road or next to the pipeline. At each access point to the pipeline, there was a sign indicating that non-motorized vehicles were allowed. We figured that included us, as we couldn't imagine they would consider Daryl's motor-mouth a vehicle. We explained that to the security officer.

"You've been camping back in the right-of-way for a week? Next to the pipeline?" he asked. The look on his face was one of sheer disbelief.

"We're not the only ones to camp by the pipeline," I explained. "I've been reading loads of journals by other cyclists; each and every one talks about camping by the pipeline. It's really the only place to put a tent around here."

"Well, I just want to let you know it's illegal to camp there and you'll probably get a citation if you do it again," the officer responded. "Folks around here take pipeline security very seriously — you would have the state police up here and that blue and white helicopter you see flying around would land right next to you. You don't want to go there."

We shook our heads and continued on.

"What's the big deal about the pipeline?" Daryl asked as we pedaled up the next hill.

"It's really an amazing thing," I responded, recognizing a teachable moment. "What do you know about the pipeline?"

"I know they built it to transport oil."

"But why? Why don't they just send the ships up to Prudhoe Bay to get the oil?"

"I dunno."

"The oil is up on the north slope," I explained. "But the ocean freezes up there in the winter, and ships have a really hard time floating on ice. That's why they built this pipeline — 800 miles down to Valdez. The water never freezes in Valdez so the ships can get in all year long."

"It's 800 miles?" John asked. "Is it really that long?"

"That's what I read before we left home. But they didn't build it that long — when they built it, it was a lot shorter. Any idea why it's longer now??

"They added more to the end?" Davy guessed

"Nope. The pipeline was cold when they built it, but oil is hot. What happens when something gets hot?"

"The molecules take up more space so it gets bigger!"

"Exactly. So when they built the pipeline, it was one length, but after they put the oil in it the pipeline expanded by four feet for each mile. Cool, eh? But the really amazing part is this — they built it with a bunch of corners so it could expand. Otherwise it would all get crammed together. Look — see there! It's straight for a mile or so, then they built a zigzag into it so it could expand. Another reason it zigzags is so it can move with earthquakes. Is that cool or what?"

"Yeah, whatever. That's really cool," the boys said with ten-year-old sarcasm.

We passed a little stream with clear water and climbed off our bikes to filter. John pulled the filter out and I pulled the pot out. The boys scampered around gathering all the water bottles from the bikes. Taking everything we needed, the four of us picked our way over and around boulders and trees to reach the riverbank below us.

I filled the pot with water and set it carefully by John's feet. He placed the intake tube of the filter in the pot and the outtake tube into a water bottle and pumped. He pumped. And pumped. But nothing happened. Nothing. No water went into the filter; no water came out. Nothing.

John took the filter apart to see what was happening. All looked well, but it didn't work. The boys and I stood over him, worried. Our filter was critical. It was one of many absolutely essential items we could not live without.

What now? We were still days away from Fairbanks. Drink water straight from the streams? How sick would we get? Was the trip over? Hitch a ride and head down to Fairbanks?

Unsure what our next steps would be, we headed back up to the road with the busted water filter. Just then a motorcyclist pulled up.

"Gads!" he exclaimed when he saw the boys out in the middle of nowhere traveling on bikes. "This is quite the story. What's up with you guys?"

"Our water filter just broke," John told him. "We have no idea what we're going to do."

"I have a filter. I've carried it all the way from California and never needed it once. I'll sell it to you if you want."

We happily forked over the money, said goodbye, and headed back down to the stream with filter in hand. We were grateful for the universe intervening just when we needed it.

Thirty minutes later another motorcyclist pulled up from the opposite direction and handed us some money. "This is from Jim — the other motorcyclist you talked with," he said. "He felt badly about charging you for the water filter and wanted to give this back to you."

Wow! Those Road Angels were everywhere.

We rode hard in order to find hamburgers. One of the few restaurants on the Dalton was a burger joint and we were on a mission to get there. I could see the big juicy burgers in my mind's eye. As I pedaled, I listened to the crackling sound of burgers cooking on the grill and smelled the hearty, meaty aroma....

Eleven days and 375 miles after we started our journey, our ragtag bunch of filthy cyclists poured into the hamburger joint and stuffed the best burgers in the world in our mouths, trying our darndest to overcome the caloric deficit we had endured for days. Wonderful, juicy burgers were just what we needed.

"This is even better than a visit to a candy shop!" John joked.

"Better than a candy shop *with* a lot of money!" Daryl added.

There were a lot of odd things about the Dalton, but one of them was that we traveled 240 miles to the first restaurant, another 135 to the second, and only four to the next. In order to take advantage of both restaurants, we ate dinner at the burger joint, then breakfast the following morning at the restaurant next to the Yukon River. For the first time in a week, we started the day with full and happy bellies.

We crossed the Yukon River and kept pedaling through the hills. From the top of one enormously overgrown hill we could see the entire gargantuan climb of the next. South of the Yukon, however, the hills were graded so we could ride rather than push our heavy bikes.

On day fourteen, we awoke with only twenty-four miles of the Dalton Highway left to pedal. Twenty-four miles. We had pedaled 390 and were so close. Nothing could stop us now!

DAY 14 It was almost as though the Dalton saved the best for last, and we struggled mightily those last few miles. Hills that never ended… very rough road surface… heat, humidity, mosquitoes…. But finally we came around a corner and could see a ribbon of pavement up ahead. The Elliot Highway! We had done it! We had conquered the Dalton. My legs were fried. They had been reduced to a trembling mass of quivering flesh, but nothing could hold me back. We had made it.

We climbed off our bikes and leaned them against a guardrail along the Elliot Highway — a ninety-mile stretch of paved road that would take us to Fairbanks. My food bags were nearly empty, but now I knew — I knew we could do it. I broke out my last bag of freeze dried banana cream pie for our celebration party and the four of us sent up a good long shout.

"WE DID IT! WE CONQUERED THE DALTON!"

Chapter 3

Buffalo and Bears and Big Horns, Oh My!

THE ALASKA HIGHWAY

"Hey Mom!" Davy asked as we pedaled out of Fairbanks. "How strong do you think I'll be when we reach South America?"

"I have a very distinct feeling this trailer I'm hauling will be on your bike by then," I replied. "And I'll *still* be struggling to keep up with you!"

We had loaded Davy's bike a bit heavier when we left Fairbanks in an attempt to equalize us. Davy had quickly proven his abilities on the bike and we no longer worried about him. He was strong, confident and capable and he handled his bike like a pro. Our only worries were of his ability to handle traffic, but that wouldn't be tested for another couple thousand miles until we reached the end of the Alaska Highway. He would break into it gradually.

We had spent a delightful week in Fairbanks with our friends, Larry, Lisa and their two daughters. The boys went kayaking, we visited Santa Claus at his home, and we ate. Lots. But the time came and we packed up and headed out.

Our confidence level had skyrocketed after successfully reaching the end of the Dalton, and we quickly settled into a comfortable pace. We woke up early, rode a few hours, found a nice spot to cook lunch, then rode some more. Distances on the Alaska Highway were long, but not nearly as long as the Dalton. For the next two thousand miles, we would be riding two to

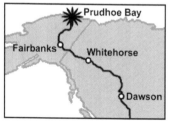

three hundred miles between towns and grocery stores. Fortunately, I now knew how much food we needed.

The Alaska Highway was hastily constructed in the 1940s after the attack on Pearl Harbor. At that time, the US government suddenly realized they had no way to reach Alaska other than plane or ship — and therefore no easy way to get troops up there to defend it in case of an attack. As they constructed the road, workers lived in camps spaced every couple hundred miles, and those camps have now turned into the only towns along the highway. Fortunately for us, the rough dirt track of the 1940s has now been paved and had, for the most part, a fairly decent cycling surface.

The mosquitoes had abated somewhat and were no longer our primary concern. Bears had taken over that role. We were cycling right through the very heart of bear country, and were conscious each and every day of the risks. We intensified our bear protection routine and hoped it was enough.

"Remember guys — no food near the tent at all!" I shouted when Davy wandered a bit too close to the tent with a granola bar in his hand.

"And don't wipe your hands on your clothes!" John added.

We went to extreme lengths to be sure we had no food smell on us or our tent. Each evening we stopped to cook dinner an hour or so before we planned to stop for the night. We cleaned our dishes very well in the abundant streams before strapping them back on my bike. We brushed our teeth for the night, then we set up our tent as far away from our cooking spot as possible.

I kept food, toothpaste, and shampoo on my bike. John and Davy had nothing that smelled on theirs. Once the tent was set up, we moved the bikes a couple hundred yards away and the food even farther. Each night we created a big triangle — cook in one spot, sleep in another, and store bikes and food somewhere else.

There were two basic types of bears we had to think about. Polar bears were common up on the northern slope of Alaska, but not during the summer so we hadn't worried about them much. Now, black bears were abundant but were typically quite docile and afraid of people. There were a few grizzlies, but they tended to hang out farther back in the woods away from the road.

Crack! I heard something outside the tent, mere inches from my head, rustling through the branches. My heart leapt into my throat and pounded like a hammer. My breath caught in my throat. What was it? A bear? Moose? Caribou?

As I lay in our tent with my darling boys on either side of me, I panicked. We had done everything we could have. We meticulously kept food smells away from the tent and had no food anywhere near where we lay. What was it? Why had it come here?

As I lay there contemplating the creature outside I wondered, yet again, if this journey was the right thing to do. What if? What if a bear came crashing through the tent a second from now? What if something bad happened?

I tried to tell myself that bad things could happen anywhere, not just on the Alaska Highway. I reminded myself that we had successfully pedaled 9300 miles through the US and Mexico when the boys were in third grade and nothing bad had happened — and within a few weeks of arriving back home to Boise I was hit by a car while cycling home from work and Daryl narrowly escaped two rattlesnakes two feet from his toes. And yet — there was something out there, and if we had been back in Boise, it wouldn't be.

"Nancy!" John whispered. "What's out there?"

"I don't know, but I'm scared spitless."

We lay quietly and listened to whatever it was lumber off into the woods.

"Should we pack up and get out of here? What if it comes back?"

"If it was a bear, do you think it would turn around and come back? Or just keep going?"

In the end, we opted to wait it out. The boys were sleeping soundly, and they needed the sleep. To wake them at two in the morning — even though it was plenty light enough to ride — seemed cruel. If there had been an immediate threat, it would have been different, but… John and I lay back down and tried to fall back asleep.

We slowly made headway as I tracked our progress on my map. Delta Junction passed beneath our wheels and we met up with the parents of a friend. We arrived into the town of Tok and spent the Fourth of July holiday with friends of a friend. We hung out in a convenience store for a day waiting out rain. We bounced and jiggled over road construction.

 Finally, we reached the Canadian border. Our first international crossing! We patiently waited in line behind the cars and pulled up to the window when our turn came. John handed over four passports.

"Do you have the boys' birth certificates?" the border official asked. "I need to prove you are their parents."

Huh? We had needed to show birth certificates in order to get the passports, but we didn't have them with us; we saw no need for them. Now what? We knew that border crossings were always a bit scary as we were totally at the whim of the official, but we never considered we might need the boys' birth certificates.

"Are these your parents?" the official finally asked Daryl.

"Yeah," he mumbled.

"And is he your brother?"

"Yeah," Daryl mumbled again.

She looked at John and me. "I'm going to let you through — I can't imagine anybody kidnapping a couple of kids and then taking off on bikes — but you really need their birth certificates to prove you are their parents."

We promised we would get the certificates just as quickly as we could, thanked her profusely, and pedaled our way into Canada.

Each time we passed through a tiny town, we stocked up on food for a week or more, knowing the next store would be hundreds of miles away. Fortunately, there were plenty of streams from which to filter water. The road was little more than a narrow path cut through dense forests and we saw more moose than people.

The kids enjoyed the freedom of the wilderness and were creative in finding games to play. One day, a pinecone war might break out and the boys busily collected pinecones during every break to throw at each other while riding. Or maybe it was a berry war, with bright red berries flying back and forth. Traffic was light and we had no worries as we cycled.

One day, John swatted a deer fly and managed to injure it. The boys picked it up and set it smack dab in the middle of an ant pile.

"Look!" Davy screamed. "The ants are attacking!"

Ants swarmed over the fly, yanking and pulling it toward their hole. The fly battled valiantly.

"They're getting it! Look at that one — he's got the wing in his mouth!" Davy said, as ten-year-olds tend to do.

"Watch the fly — see how he's fighting? I feel badly for him," Daryl added.

In the end, the fly lost the battle and the ants pulled it down into their hole. It was time for us to move on.

As we approached the Kluane region in the Yukon, I was overwhelmed by the beauty of it all. A narrow valley surrounded by some of the highest peaks in Canada. We looked out on a great big turquoise blue lake, surrounded by dense green vegetation.

The Alaska Highway in the Yukon. The stretches between towns were between two and five days - a long way but nothing compared to the Dalton.

I rode along the shores of Kluane Lake, gazing thousands of feet up at the 'hills' surrounding the valley. Their tops extended to the heavens, and yet I knew I was looking at only the foothills — the real mountains were hidden behind them. I totally understood why poets struggled to capture the grandeur and magnificence of the Yukon. There truly was no place on earth like it.

I couldn't help but feel I was the luckiest woman on earth as I cycled beneath the towering peaks. I was out exploring our planet with the three most wonderful people I knew. I had a spouse who shared my passion for biking, and two boys who were the happiest, most creative kids I'd ever seen. As I pedaled beneath the massive mountains on either side of the valley, I was overwhelmed on so many levels — life just couldn't get any better!

As beautiful as it was, we were pushing ourselves hard and getting more tired by the day. We had good reasons for that. The primary reason was that we had to get to Mexico by the time winter hit. We still had a good four thousand miles to go and winter would come early way up north. We wanted to be in Mexico by Christmas.

The other reason for pushing hard was the fact that we could only carry so much food. Distances between grocery stores dictated how much food we needed to carry while in the wilderness and big daily miles meant fewer days between towns and, therefore, less weight to carry.

Even though all four of us knew the reason for pushing hard, we were still tired. Each morning we dragged ourselves out of our tent and onto the bikes. We dreamed of Whitehorse and a couple of rest days.

As we pulled into Whitehorse sixteen days and six hundred miles from Fairbanks, we were dumbstruck. There were people — 20,000 of them. There were houses — more than twenty of them. There were stores — real live grocery stores rather than the Ma & Pa shops we'd grown accustomed to. And there was traffic — as in, cars and trucks and buses. White-knuckling our way through the city, we felt as though we were aliens that had suddenly been dropped onto a foreign planet. We had only been on the road thirty-seven days, but had adapted so efficiently to life on the road that the city was overwhelming.

We checked into a hotel, hauled all our bikes, trailers, and pannier bags up to the room, took showers, and collapsed into bed in front of the TV screen. I made a quick trip to the grocery store, but otherwise we didn't leave the confines of that hotel for three days. Running water, a toilet, a shower, soft beds…. We could have stayed indefinitely.

Our rest in Whitehorse was delightful, but we knew that every day we rested was one day closer to winter. As much as we would have liked to hang out longer, we packed up our bikes and hit the road.

 "Move 'em out!" John bellowed that afternoon after taking a break to filter water in a small stream. Everyone scurried about getting helmets on and ready to go. Everyone except Daryl, that is.

Daryl's helmet had vanished. Disappeared. *poof* All four of us searched for the wayward, bright red helmet, but it had truly vaporized.

"Did you take your helmet off back there where we met those other cyclists?" I asked eventually. "Could it be back there?"

Even though Daryl was certain he had arrived at the stream with his helmet, it was worth a shot. I ditched my trailer and pannier bags by the side of the road and pedaled five miles back to the spot John and I had stood chatting with other cyclists while the boys played. There was nothing.

During the five miles back to where John and the boys had set up camp, I formulated a plan. "Daryl!" I shouted as I screeched to a halt at our new campsite by the stream. "Get ready! We're leaving now!" To John I added, "If we leave now we should be able to hitch a ride back to Whitehorse before the stores close. I just hope like crazy WalMart has helmets."

The kids and I raced to the road to flag down a car for the forty-mile journey back to where we had just come from. The journey to town was nerve-wracking. What would we do if they didn't have helmets? The next town with any chance of a store big enough to carry them was a thousand miles away. Let Daryl ride without one? Give him mine? Take a bus to town, then bus back?

As it happened, WalMart was open and they had helmets. I gratefully pulled out my wallet and thanked the good Lord above that this happened a mere forty miles from a city. As we hitched back out to where John had camp set up for us, Daryl clutched his new helmet and we all wondered just what had happened to his old one.

The trouble with our forty-mile day, however, was that we weren't as close to Muckluk Annie's as we had wanted to be. Cyclists we had met on the road had told us about the small campground and restaurant where they served the best all-you-can-eat pancake breakfast for miles around. It was, in fact, the only *anything* around for miles.

All day we pedaled hard against a headwind in a cold, drizzly rain. "Remember the Muckluk!" became our mantra as we kept our noses down and pounded the pedals, determined to reach the campground. It was amazing what the thought of pancakes could do to the energy level of a couple of young boys on bikes.

That night I placed large steaming bowls of spaghetti in front of my sons. "I don't want to eat much," Daryl quipped, "I want to be really hungry tomorrow morning!"

The following morning we noticed the flags flapping in the wind as we made our way over to the restaurant. Flapping, that is, in the wrong direction. And it was raining. I've never seen two boys put away more pancakes than mine did that morning while we watched the flags and contemplated our options.

Should we go? Should we stay? As much as we wanted to get some miles in, it wasn't worth fighting a headwind that strong. We had learned to pick our battles carefully and fighting a headwind was one battle we nearly always lost. We might make a bit of forward progress, but it wore us out so completely we lost time in subsequent days.

By noon the wind had shifted into mostly a crosswind and we decided to head out. It was tough, slow going, but we made some sort of progress. A few miles from the restaurant, I noticed a long bridge stretching over the lake ahead of us. We had learned to be wary of bridges, as conditions were frequently very different on them than on land. I grabbed my handlebars a little tighter and braced myself for whatever Mother Nature would throw my way.

"Holy crap!" I heard John shouting ahead of me. I peeled my eyes away from the steel grid surface of the bridge just in time to see him careen wildly to the opposite side of the road. A second later, the wind picked up Davy and his bike and deposited them next to John.

I, being third in the line, learned from the other two and hit my brakes to stop before the wall of wind hit me. Even so, I was unprepared for the sheer force of it, and my bike toppled to the ground at my feet.

Daryl had jumped off the tandem and scrambled back to the side of the bridge, John and Davy were both smack-dab in the middle, and I stood at the side of the bridge with my bike on the ground.

"We can't do it!" John shouted to be heard over the howling wind. "The wind's too strong — there's no way we can ride across!" John and Davy both hightailed it as fast as they could back to the side of the bridge, man-handling their bikes against the onslaught. I picked up my bike and braced myself against the force.

Together, we walked our bikes across Teslin Lake, leaning into the wind and watching the waves dance below us through the steel grid surface of the bridge.

Shortly after crossing the bridge, however, came the most bizarre wind patterns I'd ever seen. The wind shifted again — this time into a tailwind — but we periodically got blasts from all directions. Every once in a while a massive gust from the side nearly knocked us over, or we ran into a wall of a headwind and nearly screeched to a complete halt.

With fickle wind like that, we couldn't relax at all — not even for a second. It seemed like every time I relaxed my grip, another blast hit me and I nearly toppled over. We plodded on to get our miles in for the day, then wearily set up camp late in the evening. The four of us snuggled up in our sleeping bags and fell asleep in the broad daylight.

A few hours later I woke up in the middle of the night and realized it was dark. Not completely dark — it was that almost-dark stage when you need a light to read by but you can still navigate without one. And then I thought, "This feels strange. I haven't seen dark since we left Boise."

Darkness was a strange thing. It was something I had always taken for granted, just like the fact that the sun would come up in the morning. But after being so far north for so long where there was no way to escape daylight, the darkness came as a surprise. I knew it wouldn't be long before our long summer days would be a thing of the past.

The following day we were screaming along the highway thanks to the most awesome tailwind imaginable when we saw four bright red Coke cans lined up on the side of the road. The strange thing about the cans was that only one had succumbed to the howling gale; the other three remained upright like wee little soldiers standing at attention.

"They're not open!" John shouted as he slammed on his brakes. Davy and I, cycling behind him, slammed ours on as well.

Daryl scrambled off the tandem and ran back to collect the booty.

"They're cold!" he screamed in delight.

"I wonder how they got here — it's pretty strange to find four cans of ice-cold Coke out here in the middle of nowhere."

"A note!" John pointed. "There's a note! Daryl — pick it up!"

We all crowded around to read:

> *Enjoy the ride!*
> *-Vic*

We hadn't the foggiest idea who Vic was, but those cold Cokes were one step short of heaven there on the side of the road. We never knew when Road Angels would enter our lives, and we were so very grateful for Vic and his ice-cold Cokes.

There was something magical about the Alaska Highway; the sheer remoteness of it all was beyond comprehension. In some ways, we loved that. We loved the fact that we were out there in the great outdoors with just us and Mother Nature; we were simply part of the food chain. In other ways, it was getting old.

In each town we passed, I scoured the shelves of the grocery store to find enough food to get us to the next town. When we set off from a town, my bike was loaded down with fifty pounds or more of food. My panniers and trailer were stuffed to the gills and I occasionally tied a few bags and boxes of snacks to the tandem and Davy's bike.

By the time we pulled into the next town, it was all gone. I was a master of planning food by now and knew exactly how much to pack. I could estimate with surprising accuracy how many days it would take to reach the next spot of civilization and always packed one extra day's worth of food just in case.

But still, I was dreaming of the day when we reached civilization and would pass through towns every day. What a luxury that would be! I couldn't even imagine what it would be like to buy food for only one day at a time.

In Watson Lake I meandered through the aisles of the supermarket

Liard Hot Springs was one of our favorite spots of the entire trip. For John and me, it was a chance to soak weeks' worth of grime from our bodies. For the kids it offered a new and unique playground.

stocking up for the 330 miles to Fort Nelson. When we left town, I carried food for four cyclists for eight days. My panniers and trailer were stuffed with pasta, rice, sausage, cheese, and granola bars.

And then we met Mr. Bear. Even though the food was stashed in waterproof bags, there was a distinct possibility that the bear could smell it. How hungry was he?

After being chased down the road by the bear, we redoubled our bear protection strategies and picked up a can of bear spray.

Still, the boys were unfazed. Nothing seemed to bother them. They even ate horseflies.

Davy wrote in his journal, "I ate a horsefly. It didn't taste. Mom said that she would give me ten cents not to eat it, but just watching her reaction was worth it. She looked away and shouted, '*Eeewwwwww!*' She was shivering all over. That was priceless." The joys of parenting never ceased.

We had been on the road for seven weeks and were excited to be approaching Liard Hot Springs. Many travelers had told us about the hot springs, so we planned a day to relax in the hot waters. It was just as lovely as they had said it would be.

As we soaked in the relaxing hot water, a family invited us to their RV

Homeschooling at its best.

for dinner that night. The boys spent the evening watching movies with their son, Michael, while John and I were entertained for hours by Terry's stories. Kelly had whipped up some of the best food we had eaten since Fairbanks.

But perhaps the best part of hanging out with Kelly and Terry all evening was the rain — it poured buckets and buckets — while we kicked back in lawn chairs under their awning. We started to think maybe there was something to be said for those RVs after all.

Around midnight we waddled back to our tent in near darkness.

"Who left the tent fly open?" I called as soon as I arrived.

"Not me!" Davy answered.

"Not me!" Daryl echoed.

"I didn't," John added. "Someone must have broken in."

Once we looked inside, however, it was clear that no one had broken in — nothing was taken, but LOTS of stuff was wet.

I don't mean just a few little drops of water. Our mats were floating in a huge puddle of water, one pillow was completely drenched, another one quite wet, and half of two sleeping bags were wet. It was quite a disaster. As near as we could figure, John left the fly open when he went back to our site to get jackets.

We mopped up the mess the best we could, and then piled in. Our tent

Shortly after taking this picture, a bear popped up out of the bushes.

was just barely large enough for the four of us anyway, and with one-quarter of it rendered useless, tight was an understatement.

The kids and I crammed into one half of the tent using two sleeping bags, while John curled up in the remaining part using the dry parts of the two wet bags.

It was a good lesson to always close the fly, even if we didn't think it was going to rain.

It was hard to pull ourselves away from Liard Hot Springs a day later after drying our sleeping bags in the intense Canadian sun, but we knew we had to. We rolled up the tent, lashed everything onto our bikes and headed out.

Within a few miles, we came upon a huge herd of buffalo grazing on the side of the road. We hit our brakes and ground to a halt.

The massive creatures grazed peacefully next to the highway and the four of us stood rooted in place completely awestruck. The narrow strip of cleared trees next to the Alaska Highway was only forty feet deep and it was filled with dozens of buffalo. We climbed off our bikes to sit on the side of the road and watch.

In time, we pulled ourselves away and continued pedaling. A mile farther, we were treated to yet another herd of buffalo. Again, we climbed off our bikes and hung out for a while watching the magnificent animals.

The road called, so we climbed back into the saddle and started pumping. That didn't last long.

A few miles later, we came upon a small group of bighorn sheep. Once again, we climbed off our bikes and sat on the side of the road watching the graceful animals.

We were wondering if we had entered into some kind of wildlife preserve. Every couple of miles we came upon yet another group of animals — moose, caribou, bison, or bighorn sheep. Each time we stopped for more photos and videos.

Around midday, we came upon an interesting road sign: **Buffalo on Road.** We all climbed off our bikes and leaned them against the sign. The boys scrambled on top of the sign, while John and I stood with our bikes on the ground. We set the self-timer on our camera and piddled around for a good forty-five minutes at the sign.

As we pulled away, we happened to glance over to the other side of the road — at the bear grazing in the ditch.

We thanked our lucky stars that he hadn't decided to cross the road, and kept on pedaling. I wondered how we would deal with "normal" cycling after passing through the Serengeti of the north. Day after day we shared the road with deer, caribou, moose and bears as we slowly made our way toward civilization.

We had been lucky for weeks. All the other cyclists we had met talked of daily rain and their spirits were low. There wasn't much worse for a cyclist's morale than day after day of pouring rain. Somehow, we hadn't gotten it.

The skies had been overcast for weeks, but the worst we had gotten was a light sprinkle while we cycled. One evening we had stumbled upon a small gas station with a campground in the middle of nowhere, so we set up camp there. The following morning it was pouring rain so we opted not to go anywhere. It was like the good Lord above had placed the campground there just for us.

We could frequently see rain ahead and prepared for the worst, but by the time we arrived the rain had stopped. Storms gathered off to the sides, but miraculously went around our path. "It's a good thing the road went the way it did," Daryl wrote in his journal. "If it had gone to the right, we would have been soaked. As were going down off the pass, Daddy said, 'Get ready to be cold, wet, and miserable.' I was a little wet, a little cold, and not miserable at all."

Just before arriving in Fort Nelson, our luck ended. We climbed to the top of a pass under cloudy skies and hoped our luck would hold. It didn't. A steady, cold rain fell as we plunged back down off the mountain. Our plan to make it to the city was put on hold and we made a mad dash into the woods to set up camp.

The following day we arrived into Fort Nelson and emerged from the vast expanse of wilderness. Although the population of the town was only six thousand inhabitants, to us it felt like New York City.

We were nearly at the end of the Alaska Highway. Fort St. John lay a paltry 240 miles away, after which it would be another forty-five miles to Dawson Creek and the official end of the highway. John and I wondered how Davy would deal with traffic; until now we hadn't encountered any significant traffic at all. Would he be able to do this? We knew he was physically capable of riding his bike to Argentina, but could he handle the mental stresses of dealing with traffic on a daily basis? We would find out soon enough.

Davy and Daryl were, in many respects, extraordinary. They set high goals and never wavered in their determination to achieve them. They understood the idea of breaking an enormous task into manageable chunks rather than being overwhelmed by the big picture. And yet, in other ways, they were very typical ten-year-old kids.

So far, Alaska and Canada had been nothing more than an enormous playground for the boys. Each time we climbed off our bikes they were off and running. They climbed trees and balanced on guardrails. They played soccer with discarded Coke bottles and baseball with pinecones. While John and I rested on the side of the road, Davy and Daryl ran and played just like children the world over.

Were we forcing them to grow up too soon by taking them on this journey? A handful of bloggers had accused us of taking them on a forced march, of taking away their childhood. Were we doing that? Or were we giving them a childhood dreams are made of?

Davy and Daryl were the happiest kids I'd known. They loved their lives on the road. They thrived on the challenges and glowed with delight at being outdoors. I couldn't help but feel that Mother Nature was the best teacher around and that my sons would learn life lessons that would carry them through their lives.

But still those doubts plagued me at times. Were we doing the right thing? Was it fair to take our children out of school, soccer teams, and Boy Scouts? Was it a fair tradeoff?

"You see that over there?" the manager of the campground interrupted my thoughts as he pointed toward a jet black, roiling, seething mass of clouds. "You don't want to be caught out here in that. It'll be a bad one."

"I saw it," I replied as I tied our big blue tarp securely over our bikes. "I'm just battening down the hatches here and getting ready."

"We use Room 21 as a supply room for the lodge," he told me, "but there is some room on the floor for a couple of sleeping bags. You are welcome to take refuge there if you want. I know I wouldn't want to be out here in that storm."

I thanked him for his generosity, but figured we could weather the storm in our tent. After all, we'd been through a storm or two in that thing. A few minutes later I had everything prepared — the bikes were covered, our gear was stashed, and the tent stakes firm. I crawled in the tent with John and the boys.

"I think two of us should head over to the room," John said, as he looked at the sky through the window of our tent. "Nancy, why don't you and Daryl sleep over there tonight?"

"We've always been okay in here before," I replied.

"Yeah, but it's never been this bad before. The way I see it, that storm is blowing in fast. If you're going to go, you have to go now. Once it hits, there's no way you'll be able to get your sleeping bags over there without them getting drenched."

Daryl and I clambered out of the tent with sleeping bags, pillows, and mats in hand and dashed to the supply room. A few minutes later we were sound asleep on the floor.

It seemed like five minutes later when John barged in.

"Nancy!" he called out. "What a storm! Did you see the lightning?"

"A storm?" I asked sleepily. "Did it hit?" Obviously I was oblivious to what was happening outside.

"Holy cow! Did it hit? I've never seen a storm like this! Lightning was flashing pretty much constantly for thirty minutes and rain came down in waves. It was almost like someone was standing there pouring bucket after bucket of water down on us. And the wind! Our tent poles were bending like willows in the wind. It was crazy! It let up a bit after thirty minutes or so, but it's been raining steadily all night."

As it happened, our tent leaked and there was a big puddle of water right where my sleeping bag would have been. It's a good thing Daryl and I took refuge in the supply room.

DAY 62 It was a quick hop to Fort St. John which, for all practical purposes, indicated the end of the Alaska Highway. The official end would come the following day after another short ride, but we had emerged from the wilderness into civilization. From here on out, we would be passing through at least one town each day.

I felt as Alexander the Great must have felt after he crossed the Sahara Desert and finally arrived in the oasis of Siwa, or how the gold miners felt when they staggered into Dawson City after trudging through the wilderness for weeks. Arriving into Fort Nelson felt like landing on a foreign planet.

It was a whirlwind of activity when we arrived into town. Davy and Daryl were the youngest people to cycle the entire Alaska Highway and the press was out in force. A luxury hotel agreed to host us and we felt horribly out of place traipsing into luxury as muddy water dripped off our bikes and gear.

Before we even had a chance to shower away all the muck we were whisked away for TV and radio interviews, photo shoots, and meetings with local officials. It was pretty heady stuff for a family used to being part of the food chain out in Mother Nature's world.

But we had made it! I had given us about a 50% chance of completing the Dalton Highway and then about 60% of making it to Dawson Creek at the end of the Alaska Highway. Now the long distances and remote areas were behind us. From here on out, our journey would be easier. The chances that we would reach Argentina someday were now a whole lot higher.

Chapter 4

Beauty is in the Eye of the Beholder

ALBERTA, CANADA

As happy as we were to put the long remote stretches of the Alaska Highway behind us, we were equally as happy to be heading directly into another one. Jasper and Banff National Parks lay ahead. It would be a mere 180 miles between the two cities, which we figured we could do with our eyes closed at that point. Not that we wanted to, as we had heard stories of the lovely stretch of highway.

Our no-rain streak had broken and we were plagued with near-daily rain. Most days it was just a slight drizzle, but occasionally we dealt with downpours. We kept our fingers crossed that the weather would be kind to us as we cycled what was billed as the most beautiful highway in the world: the Icefields Parkway.

As we climbed up to Jasper, a major storm moved in with high winds. "Mom!" Davy shouted. "Did you see that? The wind literally picked me up and threw me off the road!"

I was cycling behind Davy at the time and saw him suddenly dart onto the shoulder. As hard as he tried, he couldn't keep his bike from bucking. Both the tandem and my bike were heavy enough to hold their ground against  the onslaught, but Davy's wasn't. Time and time again, the wind pushed him off the road. We were grateful the wind was blowing him off the road rather than into it, but were still concerned — how long would it be before he bit the dust in the gravel shoulder?

Unfortunately, there was no place to stop, so we pushed on. We were relieved when we pulled into Jasper knowing Davy had survived the wind; in another way, we were very concerned. Although we had cycled 2500 miles so far, we hadn't dealt with much traffic at all. Davy was comfortable on his bike, but still didn't know how to ride with cars surrounding him.

John and I sandwiched our son between us as we pedaled through town. John and Daryl went first on the tandem so Davy would have an example to follow. I followed behind to shout at him if he started to make a mistake. The very first time we encountered heavy traffic in Dawson Creek at the end of the Alaska Highway we had had a near miss — Davy darted across the road after John even though the cars were too close.

"Davy!" I had screamed as cars honked their horns and slammed on their brakes. Davy pulled back to the side of the road in front of me and waited until it was safe to cross.

We had several long talks with him after that about the idea that he, alone, was in that particular time and space. He needed to be aware of where he was at all times and not blindly rely on following John in front of him.

Although our son had come a long way in his traffic awareness since reaching the end of the Alaska Highway, we were still concerned. With the wind and now heavy tourist traffic, we said a little prayer, sandwiched him between us and carefully made our way through town. Davy did fine and we breathed a sigh of relief when we rolled up in front of the local supermarket.

After stocking up with enough food for a week, we pedaled out of town to the campground for the evening. We were psyched about heading onto the Icefields Parkway through the Canadian Rockies the next day. After having heard the stories for so long, it would be a real treat to see the high peaks and glaciers up close and personal.

Twelve hours later we awoke to the pitter patter of rain on the tent.

"I vote we stay here!" Davy piped up.

"I vote we move on," Daryl chimed in. "I don't want to be bored out of my brain again."

It didn't take long before we made the decision to stay put. It was simply too yucky to move on.

A few hours later, however, the rain stopped and a few patches of blue sky shone through. We reversed our decision and quickly packed up. We set our destination as the next campground twenty-two miles away.

Seventeen of those miles passed quickly and easily as we slowly climbed into the mountains alongside a river, but then, everything changed.

"Five miles to the campground!" I called as massive raindrops pelted us. "Let's go!"

Less than a mile earlier the clouds had dropped to dangerous levels. Now, the heavens were beginning to open up.

The four of us, decked out in rain jackets, took off into the deluge trying to make it to the campground before we got too wet.

Two miles from the campsite, Davy slowed to an agonizingly slow pace. John and Daryl quickly disappeared out of sight, and it was only through sheer force of will that I didn't leave Davy behind.

With a half- mile to go, he ground to a halt.

"Mom," Davy turned to me. "I'm really, really cold." He slowly peeled his fingers off his handlebars as cold rain continued to fall by the bucket-load. "I can't go on. My hands are too cold."

Less than a mile to go, and he just couldn't do it. Our gloves were tucked away at the very bottom of my pannier, and with all the water around, the last thing I wanted to do was go digging.

But then I remembered I had a thin pair of gloves tucked away that were easily accessible. Too big, perhaps, but they worked.

Just as we pulled into the campground, the rain stopped and we spent a delightful evening sitting around the campfire chatting about what the next week would bring. Too bad we didn't have any marshmallows.

"Man, that was a real rumbler!" Davy boasted the following morning as we waited for the rain to stop.

"Code red! Code red!" Daryl and John responded frantically as they burst into action.

Sleeping bags and jackets quickly turned into fans as they wildly pushed the air away, then they both dove under their sleeping bags.

A few minutes later I heard it again — this time from John's side of the tent. "Fffffffdddddd."

"Oooh, Daddy!" Daryl cried. "How could you?"

"That was a feisty little devil wasn't it?" John grinned.

The boys — all three of them — had entered into an all-out fart war. Each one boasted bigger, louder, stinkier, or more potent farts than the others.

"Was that a machine gun? Or a fart?"

"That, Daddy, was a fart," Daryl quipped. "But let me assure you it was deadlier than a machine gun."

I listened to their banter with a fairly high level of confusion. Was this a

Break time. The warmth of the sun and the view of the Rockies made for very pleasant downtime.

"boy thing?" Or was it just a simple reflection of John's stagnation in the toilet humor stage? I never quite figured it out, but I guess the enjoyment the three of them derived from farting was worth it all.

As we climbed higher into the Canadian Rockies, it was almost as though all four of us were overcome with awe. Earlier in the day we talked and joked and laughed as we climbed steadily higher, but as the mountains surrounding us became bigger and more awe-inspiring we cycled quietly, enjoying the magnificence around us.

We camped just below the major climb to the first pass, but we were worried about the weather. We had been told time and again how windy and cold it was by the ice fields even on the best of days. If it rained while we were up there, we would be downright miserable. We hoped for the best and headed off to sleep.

The sixteen-mile climb to the Columbia Ice Fields was spectacular, to say the least. A light snow fell the night before, leaving the mountains with a thin white covering — just enough to bring out the magic.

It was cold and windy when we reached the Icefield Centre and we were all famished, so we pulled out our stove and cooked up some macaroni

Athabasca Glacier. We took a break from the bikes on the immense glacier on foot.

to fuel our bodies. Hundreds of people came and went to the visitor center while we sat huddled around our tiny stove in front of the building. I can only imagine what was going through their minds when they saw our small family cooking lunch in the bitter wind.

With satisfied bellies, we headed out to explore the Athabasca Glacier. The kids had a blast jumping over the many streams flowing out of the monstrous glacier, and Daryl managed to christen his new shoes by sinking into mud up to his ankles.

It was late by the time we left the glacier and pedaled three miles to the top of Sunwapta Pass before plunging down the other side.

As we descended into the canyon, enormous, magnificent mountains rose to the heavens on either side. At least we thought they rose to the heavens — we couldn't see the tops as they hid behind low clouds. We were grateful the rain had held off long enough for us to get over the pass.

DAY 79

We awoke to the pitter-patter of rain once again. It was just a light drizzle — but water still fell from the sky. Go? Or stay?

The problem was that we only had two days' worth of food left and fifty miles to Lake Louise, on the other side of another pass. If we hung out for the day, it would mean a long ride the next day, which we weren't sure we could do.

"I vote we stay here," John announced.

"I vote we go over the pass," Daryl added his two cents.

"I don't really care," Davy said. "Mom — it's up to you."

"I vote we go," I voted. We started packing.

It was one of those cold, wet, drizzly days. It wasn't raining enough to really get wet — just enough to make our lives miserable. Other cyclists came down from the pass and reported it continued the same all the way up — just a cold drizzle. Head up and over? Or stop at the first campground?

In the end, we stopped. It was already 4:00 p.m. when we arrived at the campground, and we feared it would be another late night on the road if we attempted the pass. We crawled into our tent and hoped for better weather tomorrow.

We awoke to rain the following morning. This time it was a definite rain — no mamsy-pamsy drizzle like the previous days. Our spirits were low. We had been five days in one of the most spectacular mountain parks in the world and all we had was rain and clouds. Valleys and mountains alike were socked in by thick, low clouds. Mother Nature teased us with glimpses of the majestic, snow covered peaks that lined the road and the clouds occasionally broke just long enough to reveal a mountain towering above us or a sparkling turquoise colored lake nestled in a valley surrounded by snow covered peaks.

And now we had more rain. I crawled out of the tent and emptied my food bags to take stock. I stared at our pitiful provisions.

4 apples
1 orange
½ bag baby carrots
1 bag granola
1 package fig newtons
13 snack packs of flavored wheat berries
Couple of handfuls of peanuts
Couple of handfuls of mixed nuts
½ bag banana chips
1 emergency meal of oatmeal and brown sugar (but no milk or raisins)

It was cold and rainy our entire time in Jasper and Banff National Parks. To protect Daryls' hands and feet, I put plastic bags on them. It worked a bit, but he was still cold.

"Okay, guys," I called to the boys still in the tent. "We've got plenty of food to get us to Lake Louise, but that's about it. We have a choice — ride in this cold rain today or wait until tomorrow and be hungry. What's your choice?"

It was a unanimous vote to ride.

Over three hours passed before we reached the top of Bow Pass. We were soaking wet and cold, but needed to push on. The kids donned their gloves, I tied plastic bags over them, and we headed down.

By that point Davy was tiring quickly, but he gamely pedaled on while John and Daryl quickly outpaced us. I was cold and my legs were continually doused by both falling rain and spray from passing cars. My feet sloshed in my shoes and my toes screamed in agony.

"Davy — speed up, will ya?" I called to my son riding ahead of me.

Davy sped up — for about thirty seconds, before slowing back down.

"I can't ride this slowly!" I urged. "I'm really cold! At this pace it'll take us two more hours to get into town. Please go faster!"

Davy slogged along and I bit my tongue as long as I could. Finally, I couldn't handle it any longer and pulled out in front.

"I need you to keep up with me, honey," I told Davy as I sped by. "I can't go this slowly."

I kept up a pace where Davy could just barely keep up until we came to another downhill stretch.

"Mom!" Davy shouted up to me as I quickly outpaced him racing down the hill. "Don't go so fast! I can't keep up!" Since his bike was significantly lighter than mine, gravity didn't help him as much on the downhills.

He took over in front and set a decent pace until we were about to pull into town.

Just then, the skies opened up and it began to pour — even more than it had all day long. And Davy was creeping along again. I pulled out in front again.

"Don't go too fast, Mom!" he called as I passed. "I'm getting really, really tired."

In time, we pulled into town, stopped at the mall, and made a beeline for the bakery. A date bar for me and a donut for Davy made all the difference in the world.

All evening we hung out in the cook shed of the campground huddled around the wood stove to stay warm. I guess that's really all we needed — date bars, donuts, and a warm fire.

"Nancy! Wake up!" John shouted at some ungodly hour the next morning. "There's a clear blue sky! Let's go!" I mumbled something, then crammed my pillow over my head and went back to sleep.

An hour later he was back. "C'mon, you guys! We're going hiking! It's a beautiful day and I just found out about a beautiful four-hour hike in the mountains. Let's go!"

I rolled over and looked at Davy sleeping next to me. "Do you want to go hiking?" I asked.

"Not really," he replied.

I looked at Daryl on the other side. "What about you?"

"Yeah," he answered. "I wouldn't mind."

Truth be told — the last thing I wanted to do was head up into the mountains with the threat of more rain and sopping wet shoes and wet clothes. There was a nice warm fire at the campsite, and I was a very happy camper to just sit and bask in the warmth.

The sun shone most of the day revealing the splendor of the Canadian Rockies. Davy, Daryl, and John spent the day hiking in the mountains. They climbed a nearby peak, where they had fantastic views of the entire region filled with towering cliffs, glaciers, lakes, rivers, and valleys. The colors were brilliant in the bright sunshine, in total contrast to the drab colors they were used to from the previous five days.

I, on the other hand, thoroughly enjoyed sitting around the campfire, drying out my shoes and typing journal entries.

"There's snow on the ground in Banff this morning."

My jaw dropped to the floor and my eyes widened to resemble the bagels I was purchasing.

"Say that again?" I mumbled.

"I hear there's three inches of snow in Banff," the supermarket clerk repeated. "At least that's what people are telling me."

I looked through the window to the parking lot. Sure enough, scattered here and there throughout the parking lot were cars covered with snow.

It was only August! It wasn't supposed to snow in August. What a birthday present!

August 31, my combination 48th birthday and 17th wedding anniversary, was our coldest day yet. We pulled more layers from our pannier bags as the day wore on. It was a cold drizzly day and we couldn't wait to get to Banff. I had planned to stock up on winter gear in Montana a bit farther south — I had figured that would give us plenty of time before the real cold hit. Obviously, that plan was flawed.

As soon as we arrived into Banff, I hit the camping stores and picked up some warm wool socks and other warm gear for all of us.

Next stop was the local Safeway where I found a chocolate caramel turtle cream pie to serve as my birthday cake and our anniversary treat.

We were seriously scared about what the fall would bring. If it was this cold at the end of August, would we be able to make it through the United States? We curled up in our down sleeping bags and figured we'd cross that bridge when we got there.

Chapter 5

Out of the Kettle, Into the Fire

UNITED STATES

My eyes were glued to my rearview mirror as I pedaled away from Banff and toward Calgary. Unfolding behind me was the most incredible, spectacular sight imaginable — the entire range of Canadian Rockies rose toward the heavens. And to think we spent a week cycling in the mountains and didn't see that glory at all.

As disappointed as we were, we set our sights ahead. The US border wasn't far away and we were thrilled to be approaching it. We had crossed Alaska and now Canada.

The Canada/US border was at the top of a major climb and we were determined to make it that day. All four of us were machines as we cranked up the mountain to Chief Mountain. We gasped and panted for breath and kept our legs to keep turning through sheer force of will.

Finally I pulled my gaze away from the road to look ahead and saw the most incredible sight imaginable — the US flag.

"Do you see the flag, Daryl?" I asked as we pedaled side by side. "Right up there — between the trees. The American flag!"

"I see it! I see it!" he shouted between gasps for air. "The United States! I can't believe we made it! I don't know how we did it — but we did. America — I'm here!"

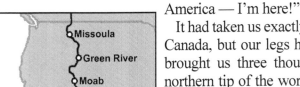

It had taken us exactly two months to cross Canada, but our legs had done it. They had brought us three thousand miles from the northern tip of the world and into our home country. Only fourteen more countries — but that felt totally within reach after having conquered as much as we had. Nothing could stop us now! Now our challenge was to get through the USA before winter set in.

But first we wanted to see Glacier National Park. As we slowly made our way through the park, we looked ahead at the road snaking along the mountainside ahead of us. Our guess was about a 9% grade, which was just on the edge of what I could pedal. I resigned myself to many miles of walking my bike. In the meantime, I kept pedaling.

To our surprise, it wasn't nearly as bad as we expected. "This is easy!" Davy exclaimed as he sped up the final approach to Logan Pass at 6,646 feet, significantly higher than any other pass we crossed. "It wasn't nearly as hard as I thought it would be."

Davy and I celebrated when we reached the top of the pass, and then sat down to wait for John and Daryl to arrive.

But they didn't make it. They had been right behind us less than a mile down — surely it couldn't take that long to climb that short distance. I began to worry. Did they go over the edge? Did they get hit by a car? Something major had to have happened for them to be delayed for so long.

Chewing my fingernails with worry, I flagged down a park worker as she drove by.

"Did you happen to see a father and son on a blue tandem?" I asked.

"Yeah," she laughed. "He said he left his camera down below, so they turned around to go get it."

At least I knew they weren't hurt.

I wandered over to my bike and took a peek in my handlebar bag — and there was John's camera nestled right next to mine. Oh crap! I sent a message down with the next driver who passed by, and settled in to wait.

It was after 6:30 in the evening by the time we started our descent to the campground seventeen miles away. It was late, but we figured we could make those miles before dark, given that it was all downhill. Besides, there was no place else to camp so we had no choice.

It was a long, slow descent as we stopped every mile to let John's rear rim cool down. His front brakes were no longer working and we were attempting to limp into Missoula where he would get them fixed, so he only used his rear brake. Slowing a heavy tandem on the massive grade created a lot of friction, and therefore generated a lot of heat. If he let it build up too much, he would blow his tire.

As we slowly made our way down off the pass, we marveled at how the sun was shining brightly on the high peaks surrounding us while we were bathed in the darkness of shadow. All was good — almost to the campground and not dark yet.

Climbing Logan Pass in Glacier National Park

But then we saw the sign:

Avalanche Campground
CLOSED

That was a problem. The next campground was seven miles away and, while still slightly downhill, it wasn't a steep downhill we could race down. We would actually have to pedal. We took off at high speed trying to make it to the next campground before darkness.

We screamed into the campground and set up camp with the last vestiges of daylight. By the time dinner got started, darkness was complete.

As hard as we tried to avoid late days and riding in darkness, it sometimes just happened. Those were the times that I appreciated Davy and Daryl more than ever — not a word of complaint, nor murmur of discontent. They rose to meet whatever challenge was placed before them, even if it meant riding way past their bedtime.

DAY 98 By the time we staggered into Missoula 150 miles away, John no longer had any brakes at all. Both of his rims had developed wide spots, which meant his brakes pulsed and shimmied whenever he tried to use them. As the brake pads slid along the sides of the rims, they bounced out over the wide spots, and jumped in for the narrow parts. John had spent many hours on the side of the road attempting to adjust his brakes, but nothing worked. There was no adjustment that would work with wavy rims.

We pedaled slowly and carefully as we entered town. John set the pace at a speed he felt he could manage, knowing the only way to stop his bike was to jump off and physically stop it with his body. Traffic whizzed past us as we slowly made our way to a bike store.

We unloaded all John's gear and handed the bike over to the mechanics, hoping and praying they would know what the problem was. It didn't take long to find out.

When they peeled away the tape inside the rims, they discovered a slit right down the middle of it. At that point, the rim had split ¼ inch in some places, which accounted for the wide spots. We considered ourselves very fortunate that we made it in before the rims totally split in two.

Our concern skyrocketed though. The rims were specially designed to handle the additional weight and stress of a tandem, but had only made it three thousand miles before splitting. We still had another 14,000 miles to go. I contacted the manufacturer to ask if our rims were appropriate for such a long trek.

We were thrilled the next day when the company responded. "Unfortunately, we had a bad batch of aluminum pass through, and it looks like you got two rims from that batch. We'll overnight new rims out and pay to have the wheels rebuilt."

At least we knew it wasn't our fault.

A few days later we were back on the road. Our trek through Montana was fairly straight forward. We were surprised when we woke up one morning to find a thick layer of snow covering our bikes and tents and we redoubled our efforts to get south quickly and pedaled hard. The clock was ticking and the pressure was on. How bad would it get before we escaped the danger zone?

"Today when we were riding it was nice and cool until the blast of cold wind hit us," Davy wrote. "Then I realized that a huge expanse of black and gray clouds was in the sky. It went over the sun and shaded us. The wind came. Without the warmth of the sun and in my t-shirt, I shivered. We stopped to prepare for rain just as the first drops of rain fell. We saw a church across the road. They let us stay there. Just like the movies, huh?"

Fall was in the air. Days were, for the most part, lovely. Crisp fall temps made for delightful cycling; down sleeping bags kept us warm at night.

Winter's here! We woke up to snow and a bitter cold morning while camping atop Big Hole Pass at 7,360 feet. None of us wanted more than to stay curled up in our nice warm sleeping bags, but the choice was not ours - we had to push on.

Days were rapidly getting shorter, cutting down on the time we could spend on the road.

Mother Nature gave us her best weather conditions as we cycled through Yellowstone and Grand Teton National Parks. Warm enough to be comfortable and cool enough to not sweat. Intense reds and yellows filled the trees, with steaming hot springs in the background. Elk and buffalo grazed by the side of the road.

We were hopeful we could slide through the US before winter truly settled in, but then came the email. "Dear John and Nancy," a friend wrote. "I'm not sure if you are aware of a massive storm moving into Wyoming, but I strongly urge you to seek shelter. They are calling for sub-zero temps and up to two feet of snow."

The next day we received yet another email from the friend whose house we were headed for. "As you know, I work at a hotel. I've talked with the manager of the hotel and she's offered to put you guys up as long as you need in order to have shelter during the upcoming storm. Would you like me to reserve a room for you?"

America's Road Angels had done it again! We hung out in the luxurious surroundings of the hotel in Pinedale while snow piled up outside. We watched TV, read books, played with beads, and backed up photos in the warm, cozy room.

DAY 126 Temperatures were still way below freezing and snow lined the roads four days later when we set off. As much as we wanted to hang out and wait until it warmed up, we needed to take advantage of every day. Fall was rapidly turning into winter and, with well over a thousand miles left to pedal before we would consider ourselves south of the danger zone, we needed to move.

We piled on every layer of clothing we owned, loaded up our bikes, and headed out. Our primary concern was Daryl. The rest of us handled the cold well, but Daryl had endured painfully cold hands and feet every time the temperature dropped. No matter how warmly I dressed him, he seemed to always be in pain when it was cold.

While waiting out the storm, I had scoured the local shops for warmer clothes for my son. The fleece gloves he had worn earlier had failed the test, so I bought him some ski gloves. I bought a great big wool sweater and threw it in the washing machine with hot water to shrink it down into thick heavy felt. We found some new leather shoes which, we hoped, would be warmer than the sneakers he had been wearing and bought them two sizes too big in order to put a couple layers of wool socks inside. He layered on two pairs of tights and his rain pants. To cover his face and neck, he wore a fleece gaiter that he could pull up to right under his eyes.

An hour later, Daryl was in tears — his feet hurt like crazy. John stopped by the side of the snow-lined road and stripped off Daryl's shoes and socks before tucking the frozen feet up under his jacket onto his warm belly.

Once Daryl's feet were warmed up, we added plastic bags over his hands and feet and headed out again. The bright Wyoming sun helped a little, but not quite enough. Our water bottles froze solid as we pedaled the rural highway, but Daryl hung in there. The plastic bags seemed to make enough of a difference that he was okay, although not comfortable.

The sun was making a rapid descent toward the horizon when we made the decision to try to get to the next town rather than camp by the side of the road. The only problem with that decision was that, as the sun dropped toward the horizon, the temperature plummeted.

Poor Daryl was in tears yet again — this time due to cold hands. We pumped hard trying to reach town, all the while listening to Daryl whimper on the back of the tandem. We had obviously failed yet again. I started wondering if it was possible to keep my son warm on cold winter days.

By the time we pulled into the ice cream parlor in Farson, Daryl was sobbing hysterically. I jumped off my bike and ran over to gently lift him off the back of the tandem and carried him into the store. After peeling away his ski gloves, I gently rubbed his hands to get the blood flowing again. His sobs slowly ebbed as TLC and warm surroundings worked their magic.

Old Man Winter finally caught us big time and dumped over a foot of snow. We hung out for four days waiting for the storm to pass.

He wiped away the last of his tears and looked at me. "Can I have some ice cream?" I burst out laughing. He'd be alright after all.

Fortunately, we never had to worry about the cold at night as our sleeping bags were very warm. While John and I set up the tent in the bitter cold behind the store, the boys sat inside enjoying pizza and ice cream. When it was time for bed, they made a mad dash to their sleeping bags and curled up in their down cocoons.

I lay in my sleeping bag that night worrying about what the future might bring. We knew from the outset that Daryl tended to get cold easily, but today could have ended in disaster. It was cold, but no colder than we figured we'd be dealing with up in the Andes once we got farther south. What more could I do for Daryl's hands and feet? I knew we had barely scraped by — another hour or two out in that cold and Daryl would have had serious frostbite in his fingers. We had tried fleece and ski gloves. Would wool be better?

The next chance I had, I picked up two layers of wool gloves for my little guy — a thin liner pair and a nice thick outer pair. Although he still complained about cold hands, he never again reached the point of pain and agony he experienced that day in Wyoming. In fact, we discovered the wonders of wool all around, and slowly started switching all our clothes over to wool.

In the evening, we turned off the road and headed back toward the mesa to camp. In addition to having such a beautiful place to sleep, the coyotes sung us to sleep!

We managed to get the cold issue more or less squared away, only to jump directly back into the rim/brake issue. As we pulled in to Rock Springs in southern Wyoming, John noticed his bike pulsing and shimmying — his rim was splitting again.

When we contacted the manufacturer of the rims up in Montana, they had informed us of the defective rims and said they still didn't have good rims in stock. They also said the general pattern had shown that the defective rims tended to hold up for around 3000 miles. Given that we were 1500 miles from Albuquerque at the time, we figured we could put more defective rims on and have the wheels rebuilt again down south. In theory, it worked.

As we arrived into Rock Springs, only seven hundred miles from Missoula, however, John started complaining about his rear wheel. We pulled into town and called the rim company.

"Don't ride on it," advised the representative from the manufacturer. "We'll overnight a new one out to Rock Springs and arrange for the wheel to be rebuilt."

With winter upon us, however, that wasn't a great option. Each and every day was critical, and we couldn't afford to hang around for three or four days waiting for the bike. We worked it out that we would make an attempt to get to Moab 350 miles away and the company would have a rim waiting there for us.

All went well for a while and our confidence level improved slightly — it was looking like the rim might very well hold steady.

But then it all changed. Nine miles from Vernal we had to stop and adjust John's brakes — the bulge had grown to the point where the wheel couldn't spin any more.

John disconnected his rear brake entirely and we continued on. He was back to only one brake, so we made sure to keep speeds slow knowing he didn't have much braking power.

We were grateful when we pulled into Moab — we had made it. Riding two hundred miles with limited brakes was nerve-racking and we couldn't wait to get the tandem's wheels rebuilt. Everything worked like clockwork. The rims were at the store, the technicians were anticipating our arrival, and they had the bike ready to go within a few hours.

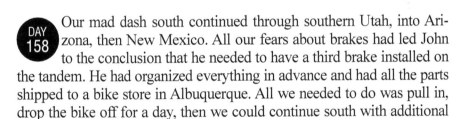 Our mad dash south continued through southern Utah, into Arizona, then New Mexico. All our fears about brakes had led John to the conclusion that he needed to have a third brake installed on the tandem. He had organized everything in advance and had all the parts shipped to a bike store in Albuquerque. All we needed to do was pull in, drop the bike off for a day, then we could continue south with additional braking power.

Or so we thought.

Just as planned, John and Daryl rode the tandem to the bike store early in the day, then headed over to the library to wait. A brand new drum brake was installed onto the rear wheel of the bike and the existing rear rim brake rewired to give it to Daryl. Everything went well and, by four in the afternoon, they were on the bike heading back to our friend's house.

And that's when the car didn't see them.

As John pulled out into an intersection, a car turned left and ran straight into them. Fortunately, both bike and car were going slowly. Daryl was able to jump off the bike and run to safety but John, his feet clipped to the pedals, went down with the bike.

The next few hours were a blur of confusion. How badly was John hurt? Was the tandem damaged? How badly?

The ambulance drivers graciously put the bike in the back of the ambulance and took it back to the bike shop it had just left, and then drove

John and Daryl to where Davy and I were waiting. We had no idea what the future held.

I was grateful my son was unharmed, but John's health was critical as well. As my husband limped around the house that evening, we talked about the implications of the accident. What if the bike was damaged beyond salvage? It would be a minimum of two months before we could get a new one. How badly was John hurt? It didn't appear that he had broken any bones, but he was limping pretty badly. How long were we out of commission?

By the following morning, once the adrenaline had passed out of John's system, we had some answers. His leg, which had appeared to be the major issue the night before, was actually okay. Both his wrists, however, were not. Sprains to both wrists would take time to heal.

News about the bike wasn't good either, but not as bad as we feared. The frame itself appeared to be fine — the shop had carefully evaluated it and found no cracks or dents in the frame and it was still true. The trouble lay in the handlebars and crank arm for the pedal — they were both bent beyond repair. We would need to wait for new ones to be shipped in.

Now what? We were staying with a friend, but she was scheduled for surgery and had made it clear from the outset that we would need to be out of her house. She had told us we were welcome before or after the surgery, but her house would be off-limits for two weeks. We had planned to be well on our way before her surgery date. Now we wouldn't.

That's when Albuquerque showed us her magic. The local TV news station ran a story about our journey and the accident. Homeschool groups found out we were in town and invited us to their events. Each and every time I opened my email I found more messages from local people offering us a place to stay or the use of their car or to take our sons to parties. The outpouring of support was overwhelming. How could we possibly repay these people for their kindness?

Since John and Daryl didn't have a bike to ride, transportation around the city was hard, so we quickly accepted the offer of the use of a car. We moved into the house of another family who also had twin boys. John babied his wrists in order to promote healing and we prayed the bike would be repaired soon. All we could do was wait — so wait we did.

Eight days later we were ready to move on. John's wrists, while still a bit sore, were healed enough that he felt he could manage the 150 miles to another friend's house in Truth or Consequences. Harry had a complete shop and our plan all along had been to spend a week there so John could completely rebuild the bikes and get them ready for Mexico. Now

Harry, Bernice (Harry's mother), Nancy, Davy, John, and Daryl in Truth or Consequences, New Mexico.

we would also be able to spend the Thanksgiving holiday with him. We packed up and continued south.

Our time in the USA had been marked by wheel and brake troubles. John had spent countless hours on the side of the road fixing one thing or another. Now, after having cycled a total of 5000 miles, we had a pretty good idea of what worked on our bikes and what didn't. John and Harry locked themselves away in the shop to get all three bikes in tip top shape.

All along, our goal was Truth or Consequences before winter and we had made it. We were far enough south that we no longer worried about winter. Even if temps dropped, they wouldn't stay down for weeks. We might end up with a few days of very cold temps, but we could fairly safely say we were out of the danger zone. Our mad dash to stay ahead of Mother Nature was over.

From here it was just a short hop over the border into Mexico. Or at least that was the plan.

Chapter 6

The Search for a "Safe" Crossing

TEXAS

All four of us were giddy with excitement. A new country. Another border crossing. We were making progress.

It was only a few miles from Truth or Consequences to El Paso, where we planned to cross into Mexico. John had all three bikes in tip-top shape and we had purchased everything we figured we would need. We were ready for a new adventure south of the border.

And then it stopped before it even got started.

We had been receiving emails from our blog readers for a few weeks expressing concern about us heading into Mexico. Would we be safe? How did we plan to avoid all the drug violence going on in the country? John and I had talked about the concerns for hours, and come to the conclusion that people were blowing the situation out of proportion. We were fairly certain we would be fine.

We pulled into El Paso and pedaled up to some friends' house. Patty and Roy welcomed us in and our conversation immediately turned to Mexico.

"Things are pretty tense in Juarez these days," Patty told us. "I work

across the border and go down there every day. There were sixteen killings last week."

John and I looked at each other, not quite sure what to say.

"Do you think we should cross here?" John asked.

"Oh, sure!" she responded. "It's tense, but

the killings are targeted. They're killing judges and police and other people involved in the drug trade. They're not killing bicycling families coming through the city."

In the three days we stayed in El Paso, we changed our minds fifteen times. We'll cross here. No, it'll be better to cross somewhere quieter. We'll be perfectly fine here. Another crossing is safer.

"What about the people out there who are criticizing us for doing what we're doing," John asked me one evening. "They're already blasting us. If we cross here when all these killings are going on, we'll just be handing them fuel for the fire."

He had a point. Shortly before we set off from Alaska, a few very vocal people had started criticizing us. They claimed John and I were selfish parents only looking at what we wanted, not what was best for our sons. They wrote blog entries and put out the word anywhere they could that we were using and abusing our children by taking them on a "forced march."

They even went so far as to say that the reason we had raced through the United States was to stay one step ahead of the Child Protection Agency. In their opinion, we were terrible parents inflicting a nightmare upon our children.

If we crossed the border in Juarez, a city greatly feared by many Americans, we would just be feeding them. We caved under the pressure, conceded to public criticism and made the decision to continue south along the border to a smaller, perhaps safer, border crossing.

As we cycled out of El Paso, we followed the border. Through a simple chain link fence, we watched the Rio Grande meander between the two cities. On the other side of the water, we watched Mexican children run and play through their neighborhoods. It felt like it was a world away, and yet so close.

Before long we were out of the city and into farmland. Cotton, pecans, and other mystery crops lined the roads. Traffic was minimal and we relaxed into a comfortable pace.

When evening approached we camped in a dry river bed under a bright half-moon. "Today we left El Paso," Daryl wrote in his journal. "I saw Mexico. We've come a long way since Prudhoe Bay. The Dalton Highway, the Alaska Highway, Canada, and now the US. We are camped in a riverbed, specifically a little outcropping of the wash. There was a steep dirt wall halfway around it. Davy and I climbed on it."

As I curled up in my sleeping bag in our cozy tent, I realized that quiet evenings like this one were one of the most special things about our journey. After being outside and active all day, crawling into our tent to read and relax for a few hours while listening to the coyotes sing in the distance

There's Mexico! We cycled along the fence for about five miles in El Paso. The fence was all that separated Texas from Mexico.

was magic. How could anyone feel we were abusing our children by giving them such a gift?

The following day started off normally, but by mid-morning a strong wind had kicked up and it looked like rain was imminent. We took shelter under a bridge while the wind gained strength until it was howling past us. A few raindrops fell from the sky as we prepared for a downpour.

I unstrapped our jackets from where I had earlier lashed them on Davy's rack and, as soon as they were freed, the whole bunch sprouted wings and flew away. Davy quickly sprinted after them while I hurriedly opened a dry bag to cram them in.

Every tiny task became an enormous chore as the wind stuck its sticky fingers into every nook and cranny and pulled items out. If it wasn't securely lashed to a bike, it was soon flying across the road.

"Let's go!" John shouted once we had the bikes prepared. Our flags and jackets whipped furiously in the wind. "Take advantage of this tailwind for once!"

We climbed on our bikes and took off with the wind at our backs. As the wind howled, we barreled along the road at top speed — until the next curve in the road.

When we turned, the wind became a force to be reckoned with as it blew us off the road. Our bikes leaned into the wind as we struggled to maintain a semi-straight line.

The wind blew and we bounced around the road like pinballs in a pinball machine.

The road curved again for the last five miles into Sierra Blanca and the wind blew us into town. By the time we got there, a cheap motel sounded like a much more attractive option than our tent. We checked in and called it a day.

We snaked our way through the mountains in southern Texas battling headwinds and crosswinds and taking advantage of tailwinds. If we had learned anything about Texas it was that the wind always blew — from somewhere. When we were lucky enough to have a tailwind, we pedaled furiously. When we had headwinds or crosswinds, we pedaled slowly taking plenty of breaks.

Each time we climbed off the bikes, the kids were off and running, exploring tunnels under the road, throwing snow balls, climbing trees, or jumping from one boulder to another. There was no end to the games they created. I sat at a rest stop on the side of the highway watching the pure uninhibited joy in my sons and wished I could be like them. I wished I had the creativity, the energy, and the free spirit they had. I wished I could have so much fun so simply. Why did we have to grow up?

"I wish a rancher would pull up and invite us to camp on his land," John mused.

We had wanted to stop for the day for ten miles, but hadn't seen a single place to pitch a tent. Fences lined both sides of the highway with no break in sight. It was 5:00 in the afternoon and we figured we had thirty minutes, at best, to find a spot for our tent.

Not more than five seconds after John's wish for a rancher, a black car pulled into the rest area. The window rolled down and a friendly face appeared.

"Where are you headed?" the woman asked. "Where will you sleep tonight?"

And so it was that we found ourselves bouncing along a rough dirt road to a small ranch house a mile off the road.

"Welcome!" Gene, the father of the family, greeted us as we leaned our bikes against their fence. "We're glad you're here."

"So are we!" John responded.

"My grandfather bought these 20,000 acres back in 1962 and it's been in the family ever since," Gene continued. "This is my favorite place in the whole world! Unfortunately, we only get out here three or four times a year — the rest of the time we live in Austin."

John and I spent a delightful evening swapping stories with Gene and Mary, while the boys had a blast playing with their four kids. We stuffed ourselves with chicken and spaghetti, garlic bread, and salad, then headed out by the campfire where all the kids collaborated to light fireworks.

We set up camp behind the ranch house in a dry pond basin where the ground was flat and soft and we were protected from the howling wind. As I lay in my sleeping bag I thought back upon the day and about our nervousness at finding a place to sleep. There was nothing out there but miles and miles and more miles of Texas. The highway was lined on both sides by continuous fences, leaving nowhere to pitch a tent.

It could have been a horrible night, but it wasn't; it was delightful instead. Somehow, call it a God-moment or serendipity, but help came just when we needed it. We had been on the road for six months now and had met more Road Angels than I ever dreamed existed, yet we were still humbled and honored by each and every act of kindness they extended.

DAY 196 We awoke the following morning to sounds of what appeared to be gale-force winds. Down in our pond basin, sheltered from the winds, we didn't feel them at all, but we listened to the howling in the trees above us and could only hope and pray the wind was going in the right direction.

We packed our bikes and headed up to Gene and Mary's ranch house for breakfast. "The wind typically comes from the west," Gene told us, "but after a storm it shifts and comes from the east for a day or two. I have a feeling you'll have a headwind today."

He was right. When we got out on the road, we faced the worst headwind we had dealt with yet. Langtry was thirty miles away and we knew we had no choice but to make it there; it would be thirty miles of solid, unbroken fence lines on both sides of the road until we got to the town.

In addition to heading straight into the wind, it was cold. The forty-degree weather seemed to be in the 20's because of the wind chill factor. We were bundled up in our winter garb and looked like Michelin men pedaling down the road.

"I can't do it, Mom," Davy murmured early in the afternoon as he stood straddling his bike and resting his head on the handlebars. He tried to catch his breath and summon up a bit more energy. "There's no way I can make it ten more miles."

"I'm exhausted too, honey," I commiserated. "Let's try to catch up with Daddy."

A mile later we pulled up to where John and Daryl rested on the side of the road. "I just talked with the border patrol," John told us. "He said it's private property all the way to Langtry; there's no way we can camp here. How fast are you guys going?"

"Three miles per hour uphill; four down. This headwind is killing us," I complained.

"That means it'll take at least two hours to Langtry. It'll be dark by then, but we have no choice."

We dug out our blinky lights and strapped them to the bikes, and set off into the wind.

Mother Nature mobilized her entire contingent of Wind Warriors against us as Mr. Sun made a rapid nosedive toward the horizon. The four of us raced against time as we frantically pushed on toward town.

One mile from town we passed a dirt road heading down into a canyon under a bridge — and we turned in. After clearing a spot in the mesquite bushes in the growing darkness, we quickly set up the tent, covered the bikes with our plastic tarp, then dove into our tent to eat our dinner of crackers & cheese, beef jerky, and M&M's.

All four of us were beat after a full day of fighting our worst headwind yet and were ready to collapse into our sleeping bags. Even as tired as I was, my heart swelled with pride at seeing my young sons rise to the challenge and tackle a job harder than most adults were willing to face. Davy and Daryl were so determined, so motivated to reach Argentina, they never wavered in the face of adversity. No matter what obstacles were thrown in their path, they climbed over them with nary a thought. If they could battle winds like this, what else could they accomplish in their lives?

"It sounds like the wind has died down," I said the following morning as I sat in our tent packing my sleeping bag. "I hope it's a good day — we've got twenty-five miles to the state park."

A few minutes later I climbed out of the tent and into a drizzle. It wasn't much, but a very slight drizzle descended from the very heavy clouds overhead.

"Let's move!" I shouted. "Let's get everything packed before it really starts to rain!"

We were determined to make it to Seminole Canyon by that afternoon as we had agreed to meet some newfound friends there. We hoped to spend the afternoon on the Rio Grande visiting ancient petroglyphs.

Fortunately, once we hit the road, the drizzle petered out, but as it did, the temperature plummeted. We pulled out extra socks and gloves and

The inhabitants of Seminole Canyon sketched these pictographs some 4,000 years ago. An acquaintance brought us out to these remote caves on the Pecos River in his boat. Here Davy points them out to Daryl.

continued on. Just as we reached the turnoff to the state park, our friends drove up with their boat. Perfect timing!

John and the boys headed out on the river with Glenn and Sam while I enjoyed a lazy afternoon in the campground. As it was bitter cold outside, I enjoyed a few hours in the heated bathroom, taking a long, leisurely hot shower, and then reading a good book while resting on the bathroom bench.

I started to think that sometimes it wasn't so bad to be left out of all the activities.

It was Christmas Eve and one of those days when we would normally be thrilled to be on the road. Temperatures got up into the 70's, the sun shone brightly, and the sky was crystal clear. In short, the day was an absolutely perfect cycling day, but all four of us were totally worn out from climbing hills against brutal headwinds in the frigid cold the past few days, and just wanted to rest.

We plodded along to get to Del Rio, not enjoying the ride *per se*, but dreaming of a hotel room. We were learning quickly that it didn't take much to please us. After days of camping out, a simple roof over our heads was the pinnacle of delight. And the fact that Christmas would not be spent in our tent made it even more special.

When we left El Paso 365 miles earlier, our plan had been to cross into Mexico at Del Rio. Now that we were there, the outcry continued. We made the decision to carry on along the Texan border, looking for a small, sleepy border crossing. We enjoyed a couple days feasting on turkey and ham before pushing on.

"TAILWIND!" Daryl shouted once we were out of the city and realized just what we had. The wind was ripping through the trees and creating dust storms in the desert, but it happened to be a tailwind.

One of those laws of nature we had all learned well was that a flag attached to a forward-moving bicycle would flutter backwards. That was just the way it was. Until the day we cycled out of Del Rio, that is.

I had spent many an hour staring at the American flag on the back of Davy's bike, and for every single one of those hours that flag fluttered back toward me. Occasionally it waved to one side or the other if we had a strong crosswind, but mostly Old Glory just reached out towards me as I rode behind my son.

But that day the flag did everything it could to get away from me. Rather than fluttering out behind the bike, those stars and stripes spent the day trying to reach Davy's handlebars — even though we went faster than we had ever gone before.

We got our payback for all those hours we spent fighting headwinds that day. Payback for the agonizingly slow miles we spent crawling through the desert to get to Del Rio. We flew.

The terrain was fairly flat and the wind pushed us from behind like a kid pushing his brother out of his room. I was sorely tempted to rig up a sail to catch the air.

A mere four hours after leaving Del Rio we pulled into Eagle Pass sixty miles away. We raced into town with our eyes peeled for a cheap hotel when a man flagged us down. We hit the brakes to see what he wanted.

"You're welcome to stay here in my house tonight," Von said. "My house isn't anything fancy, but I've got some space on the floor if you want to throw down your sleeping bags."

The kindness of strangers never ceased to blow me away.

A few days later, we faced another long day on the road. It was nearly sundown when we arrived into town and pulled into the RV Park. I quickly dropped my gear and made a mad dash to the grocery store for dinner. I ran around the store frantically grabbing provisions for the next couple of days, racing through the aisles throwing things in my cart so I could get back to the campground before it got totally dark. My mind was a blur of all the things I had to do in a short period of time.

Suddenly it dawned on me how that pace used to be normal. I used to race into stores to quickly grab what I needed before hurrying back to my car to race to my next stop. I ran from one meeting to the next, hurriedly filling out stacks of paperwork in between them all. Drop the kids off at school, fight the morning traffic getting to work, sprint to the bathroom between classes, ferry the kids to soccer practice. It seemed like it never ended. That was just how life was.

On our journey I had grown accustomed to a slower pace of life. I had gotten used to taking time to smell the roses and tell my boys how much I loved them. Even when we were battling headwinds or climbing hills that never seemed to end, time was on our side. I had come to the point where I was taking that for granted.

I couldn't help but wonder how society would change if humankind could just have time, if we weren't so busy hustling and bustling from one activity to the next. What would happen if all of us decided that time with our family was a bit higher on the priority list?

I think the world would be a different place. Maybe that's not a bad thing.

We headed out from Carrizo Springs bright and early in the morning knowing we were heading into no-man's land. We had been warned about the miles and miles of nothing. That part was okay; we could deal with that just fine.

The tough part was camping out. That particular stretch of no-man's land was actually ranchers' land — mile after mile after mile. Fences lined both sides of the road for hours on end. Although we knew each ranch had a house tucked away somewhere, we had no idea if they were a mile off the road or ten. In short, there was no place to camp and absolutely nobody to ask.

As evening approached, we diligently looked for a place to camp for ninety minutes, but there was nothing. Nada. Zippo. Just fences ten feet from either side of the road. We prayed for a Road Angel to show up or some divine intervention while contemplating the idea of jumping the fence to camp on private property.

I had heard of other cyclists doing that, but we had never needed to —

never. We had always managed to find a dirt road heading back from the highway or a friendly face to ask permission from. But that day there was nothing.

Just before dark we passed through a border checkpoint and asked the guards about a camping place. They simply confirmed what we already knew — there was no place. One of the guards suggested climbing the fence and camping in a field.

With the sun saying its final farewells of the day, we made the decision to camp illegally — to scale a fence and camp on some rancher's property. Working together, we manhandled the bikes and trailers over the gate and set up camp just inside the property. It was unsettling camping on private property without permission, but we knew we had no other option. We could only hope nobody would mind.

Early the following morning, we climbed out of our tent and quickly packed up. We wanted to get off the private property as quickly as possible in case the rancher appeared. There was no telling what someone might do when they found a family camping on their land.

We stuffed our sleeping bags, took down the tent, and hauled everything over to the gate. Working together, we lifted the trailers up and over, then Davy's bike, then mine. Just as we were finishing getting my bike over, a great big monster truck pulled up in the driveway.

Your stereotypical Texan rancher with cowboy boots and great big hat stepped out of the truck. "What's up?" he asked.

"We're just trying to get back on the road," John apologized. "There was no place to camp last night, so…."

"I tell ya what," the rancher said. "Let me open that gate. It'll be a whole lot easier to get them bikes out that way."

All our fears were for naught. He didn't care in the least that we had camped on his property.

As I cycled away, I started thinking about something I had read earlier. Researchers had found that about 40% of the things we worry about never happen, 30% are in the past and can't be helped, 12% involve the affairs of others and are not our business, 10% percent relate to sickness, real or imagined. That meant only 8% percent of the things we tend to worry about are even likely to happen.

And we had just learned that we didn't really have to worry about most of that 8% either.

DAY 210 "Hey Mommy, do you remember that lake I jumped in up in the Arctic tundra?" Daryl asked as we pedaled along a remote Texan road in the afternoon.

"You mean the one with ice still floating in it?" I questioned.

"Yeah, that one. I wouldn't mind jumping into that lake right now. I'm hot!"

Our bodies were sorely unprepared for the heat and humidity we encountered as we approached the tip of Texas and we were struggling big time. The kids, after one of their Coke-bottle soccer games at a rest area, were dripping with sweat. It seemed so odd, so foreign after months of cool, dry weather.

After a long, hot day, the sun eventually began its descent toward the horizon and it cooled off a bit. "Ah," I thought as we pulled into Roma. "Finally! It's actually quite pleasant!"

Then I saw the bank sign flashing ahead of me: **5:22 85°**.

Eighty-five degrees? And that was the cool, pleasant temp? I wasn't sure I wanted to know how hot it got that day. And we knew it would only get hotter as we moved farther south.

"Do you realize this is our last riding day in the USA?" John mentioned as we pedaled southward.

Daryl getting interviewed by Channel Five of McAllen while riding in a community awareness bicycle ride. He was very shy when a camera was pointed at him.

It seemed unreal that we were actually at our crossing point after following the Rio Grande for weeks. We had cycled through our second country — two of the largest ones we would pass through.

As we pedaled into McAllen, fifty miles from the very tip of Texas, we were surprised at the reception we received. We cycled into town and car after car whizzed past giving us friendly toots of their horns, waves, and thumbs up. Many people shouted out their car windows. "Way to go!" "Good job!" It was like the whole town was populated by cyclists cheering us on.

It wasn't until later that we discovered we had been on the local news the previous night. They had been alerted that we were coming and had taken some pictures off our website to announce our arrival into the city. That was just the beginning of the warm welcome McAllen gave us.

We had been in contact with the bicycling club in McAllen for a few weeks, and they welcomed us with open arms. They arranged for us to stay with one member, treated us to an evening at a professional hockey game where the boys got to ride on the Zamboni to clean the ice, and hosted a marvelous barbeque with the entire club. We celebrated the boys' eleventh birthday on the shores of the Rio Grande during a picnic open to the entire town.

As wonderful as all that was, perhaps the biggest gift McAllen gave us was an introduction to Claudio. Claudio, who lived across the border in the Mexican town of Reynosa, ended up being perhaps our most amazing Road Angel of the entire journey and helped us tremendously throughout Mexico. We couldn't wait to cross into a new country at last.

We celebrated Davy & Daryl's 11th birthday in a park along the Rio Grande.

The trouble now was that Davy's bike no longer fit him. Davy had gone through a massive growth spurt in the past few weeks and, as I watched him riding into McAllen, I noticed just how small his bike was. He looked like a massive giant riding a tiny kid's trike and I knew he would only get bigger.

We searched the stores in McAllen for something that would work, but there was nothing. They had mountain bikes and road bikes, but nothing that would work as a loaded touring bike.

The day before we were scheduled to cross the border, I rented a car, threw the boys in, and headed out for the five hour drive to Austin. We pulled up to an REI store, bought the same bike Davy had been riding but a couple sizes larger, loaded it in the rental car and drove back south.

The following morning we moved Davy's panniers from his old bike to the new one and we were ready — for a Mexican escapade.

Chapter 7

The Mexico the Mexicans Know

MEXICO

I stood, straddling my bike, facing the paparazzi in Reynosa. Flash bulbs flashed, video cameras whirred, dozens of microphones gathered in front of my face. I stammered and stuttered trying to remember my Spanish from twenty-two years ago. I never expected this kind of reception in Mexico.

Claudio, the contact we had met in McAllen, had arranged an amazing welcome to his country. We cycled through the streets of Reynosa escorted by four members of his motorcycle club, two police motorcycles, and a police car. They zoomed past us to the next intersection to stop cars so we could cycle through without even looking.

We rounded the corner of the town plaza and came face to face with reporters from every newspaper, magazine, radio and TV station in the area. John and the boys, who didn't speak a word of Spanish, stood back to watch while I fumbled about trying to explain what we were doing and why. My brain was stretched trying to remember words I hadn't used for decades.

Claudio had us on a strict time schedule and before long he cut off the reporters and we were whisked off to another spot on the plaza where the mayor of town officially welcomed us to Mexico and sent us on our way.

As we slowly made our way through the border town, we had an entourage suitable for a world-renowned rock star surrounding our rag-tag little family on our travel-worn, dirty bikes. I wished I'd taken the time to

comb my hair at the last stop or at least put on my cleanest holey t-shirt. And was there actually a *hole* in the back of John's bicycle shorts?

I was amused to see the huge cameras sticking out the windows of cars driving alongside us, recording our every pedal stroke.

We made our way to a local school where all the kids lined the edges of the gym. We pulled in on our bikes, made a quick loop around the gigantic room, then stopped to be welcomed and congratulated by the principal.

From there we headed to a museum, where the cameras caught our every move. We looked over memorabilia from the past century before climbing back on our bikes.

At some point in our journey out of town I realized two things: I had neither Mexican pesos nor any food. We were heading into what looked on the map to be a quite rural area and I knew I needed those two items.

"Claudio," I shouted to be heard over the roar of his motorcycle the next time he pulled up beside me. "I need to get to an ATM!" He nodded and zoomed off to tell the rest of our escorts.

A few minutes later we pulled up to a bank and I climbed off my bike to hurry inside to get money. John and the boys waited outside with the crowd.

When I came out with money in hand, I sheepishly approached Claudio again. "I'm going to need to stop at a supermarket as well. I don't have any food to get us to Tampico."

I walked out of the supermarket a few minutes later. As I took in the scene in front of me, I burst out laughing. John and the boys, dressed in their tattered touring clothes, stood around our bikes loaded down with enormous amounts of gear making them look like little more than homeless drifters or quintessential bag ladies. Surrounding them with their shiny powerful motorcycles stood a crew of Mexican men dressed in their finest leathers. I couldn't help but think it looked like some scene straight out of Hollywood.

Giggling about how incongruous this all was, I hurriedly stashed my food and got ready to hit the road for good.

Ninety minutes later we arrived at the city limits where the police had to turn around. Claudio and his group offered to escort us farther, but we figured we were good — the road was nice and wide, and there was very little traffic.

As we said our goodbyes and thank-yous, Claudio reached into his pocket and pulled out a cell phone. "This is for you," he said as he handed it to me. "I've got it preprogrammed with all the numbers for the presidents of the motorcycle clubs in the cities you'll pass through. See here: I've got this one listed as Tampico Alejandro. When you are a couple days out of

Claudio met us at the border crossing in Reynosa, Mexico. He arranged motorcycle escorts through every single Mexican city we passed through.

Tampico, give Alejandro a call and he'll get the motorcycle club organized to help you get through the city. You'll find a number in here for every city along the eastern coast of Mexico. If you decide to change your route, contact me and I'll get you other numbers."

We thanked Claudio and the whole crew, stashed the cell phone in a pannier, and we were on our own. We were grateful they had gotten us through the madhouse of the border town, but it felt great to be back to just the four of us on a quiet rural road.

All too soon, the sun began to make its descent and we needed a place to pitch our tent. John found a beautiful little field off the side of the road, and I went to a nearby house to ask about the possibility of camping in it. "I don't know about over there," the man said, "but you can camp here if you want — anywhere around the house is fine." We pitched our tent in his yard and enjoyed a quiet evening with a rural Mexican family after a hectic day.

The following day found us cycling through remote Mexican lands. We were stunned at how quickly we transitioned from the busy border town to rural desert with five or ten miles between houses. Late in the afternoon, as the sun drew closer to the horizon and we had no place to camp, we started to worry.

Although we had wild camped many nights in the USA and Canada, we had decided to stay close to people in Mexico. The way we figured it, there was safety in numbers. As evening approached we started looking for a house to ask permission to camp.

But, as seemed to happen all too often, once we started looking for a house to ask permission, there weren't any. We pedaled and pedaled but saw nothing but empty farmlands.

Just as we were about to accept the fact that we would have to go back into a field and set up the tent, a small store appeared. And not just any small store — one with a bunch of kids.

We had barely gotten the tent set up before a soccer game started and more kids magically appeared. Davy and Daryl were right in the middle of the mayhem.

"Yay!" Daryl shouted as he threw his arms in the air in victory after scoring a goal.

"Good one!" Davy added.

Their teammates gave them high-fives and cheers in Spanish, none of which Davy or Daryl understood. None of that mattered — soccer was an international language.

John and I sat back and watched the boys play. We could tell it wouldn't be long before they were speaking the new language.

Days blended together as we slowly worked our way south. One day after fighting headwinds for hours, we were all more than ready to call it a day by late afternoon. We pulled into a small town 175 miles south of the border and headed directly to the only hotel in town.

"Mommy! Mommy!" Daryl shouted as we pulled into the parking lot. "They have tamales! They have tamales!"

I glanced over to the pickup truck parked in front of the hotel and noticed the big TAMALE sign, before refocusing my attention on the hotel. I climbed off my bike and headed out in search of the office to see about a room. I was hot and sweaty, and wanted to find a place to stay for the night. Food could come later.

"Mommy! They've got tamales!" Daryl danced with excitement around me. "Can we get some? For dinner? Please?"

Daryl was in heaven — they had tamales, his favorite food in the whole wide world. Davy had been good since we arrived in Mexico — his favorite food was tortillas and beans — but Daryl had been searching high and low for tamales since we crossed the border. He finally found them.

I handed him some money and told him to go buy some.

Our motorcycle escorts waited for us at a grocery store while we stocked up for the next leg of the journey.

"Will you come with me? I don't know how to buy them," he begged.

"Nope," I replied. "You can do it. Just go tell the man *'Quiero tamales'* and you'll be fine."

"But what if he starts talking jibberish back to me? I won't know what to say."

"You'll figure it out, or you won't get tamales. There are only two possibilities here."

He took the money and headed out. A few minutes later he returned triumphant with tamales in hand.

He was well on his way to fluency in a new language.

"I've been thinking," John said the following day as we took a break amongst the tall grassy weeds along the quiet country road. "You know that saying 'The world is our classroom and the journey is our textbook'?"

"Yeah, I've heard that before."

"That's really true for Davy and Daryl. It's amazing how much they're learning. It's not like we're actually teaching them all that much but yet they're learning. Maybe we should change the saying to add that Mother Nature is their teacher."

As we pedaled through the Mexican countryside, I thought about John's words. Our sons had learned so much in the seven months we had been on the road. We had pedaled 6000 miles and already had a lifetime of adventures. I could only wonder what affect our experiences would have on the boys. Only time would tell.

"Hey, Nancy," John said as we ate tacos at a tiny taco stand by the side of the highway. "What's this in my armpit?"

I pulled out my glasses and took a close look at the tiny black dot.

"It's a tick. And there's another one! They're embedded into your skin."

As we took a break in the deep grass earlier we had seen lots of itty-bitty ticks climbing around, but we had somehow hoped they weren't ticks as we knew them. We were wrong.

Within the next few minutes, John had found one on his arm and another on his back. They were tiny — no more than two millimeters in diameter. It was very easy to mistake them for a small mole or freckle.

"Is this one?" he asked, pointing to a spot on his belly.

"Yep!" I replied after close inspection of the spot.

"And this one?"

"Yep!"

As soon as we arrived at a hotel that evening, all four of us had close inspections for wayward ticks. For the record, I won with twenty-six ticks attached to various parts of my body.

We had been in Mexico for a week and were approaching our second large Mexican city. As we pedaled into the city, traffic grew heavier. After so many days of cycling remote, rural roads with very little traffic, we were unaccustomed to the cars barreling past us. It was unnerving to have cars and trucks and buses blasting past just a few feet from our sides.

A short while later John glanced behind us and noticed a horse cart approaching. We slowed down to allow him to catch up, then we fell in behind him. His cart was wide enough that car drivers had no choice but to go out and around, leaving us a very wide berth.

Pedaling slowly behind the horse cart, I pulled out our cell phone and called our motorcycle club contact in Tampico. "Hey Alejandro!" I said, "We're just now coming into town."

"Keep going a few more miles and I'll meet you at the *barquito* (little boat)," he replied.

A few minutes later, we found the *barquito* on the side of the road — an old boat that had been erected as some sort of monument. Alejandro pulled up in his red pickup and emerged with a big smile on his face.

Welcome to the big city of Tampico! The president of the local motorcycle club met us with his red pickup truck to guide us to his office. I don't know how we would have found our way through the city without him!

"Welcome to Tampico!" he greeted. "Follow me to my office — it's very near."

Well over six miles later, after weaving through dense traffic, we arrived at Alejandro's office where he swapped out his pickup for his motorcycle. "Now we're the same," he grinned.

After a quick stop at the TV station and a few newspaper offices, we made our way to the southern edge of the city to a hotel right next to the bridge leading south to Veracruz. Our faces were covered with a thick layer of black soot from the exhaust of thousands of vehicles and I was mentally fried after navigating the packed city streets.

"Maybe we should rethink our decision not to go to Mexico City," John told me later. "Getting through the city wasn't that big of a deal with the motorcycle helping us. I bet there is a motorcycle club in Mexico City that would help us!"

I vetoed that idea pretty quickly. Remote country roads sounded like a much better idea than cycling through the largest city in the world. Even with motorcycle escorts.

DAY 230 "What can you tell me about the road along the lagoon?" I asked the TV camera crew who accompanied us the following morning.

"The what?" they asked.

"Our map shows a secondary road right along the lagoon," I explained. "We're thinking of taking that in order to escape some of this traffic."

"I've never heard of such a road," said Sandra, the assistant.

"I vaguely remember hearing about that road," Edgar the cameraman told us. "But it's very bad. If you want to go south, you should take the main highway."

We should have listened to Edgar.

The camera crew stayed with us until we reached the small town of Tampico Alto, then we were on our own. We stopped at a bus stop for a break.

"How do we get to the road south that follows right along the lagoon?" I asked a group of people waiting for the bus.

"The what?" came the response. "If you want to go south, this is the road."

We should have listened to them too, but we weren't convinced. Our map showed a paved secondary road following the lagoon, and that sounded like a much better option than dealing with heavy traffic on the narrow main highway. I headed out to find a taxi driver.

"Yes, there is a road there," the taxi driver told me. "Some parts are good, and some bad."

"But the road goes all the way to Hoconcitos?" I asked.

"Well, yes… But it's *feo, muy feo* (ugly, very ugly) down there."

At least we knew the road existed. We pedaled off toward the lagoon. We had learned a thing or two in all those miles we had pedaled and one of them was that roads that motorists consider terrible are very frequently great for cyclists.

"This is great!" John exclaimed once we reached the lagoon. "I'm glad we came this way — it's much better than fighting the traffic on the main road."

"The taxi driver told me there were good parts and bad parts. I'm guessing this is the good," I replied.

A few minutes later our smooth-as-ice pavement broke up and the road was cratered with potholes.

"If this is the bad part, it's not too bad," John said as he bumped along.

A little while later we encountered sand. Loose, deep sand. There was no way to ride the bikes through it. We got off and pushed.

"He said the road got ugly. I guess he knew what he was talking about," I said as I laboriously dragged my bike through the sand.

"Maybe we should have taken the main road after all," John added.

We took a scenic detour to get off the main road and ended up riding for miles down a sandy, muddy road.

But the worst had yet to rear to its ugly head. A short while later we encountered mud. Great big mud puddles filled the road, rendering the whole path nothing but a muddy, mucky mess. We started pushing our bikes through.

"Push!" John shouted. "Come on, Daryl — push! Harder!" Both of them slogged through the deep mud pushing the heavy tandem.

Davy followed behind.

"Keep going, Davy!" I shouted from behind him. My shoes were already completely submerged in the deep mud and I hadn't even entered the really bad part yet. "Don't stop — you'll get bogged down."

Davy pushed as hard as he could, and made it through the muck.

I took a deep breath, braced myself against my heavy bike and headed in. *Schloop!* The mud sucked my bike in. It wasn't going anywhere.

Davy found a relatively solid spot in the mud to lay his bike down and came back to help me. The two of us leaned into my bike with all our weight and managed to dislodge it, but not before we were completely covered in mud up to our knees.

For the next six miles we bounced over the best sections of the bad dirt road, pushed through the sand patches, and slogged through mud puddles. Until we came to an intersection.

In the middle of absolutely nowhere, after fifteen miles of a *muy, muy feo* road, there appeared a brand new, perfectly paved road heading off to our left that wasn't on our map. We had no idea where we were. We sat down to wait.

In time, a motorcycle showed up and told us exactly what I didn't want to hear — we had to continue down the bad road. The good news was that Hoconcito was only two miles away.

It was nearly dark when we finally straggled into the small town at the junction of the road we had chosen and the main highway. We were covered with muck, but there was no hotel to take refuge in. We found a family who allowed us to set up our tent in their yard, bought a few bottles of water to slosh on our legs to get the worst of the mess off, and called it a day.

The next day we rejoined the main highway. It appeared as though it was the lesser of two evils.

We were approaching Poza Rica, our next major city. A couple of days earlier I had whipped out our cell phone, dialed the magic number, and arranged for an escort through the city. Juan de Dios was going to come meet us on the road and guide us in.

A few miles out of town, we stopped to check the map. John and I stood straddling our bikes, heads huddled together studying the map spread out on my handlebars.

"Hello!" a man called to us through the open windows of the run-down building we had stopped in front of. Windows was a misnomer; there were simply gaping holes in the side of the building with old weathered planks nailed in place over them. "Come on in and eat!" he said. "*Yo les invito.*"

Juan de Dios would be coming soon on his motorcycle, but we figured he would see our loaded bikes in front of the restaurant, so we climbed off our steeds, leaned them together against the rough wooden wall, and headed inside.

Hijinio, proud owner of the restaurant, soon delivered a massive mound of fresh fried pork and a bowl of beans to our table. His wife and daughters cooked a bottomless pile of tortillas for us and kept them carefully wrapped in a towel to keep them warm.

We dove in and hungrily set about devouring the feast set before us.

A few minutes later, Juan de Dios walked in with two of his friends. They joined us at the table and Hijinio delivered yet more pork and tortillas. We talked, we laughed, we relaxed. And a few hours later we stood up to waddle back to our bikes for the ride into town.

I pulled out my wallet to pay Hijinio for the delightful meal, but he re-

The owner of this restaurant invited us to lunch. He served us a bunch of pork and beans and a bottomless stack of tortillas. When we went to pay after eating, he wouldn't even hear of us paying.

fused to take payment. "I invited you," he said. "When I invite you, you don't pay."

We had only been in Mexico a few weeks, but had already been on the receiving end of random acts of kindness dozens of times. As we rested at a bus stop, a couple of kids ran up and handed us a bag of apples one day. Another day a family handed us a bunch of chocolate bars as we cycled along the highway.

As we pulled in to a small town one day a man stopped in his car and offered to guide us to a hotel. For the next two days he stopped by the hotel three times a day to make sure we had everything we needed. He happily served as tour guide for the local sights, taxi driver for trips to the supermarket, and waiter at his own home where his mother served us fresh tamales.

We had been blown away by the generosity of the Mexican people we met. After listening to American media making it sound like Mexico was filled with nothing but thieves and drug dealers, we were thrilled to see the other side of the Mexican people.

As we moved farther south in Mexico, the temperature had soared. We quickly discovered the only time we could make any kind of mileage was early in the morning — but most mornings that idea was nixed by heavy fog. It wasn't until nine or ten before the fog burned off so we could get safely get on the road, and by then it was hot.

"Nancy! Nancy!" John awoke me bright and early one morning. "It's crystal clear out — no fog at all. If we want to take advantage of the morning cool, we can do it today!"

We scrambled around packing our bikes and hoped we could get a decent day's distance in. Once we got on the road, we discovered that not only did we have the morning cool to help us along, but an awesome tailwind as well. We flew. By noon we had covered over thirty miles.

"What do you think, guys," I asked as we ate beans, fried eggs, tortillas, and fresh pineapple in a roadside restaurant. "We could break our record today. It's pretty flat and we've got this tailwind to help us. Whaddaya say?"

Davy wasn't at all convinced he could do it until we reached the fifty-mile mark by three in the afternoon.

"Let's do it!" he said as he climbed back on his bike after a break. "Let's bust that record to you-know-where!" All four of us set off pumping like mad.

John and I were growing wearier by the mile, but Davy was a determined machine; he pedaled fast and furious without a break at all. John and I lagged behind and only caught up on the downhills where the extra weight on our bikes gave us a distinct advantage over lightweight Davy.

"We're tied for second place!" I called when we reached 64 miles — our second longest day yet. "Only seven more miles to go before we've broken our record!"

We pushed on.

Perhaps there should have been some kind of celebration when we made that 71-mile mark, but we were all too exhausted. We passed high-fives around, and collapsed onto a bench at the toll booth.

The last three miles to the gas station where we would pitch our tent for the evening were agonizing — and way slower than the previous seventy-one. We slowly ground out the pedal strokes until we reached the local Pemex station where we planned to camp.

As soon as we pulled into the parking lot we were greeted by a Canadian family who was spending the night at the station in their RV. Davy and Daryl climbed off their bikes and headed out for a game of tag with their six kids.

John and I collapsed into lawn chairs in front of the RV and watch the children run and play. How in the heck did they do it? I was more th happy to sit and watch.

As we moved south through Mexico, we cycled through the orange capital of North America where hillsides were slathered with orange trees, then moved on to pineapple country where we enjoyed tall glasses of fresh-squeezed pineapple juice on the side of the road, and eventually into sugar cane territory. I enjoyed watching the changing landscape, but the heat never seemed to change.

Day after day we arose early in the hope of getting on the road before the temperature soared. Once it got really hot, our pace slowed tremendously and we struggled to make much forward motion at all. Sweat poured off our bodies and mingled with road grime flung up by passing trucks.

As much as we wanted showers after a long day on the road, there were many nights when it didn't happen. If we camped in a hidden spot off the road, we had to conserve what little water we had in our water bottles. Occasionally we camped near roadside restaurants where we could sponge off, but it wasn't like standing under a shower watching layers of grime float away.

All that changed when we neared the Yucatan peninsula. Suddenly, we found small rivers and streams for the first time in ages. The kids hurriedly changed into the bathing suits and jumped in. John and I sat in the cool water and relaxed. After so long without water, the small streams were a pure delight.

I always marveled at what the boys wrote about in their journals. "While we were in a restaurant, a little chick got in, but it couldn't get out," Daryl wrote. "I saved it and brought it out to its mommy. It was a really cute chick. Then we left. The day was pretty uneventful except at the end when me and Davy went swimming in a river behind another restaurant. It was fun."

It was 250 miles across the southern edge of the Yucatan toward Belize. As we cut through the dense jungle I was amazed at the diversity of landscape. It seemed like each and every day we found new discoveries around each bend in the road.

DAY 277
Dense green jungle was a constant, but now we regularly came across huge flocks of stunning white birds in small ponds on the side of the road or massive Mayan ruins peeking up above the trees. Although we were close to the famous ruins of Chitzen Itza and Palenque, these ruins were unexcavated. We enjoyed taking breaks throughout the day to scramble on the ancient stone structures.

We pedaled, we sweated, we climbed ancient ruins and suddenly we

Riding through the Yucatan jungle.

were in Chetumal, on the Belizean border. We had cycled 7,410 miles from the tippy top of North America to the southern end and were about to enter a new phase of our journey.

Central America was just a hop, skip, and a jump away.

Chapter 8

Don't Believe Everything You Hear

BELIZE & GUATEMALA

"Avoid Belize at all costs," numerous cyclists had told us. "It's boring and horrible. Stay away."

Seeing as how we had some friends waiting for us in Honduras, we made the decision to heed their advice and make a beeline through Belize. We planned to ride long days with few breaks in order to get through the country as quickly as possible.

That plan came to a screeching halt a few minutes into the country.

We crossed the border and stopped at the first place we saw where we could get come money from an ATM machine. While the kids and I wandered around looking for a bank, John stayed at the plaza to watch our bikes.

By the time we got back with money in hand, John was deeply entrenched in a conversation with a local Belizean. Although they were speaking English, I had a hard time understanding him due to the deep accent but John was ecstatic — he had found someone he could communicate with.

John's new friend filled us in on the history of his country. "Belize was first populated by the Mayans," Albert told us. "Archaeologists estimate there were between one and two million Mayans in Belize at one point. Around 1000 A.D. the Mayan civilization ended, but nobody really knows why.

"Around about the time Christopher Co-

Central America!

lumbus sailed to America, various bands of ship-wrecked sailors, bucca-neers, and pirates started living in Belize. Before long, they started logging the rich mahogany forests of the area to send wood to England to sell.

"In the 1840's we became an official British territory. They called our country British Honduras. A hundred years later our people protested and we finally became an independent country in 1980. We changed our name to Belize in 1981."

We had been in the country a grand total of a few hours, and were already in love.

The twenty miles to Orange Walk passed quickly and the four of us rolled into a riverside resort and piled our bikes together against the wall. John headed off to talk with the owner to arrange for a place to camp while I headed off to check out the restaurant.

"Congratulations!" I heard as I mounted the steps to the outdoor gazebo that served as both bar and restaurant. "You are the most amazing woman I've ever met!"

I glanced around at the few tourists scattered about. Every one of them was applauding... for me!

"I am so impressed with what you're doing!" Stacy said. "Absolutely incredible!"

"I've never seen anybody travel on bikes through here with kids before," added her husband, Jack.

96

Jack and Stacy were cattle ranchers with organic ranches in both the UK and Oklahoma. They had fallen in love with Belize and headed there every chance they had. We were fortunate enough to arrive at the riverside retreat at a time when they were there.

As I walked to the bar, the crowd bombarded me with congratulations and questions. I pulled up a stool at the bar and ended up spending a delightful evening talking with our newfound friends next to the New River.

A couple hours later, I noticed the boys were missing. They had been playing basketball before I headed to Stacy and Jack's room for a shower, but were nowhere to be seen when I came back.

"Have you seen my boys?" I asked.

"They're in the room," came the reply.

"What room?"

"Room 1 — where you guys are staying."

"But we're camping," I responded.

"No you're not," Stacy replied. "We got you a room. You deserve a bed!"

How does one respond to such generosity? How do you say thank you to people who see a need and respond without being asked? I couldn't help but think that it was people like Jack and Stacy that made the world a better place. I could only hope that someday, somewhere, I would be able to pay their kindness forward.

"Look! A monkey!" Davy shouted as he pointed to a tree overhanging the waters of the New River. "And iguanas!"

We were crammed tightly into a tour boat navigating narrow channels of the New River. As we raced upriver, we passed crocodiles, iguanas, and birds by the hundreds. Our guide pulled up beneath a tree and handed Davy and Daryl bananas so they could reach up and feed the monkeys.

"That was fun!" Daryl grinned as he took his seat again. "Did you see how the monkey took the banana from my hand?"

Jack and Stacy had insisted we stay another day in Orange Walk in order to take a tour to some Mayan ruins hidden in the jungle. The two hours spent in the boat to get there passed quickly and before long we arrived at the ancient Mayan city of Lamanai.

It was a relatively cool day, which made wandering around the old stone buildings delightful. Our guide led us from one pyramid to another, explaining the significance of each.

"I bet the Olmecans lived here before the Mayans," Davy said as we approached one particular pyramid. "See that face? That's just like the heads

The High Temple at Lamanai Mayan Ruins is the highest temple in Belize. We all climbed up - it was a long way up! It was interesting on the top as only one side of the pyramid had been excavated. The whole back was still covered with jungle.

we saw up in Mexico. Remember, Mom? Remember how they all had that same kind of teeth? This face is just like those heads."

I was stunned.

Davy, at eleven years old, had connected ruins found hundreds of miles apart by the similarities in style of the carvings.

"Is that right?" I asked our guide. "Did the Olmecans live here before the Mayans?"

"They did," he replied. "This temple is a very special temple — it's the only one they've excavated beyond the surface. For all the other temples around here, they've excavated all the dirt and trees and stuff, but once they reached the stone of the temple, they stopped. This one, however, they continued taking off layers. Archaeologists wanted to know what was inside the pyramid.

"When they had taken off three layers, they found this face from the Olmecans. It shows that there were civilizations in the area before the Mayans. Scientists think that each successive civilization built upon the

98

temples from the previous ones. They decided not to go any farther than this, so we don't know what's inside the pyramid."

"See Mom," Davy grinned, "I told you it was the Olmecans."

Belize continued to wow us with hospitality as we made our way through the country. One night we camped in the yard of a Christian center, another night a missionary couple offered us the use of the Baptist conference center. Cycling was easy and we made good time through the country. All too soon, we met up with Helmut and Anna, whom we had met in Mexico.

"Are you sure you don't want to put the bikes in the garage?" Helmut asked.

"Nah," John replied. "Everyone's waiting in the car. I'll just cover them with the tarp; it'll be fine."

We had arrived into Spanish Lookout a few hours earlier and piled our bikes against Helmut and Anna's RV. Now we were ready to head out for pizza, but a big ol' black rain cloud loomed off in the distance. John and I covered the bikes and we set off.

Sure enough, the cloud delivered just what it had promised — the biggest rain we had seen yet. Rain poured down by the bucketful, wave upon wave of water fell in the torrential downpour. Rivers quickly formed in the streets and the ground turned to mud.

We sat in the pizza parlor with Helmut, Anna, and their six kids watching as the sky unloaded its heavy load.

Once the rain had passed, we all piled back into the car and returned to the RV and our bikes. Panic set in deep in the pit of my stomach when I saw that the tarp had come off.

We were lucky that time; the damage was slight. We had a bunch of wet clothes and John's pillow got a soaking. A few books were slightly damp, but it was frustrating as it so easily could have been avoided.

John and I stashed that experience in our brains, hoping it would remind us of the intensity of Central American rainstorms and the necessity of properly protecting our gear. We lucked out this time, but wet gear could, under certain circumstances, lead to dire consequences.

DAY 286 Shortly after a hearty breakfast of oatmeal and toast, all twelve of us piled into Helmut and Anna's Suburban and headed for the hills. Our destination was a river somewhere in the jungle. We weren't exactly sure where we were going as Helmut had received only vague directions. We figured it would be an adventure even if we got lost.

"You can go upwards from Five Sisters falls until you get to a small waterfall," Helmut's friend had told him. "Then you can hike along the river back to Five Sisters."

"Hike" isn't exactly the word I would use to describe the day's adventure. We slowly made our way down the river, sometimes swimming, other times scrambling over rocks. From side to side we passed, carefully choosing our way around the many waterfalls and other assorted obstacles.

Davy and Daryl were determined to swim every inch possible, so they climbed out of the water only to avoid the worst of the waterfalls. If it was humanly possible to stay in the water, they navigated small waterfalls without getting out of the river.

Late in the day we arrived at a unique feature in the river. It wasn't a waterfall, but it wasn't rapids either. It was a narrow channel, perhaps three feet wide, where the water slurped over a rock and poured into a deep pool on the other side.

"Don't go through it!" I told the boys. "We have no idea if it's sa…"

I was too late. Daryl had been sucked in.

I stood by the edge of the water and watched as his body submerged a few inches under the surface of the water, he slipped through the cut, and disappeared into the depths of the pool.

My heart skipped a beat or two as I waited for him to reappear, hoping against hope that he'd appear unscathed.

It was one of those moments that, in reality was only a few seconds but in my mind stretched to hours. And finally he popped up.

"That was AWESOME!" he shouted. "The water shoved me way down and I couldn't get up, but then it brought me up here. I wanna go again!" He scrambled out of the water to get to the head of the shoot again.

We quickly dubbed the shoot the "Whirlpool Slide" and spent a good hour going through it over and over. As we slowly made our way toward the mouth of the slide, the current suddenly grabbed hold of us and slurped us up. It threw us through the slide and sent us plummeting to the bottom before finally releasing its hold, and we bobbed to the surface.

"The best part of the day was what we call "The Slide," wrote Davy that evening. "There would be a little 'schlurp' that would shoot large amounts of water in a little time and we could go with that water. You would start slow and get a bit faster. And all of a sudden, whoosh! You're down, being pushed this way and that under water. It took several seconds before the current only started to slow. We went down the Slide lots of times. When you're in the 'tunnel' it looks like you're frozen. That's why

Part of our river hike through the jungle of Belize. We named this waterfall "Whirlpool Slide" because you just slide over the edge, then get caught in a whirlpool. Here, Davy goes over it feet-first.

we call it the Iced Zone. We went in feet and head first. It was awesome!"

It was dark by the time we finally arrived back home. All twelve of us were tuckered out but, as it turned out, that river hike was one of the boys' favorite experiences of the entire journey. It was a day we wouldn't forget.

"I don't feel good," Davy mumbled as we approached the border with Guatemala. He was moving in slow motion as I cycled behind him.

"We're almost to the border, honey," I told him. "Can you make it there?"

He had slowed to a snail's pace. The day had started off normally but within an hour, he was crawling.

"My tummy hurts," he said.

We rolled up to the border post and leaned our bikes together outside the immigration office. I dug through my pannier bag to get the passports out, while Davy curled up on the floor of the building.

"I don't feel good," Daryl said as he went over to lie down next to his brother.

Locals and tourists scurried past us trying to get their border formalities out of the way. John and I looked at our sleeping angels and wondered how we were going to deal with this one. The nearest town was only three miles away, but three miles is a long way to pedal when you're sick.

With new stamps in our passports, we roused our children and urged them back on their bikes. Daryl, on the back of the tandem, wasn't too much of a problem as John could carry him along. Davy, on the other hand, needed to propel his bike forward on his own. He could barely keep his head up.

"Come on, sweetie," I urged. "We need to get into town and find a hotel."

It was the slowest three miles on record, but we finally arrived into town and stopped at the first hotel we found. By then, Davy's fever had shot up like a rocket. He nosedived into bed. Daryl followed close behind.

Three days passed. The kids got better, then sick again, then better. Our hotel was hot, sticky and dusty. The water system was broken, so getting water to flush the toilet or take a shower involved a major hassle of rounding up the maintenance man and having him turn on the pump. Washing clothes was next to impossible. We were more than ready to move on.

We weren't completely convinced the boys were over whatever it was that afflicted them, but Flores was only sixty miles away and we figured we would be way more comfortable there than in the border town. As a family, we made the decision to move on.

Morning rolled around and we sprang into action. Davy appeared to be completely better, and Daryl felt fine, other than frequent dashes to the bathroom.

At five in the morning I rounded up a bucket of water to wash the five pairs of bike shorts that had been soiled in the night, strapped the clean, but sopping wet, bike shorts on the back of my bike, and we set off.

We had been amply warned of the first fifteen miles of our journey. It would be a dirt road with dust. Lots of dust. The road was decent as far as dirt roads go, but it was still slow going.

The main problem was the dust. Each truck that passed sent thick, soupy clouds of dust billowing into the air which limited visibility to about fifteen feet at times.

And all that dust came back down eventually — on our sweaty bodies and on the five pairs of bike shorts strapped onto my bike. Mud covered our bodies from head to toe. Sweat dripped down my legs forming little rivulets in the thickening layers of grime. And the clean bike shorts were far from being clean anymore.

But even so, all went well until we approached the final three-mile climb to the pavement.

"Daddy!" Daryl cried just as we hit the incline. "Stop!"

John hit the brakes. Daryl jumped off, ran to the side of the road, and dropped his drawers.

A few seconds later, we were on our way.

"Daddy!" Daryl cried again. "I've got a bloody nose!"

John hit the brakes. Daryl jumped off and lay down in the dust to stop the flow of blood.

A few minutes later we were underway again, but then the road started climbing in earnest. I got off to walk. Then Davy started walking. Eventually, John realized he couldn't make it up either. He started walking for the very first time on our entire journey.

"Push, Daryl!" John shouted. "I can't do this by myself!"

Daryl pushed as hard as he could.

"The bike's going backward! Push!"

John and Daryl struggled with the tandem, stopping periodically for Daryl to make a dash to the bushes or to lie down to stop his bloody nose. I slowly made headway up the hill, counting steps. The hill was so steep and the road surface so bad it took everything I had to move upward. I forced myself to take twenty-five steps before stopping for a breather. My shoulders ached. My legs were trembling. I feared I would never make it to the top.

"Davy, come help me," John instructed. "Daryl's not strong enough, and I can't get this bike up by myself."

Davy headed over to the tandem, and Daryl attempted to push Davy's bike. Daryl and I crawled up the hill, stopping every fifteen feet to rest.

"Put the bike down, Daryl," I told him finally. "Just put it on the side of the road and come help me push."

Daryl and I played a bizarre sort of leapfrog getting up the hill. The two of us pushed my bike thirty or forty feet, then Daryl held my bike in place while I went back down to get Davy's bike and take it thirty feet ahead. Both of us pushed mine… I got Davy's… both pushed mine… I got Davy's….

By the time we reached the top, all four of us were wiped out. It was hotter than blazes — our hottest day yet by far — and we were exhausted. The good news was that we had finally reached pavement. We pushed on.

A few miles later, we found a small village and took refuge in a shop for the afternoon. It had taken us six hours to make twenty-five miles, and there was no way we could ride in the heat of the day. We hung out and drank buckets of water and soda, trying to replenish what we had lost in the morning.

It was 4:30 in the afternoon when we hit the road again — or tried to, anyway. Just as we climbed on our bikes, Daryl got another bloody nose.

"You guys go on ahead," John told us. "I'll take care of Daryl and catch up."

Getting through Guatemala was hard. Both kids got sick at the border and then were sick on and off for the next couple of weeks. Sometimes, we had to pull over to rest on the side of the road. We quickly realized that taking a siesta during the hottest part of the day was a good thing even if the kids weren't sick.

Davy and I rode away.

"Mom!" Davy called out a while later. "I just messed my pants!"

I pulled out one of the now-dry, mud-caked pairs of bike shorts and cleaned them off the best I could, and Davy changed by the side of the road. Just as we were readying to take off, John and Daryl pulled up.

"We're going to have to get Daryl's nose cauterized," John said. "He's had three bloody noses since you guys left."

Just as the sun was setting, we limped — absolutely, completely, totally exhausted — into a small village by some lake in northern Guatemala after cycling a measly thirty-five miles. We ate a quick dinner at a local roadside stall, jumped in the lake to rinse off, and fell asleep on the patio of a generous family who offered to let us sleep there.

As I dozed off, I sent up a small prayer that days like this would be kept to a minimum. I was strong, but not strong enough for this.

We were giddy with excitement about getting to Honduras as we had friends waiting for us there. The Verhage family, including Jesse and Sammy who were near Davy and Daryl's age, were also cycling the Americas and had made their way down from Los Angeles. We had been in contact via email and Skype for five months and couldn't wait to meet in person.

We were so close, yet so far.

The boys' sickness came and went. One day they were fine, and the next sick. Davy sick one day; Daryl sick after that. We feared getting on the bikes as we didn't know what might transpire during the day, but were so antsy to meet up with Jesse and Sammy that we did it anyway. As much as wanted to make a mad dash through Guatemala, we couldn't do it. We cycled as much as we dared, and took many days off to let the boys sleep.

When we cycled, we pedaled past small picturesque villages and green countryside. I enjoyed watching daily life unfold in front of me as I rode by. I loved watching men carrying their machetes out to the fields early in the morning and then back home in the afternoon. Women washing clothes. Corn piles drying in the sun. Thatched roof huts. Kids in school uniforms waiting for the bus. It was simply daily life in Guatemala, yet I was fascinated by it all.

It took us eleven days to ride less than 250 miles, but we finally did it. We were at the border with Honduras. The very next day we would cross into our sixth country and meet another cycling family.

Chapter 9

New and Old Friends

HONDURAS

"How far have we gone?" Davy asked as we pedaled along the remote Honduran road.

"Fourteen miles," I told him.

"Only 29 to go…" he murmured. "I can't wait!"

We had crossed the border a few miles earlier and were headed to Omoa, where we would meet up with the Verhage family. We planned to hang out together for a few weeks and perhaps cycle together. All we knew for sure was that Davy and Daryl couldn't wait to meet up with them.

A few minutes later Davy came up beside me. "How far now?" he asked.

"Sixteen miles."

"Twenty-seven more! We're getting there!"

"And now?"

"Seventeen, honey."

And finally — with eleven miles still to go, they showed up! The entire Verhage family came out on their tandems to meet us on the road.

"I can't believe we finally caught up to you guys!" I exclaimed as I hugged Ciska. "It's so good to finally meet in person!"

The four boys bonded immediately and became fast friends. We stood  around on the side of the road talking in the blazing sun for a few minutes before heading off to a better place — a river a couple miles away. The four kids stripped down to their bike shorts and jumped into the water while we adults chatted on the banks.

It was wonderful to meet up with them after five months of trying to catch up. We first heard from Ciska way back in Utah and had been diligently trying to close the gap since then. It was such a treat to meet up with another cycling family.

All eight of us, on three tandems and two single bikes, paraded along the road toward Omoa, a Honduran resort town on the northern coast of the country. Holy Week was just beginning and accommodations were hard to find. Fortunately, the Verhage family had reserved space for us.

"Let's go on the banana boat!" Jesse suggested as we climbed off our bikes. "It's so much fun!"

Davy and Daryl had no idea what a banana boat was, but were game for just about anything. All four boys took off for the beach.

Normally a sleepy place with little activity, the beach was packed for the holiday. Every type of entertainment possible was there and the boys raced from one to another. They rode a rickety old ferris wheel most likely left over from carnivals in the USA sixty years ago. The ride, powered by an old car engine, went faster than any ferris wheel I had ever seen, and the boys whipped around at tremendous speeds. "Davy thinks wrongly that the reason the U.S. sold it to Honduras is because it was too fast," Daryl wrote in his journal. "The real reason is that it was too old. It just goes fast because the people who work it hooked up a car engine to it. Anyway IT WAS AWESOME."

The four boys played craps and shot rifles at cowboys to win prizes at the midway. They jumped off the town pier, played ping-pong, and swung in hammocks. Hanging out with two other boys was magical.

John and I enjoyed quiet evenings hanging out at the hotel chatting with Michael and Ciska. After being the anomaly for so long, it was great to be around others just like us.

"I want a hamburger!" Davy said as he tied his shoes.

"I want French fries!" Daryl added.

All four kids were looking forward to celebrating Sammy's birthday in Puerto Cortez ten miles away. Our whole crew descended upon Burger King, where we ate until we couldn't eat any more. Ice cream sundaes finished off the feast.

We stopped at the supermarket for some pasta and butter, followed by the meat market for beef. I was looking forward to cooking real food as we had access to a kitchen for the first time in ages. I couldn't wait to cook without having to huddle over a tiny camp stove on the ground. After a quick stroll through the market for fruits and vegetables, we headed back to the bus stop for the return trip.

An old school bus that had long ago given up the ghost in the USA had been revived in Honduras and was parked in a large gravel parking lot. We climbed aboard to await its departure. Shortly after we claimed seats, a young boy about eight years old climbed up the steps carrying a plastic tub full of bottles.

"*Refresco! Refresco!*" he shouted as he made his way to the back of the bus. "Sodas! Sodas!"

A couple seconds later, a teenage boy came in. Plastic bags filled with various vegetables hung from his shoulders and arms. More bags were tied to his belt loops and dangled around his knees.

"*Chiles! Tomates! Cebolla!*" he cried, competing with the soda vendor in volume. "Ten *lempira* per bag! Only ten *lempira*!"

Then came an older woman with an apron wrapped around her waist. "Mangos!" she called. "You want mango? With salt and chili?"

The vendors worked their way through the aisle of the old bus, selling their wares to whoever indicated the slightest bit of interest. Passengers squeezed past the throng of humanity crowding the aisle to take their seats.

Jesse and Sammy, who had been riding local chicken buses for quite a while, ignored the mayhem. Davy and Daryl, new to this novel method of transport, watched with wide-eyed amazement.

A man climbed aboard and stationed himself a short way from the doorway. "Ladies and gentlemen!" he announced in Spanish. "I've got here the most unique, the most effective, the best program for learning English you've ever seen. What makes it so unique, you ask? It is unique because this program not only gives you the English word for things, but also has those words written phonetically in Spanish…." All the people on the bus listened to the salesman with rapt attention.

Once the English language vendor had finished his spiel, he made his way through the bus and numerous people bought his program.

He pushed and shoved through the other vendors to get back to the front of the bus, carefully stashed his fabulous, unique English program in a bag and pulled out a small container of cream.

"Ladies and gentlemen!" he hollered. "I have here the most amazing, the most remarkable cream…."

By this time, we were in stitches at the mayhem, commotion, and sights and sounds around us. Even though we wanted to get back to Omoa, we couldn't help but relax and enjoy everything going on.

The whole time the English/cream salesman was talking, another man was quietly waiting in the stairwell of the bus. In time, the cream spiel ended, he collected money throughout the bus and departed — and the other guy took his spot.

108

Daryl, Davy, and Sammy enjoy the fair in Omoa. This ferris wheel was hooked up to an old car with its body taken off. The operator simply sat on the driver's seat, put it in gear, and pressed the gas pedal with his foot. The harder he pressed, the faster the ferris wheel spun. It spun fast once they got it going!

"Brothers and sisters!" he announced as another soda kid squeezed past him. "I am here to tell you about the love of God." After preaching to the crowd for a few minutes, he pulled out a pile of nail clippers. "And to remind you that God loves you, I've got some nail clippers here for only twenty *lempira* each. Each nail clipper has a picture of the Virgin Mary on it, so every time you clip your fingernails you will be reminded of God's love. And furthermore, these nail clippers come complete with a bottle opener so each and every time you open a beer bottle you will be reminded…,"

Right about then, the bus left the parking lot. Two blocks later, the bus stopped.

The nail clipper preacher climbed down the steps to leave the bus; a soda vendor climbed on. "Sodas! Cold sodas!"

A vegetable vendor climbed on carrying plastic bags draped over his shoulders. "Tomatoes! Onions! Ten *lempira* per bag! You want tomatoes?"

It took well over an hour to ride the ten miles back to Omoa, but it was the most entertaining hour we'd had for a long time.

Semana Santa (Holy Week) was over. It was time to move on. Rising well before sunrise to pack our bikes and get organized, all nine cyclists staying at the hostel scurried around getting ready. As the first rays of daylight illuminated the roadway, we pulled out of the gate in hopes of arriving in San Pedro Sula before the mercury exploded.

Our two families had been joined by a German cyclist, Anya. We were now nine people on six bicycles with three trailers, and we formed an enormously long caravan on the side of the road.

By eight in the morning it was blazing hot. By 8:30 it was blistering. By nine it was downright brutal. We stopped every thirty minutes for water to replace what poured out of our bodies.

At one in the afternoon we pulled into the city and made a beeline for a hotel with air conditioning. And we thought we could cycle in that heat? What were we thinking? We still had two thousand miles before we would reach the equator. Could we possibly do it?

One of my favorite places in Honduras, when I worked there as a Peace Corps Volunteer back in the 80's, was the Bay Islands off the northern coast of the country. I headed up to the islands every chance I got and spent many wonderful hours scuba diving and snorkeling on the wonderful coral reef. I couldn't wait to get back.

We locked our bikes in the hotel storeroom, hopped on a bus to La Ceiba, and got ready to take a boat to the island. But first, we figured we needed some sandals. Seeing as how our plans called for ten days of playing on the coral reefs of the Bay Islands, we figured sandals would be a good thing to have.

The streets were lined with dozens of shoe stores, one after the other. We randomly chose one and walked in. The entire room was packed with rack upon rack of shoes, all randomly piled on the racks with no manner of organization whatsoever. Tennis shoes in size 11 next to size 5 sandals next to fancy high heels in size 8. It was sheer chaos. We started wandering.

Within a few seconds, a clerk approached and we explained what we were looking for. "What about these?" she asked as she grabbed a pair of small sandals that might fit Daryl.

We wandered on to see what else we could find. The clerk somehow knew where each and every pair of small water sandals was hiding; for us it would have been like finding the proverbial needle in the haystack. The funny part was that she insisted on returning each pair we declined to the exact spot it was before as though it had an assigned spot in the randomness.

We managed to find a couple pairs of sandals that would work and headed to the front of the store to pay. We figured it would be a simple enough

On the road with the Verhage family. We took many breaks from the 117-degree heat. When it was that hot, 'stay hydrated' was the key phrase!

process — the clerk writes up a receipt, we hand over the money, and we're gone.

We were learning quickly that things didn't work the same way we were used to.

The clerk did, indeed, write up the receipt and told us the amount. I pulled the appropriate amount of money from my fanny pack and handed it to her. "You pay in the back of the store at the cashier," she told me.

We walked past all the racks piled high with the vast array of shoes, found the *caja*, handed over the money, and she returned the receipt to me with a bright red "Paid" stamp on it. We headed back to the front of the store.

We grabbed the shoes and headed out, but were stopped five feet later. The security guard had to inspect the package, despite the fact that he had been standing there watching as the shoes were placed in the bag. We waited.

As we finally stepped outside onto the sidewalk, I marveled at the sheer number of people it had taken to complete the transaction. How could they possibly employ that quantity of human beings for something so simple?

"May I see the bag?" a woman stationed just outside the door asked. "And the receipt?"

We handed over our shoes and she dutifully inspected the receipt and shoes to make sure they matched, then wrote a complete description of what we were taking from the store into a gigantic notebook. Did she really write down each and every purchase made in the store?

"That's one way of lowering the unemployment rate," John told the boys. "I'm not sure how efficient it is though."

I thought dealing with inefficient stores was difficult, but it had nothing on the culture shock of being thrown into a tourist destination. We had been traveling for ten months and had been off the beaten path nearly the whole time. Every once in a while we jumped onto a tourist route for a few days in Jasper and Banff, Yellowstone, or Moab, but the vast majority of our time had been spent out in the real deal. We had spent our time in your basic, normal hometown America or Mexico or Belize.

Early in the morning we taxied to the dock for the ferry to Utila. What a surprise! Foreigner city. Gringo town. Tourists of every conceivable variety hung around waiting for the boat. Budget travelers and not-so-budget tourists alike crowded into the waiting area.

After being surrounded by local people for so long, it felt odd to be one of many tourists. We didn't even have our bikes with us to set us apart.

There were, however, advantages to being in a tourist town — the main one being food. Although basic food had been available everywhere we had been, in Utila we could get just about anything we wanted. My shopping cart was filled with parmesan cheese, Nutella, cheese, and olives. A walk around the supermarket was the highlight of my day.

The supermarket and snorkeling on a gorgeous coral reef, I should say. I figured being a tourist for a while wouldn't be a bad thing after all.

For the next two weeks, the boys had the run of the island. It was a small, protected place, so there was no way they could get lost or into trouble. The four of them headed out every morning and we saw them only occasionally when they came back for food.

They snorkeled and played tag with local kids. They made sand castles at the beach and jumped off the dock. Every day, they found some new way to entertain themselves.

We arranged for scuba lessons and they enjoyed seeing the underwater fantasyland, including a massive sea turtle. John and Michael took the boys out to an old abandoned ship where they jumped off the deck forty feet from the surface of the water.

The four kids had a blast hanging out on the island of Utila. It was such a small island we let them have free reign of it.

It was a magical couple of weeks away from the bikes and all four of us were rested and recuperated from the many miles we had pedaled. Even so, we were getting antsy to get back on the bikes. We just had to figure out a way to fix the tandem.

If I learned anything from pedaling those thousands of miles, it was that sometimes the unreasonable actually made sense. If you had asked me a few years earlier if it made sense to fly back to the USA in order to pick up a brake lever, my response would have been, "Are you bloody nuts?"

In today's age of communication, where jet planes fly to the remotest corners of the planet on a daily basis, where FedEx and UPS ship packages overnight to anywhere in the world — did it make sense to fly back to the USA to pick up a bike part?

We came to the conclusion that the answer to that question was yes. Sometimes.

As we cycled to San Pedro Sula from Omoa, John's shifter lever had snapped. The hard plastic lever had completely broken off and he was no longer able to shift his front derailleur. We had searched the bike shops in San Pedro Sula for a replacement, but didn't find what we wanted. "If only we could get one from the USA," we thought. "This handle is still under warranty so it would be replaced for free."

We debated for hours whether to fly to the US to pick up a replacement or to have it sent down or maybe to completely redo the tandem's braking and shifting system. There were pros and cons for each.

Festival de los Pinos in Siguatepeque. The boys were right there in the front row trying to catch candies and other goodies that were being thrown from the floats.

Having something sent down had the advantage of us being able to stay in Honduras, but we could be stuck in Honduras for a long time as the mail system was unpredictable at best. In addition, we would need to consider customs duty, which could quite easily be 100% of the value of the item or even more.

If one of us flew to Miami, it would be safer. We could pick up the shifter handle, as well as a number of other items we wanted. With plane tickets costing only $220, it seemed to make sense to fly north.

I left John and the boys in Utila and made my way back to the mainland and to the airport. A friend had invited me to stay with them in Miami, so we chatted and relaxed and shopped for what I needed.

Two days later I flew back to Honduras where the entire crew was waiting for me in San Pedro Sula. The unreasonable had definitely made sense.

It wasn't long before John's bike was fixed and all our new gear was safely stashed in panniers. All eight of us climbed onto our bikes and took off to head south. Davy and Daryl were thrilled to have friends to cycle with. Our enormous rolling train filled the side of the highway with our bright red and yellow bags and, no doubt, we caused quite a commotion amongst Honduran drivers.

We spent our first night camping at Lago Yojoa, the next in Siguatepeque. Our plan to race down to Tegucigalpa came to a halt when we checked into a local hotel in Siguatepeque.

"We're getting ready for a big fiesta," the hotel owner told us. "Tomorrow is our village's annual Fiesta de los Pinos. It'll be a huge celebration — your boys would enjoy it."

114

We were always up for a party.

The best part was the parade; every organization in town took part. The streets were lined with people eagerly watching the bands and floats pass by. Kids sat on dads' shoulders eating cotton candy or ice cream. I guess some things are international.

Davy, Daryl, Jesse, and Sammy stationed themselves right in the front of the crowd, vying for candy and other goodies being thrown from the floats. In the evening, there was supposed to be a huge party at the main square with music and dancing, but pouring rain put a damper on that.

Back in Utila, we had met a few foreigners on vacation from their job in Comayagua and they invited us to the home for street kids where they worked. Their hope was that we could share a bit of the world with their kids; we wanted to expose our children to an unimaginable situation.

All four boys climbed off their bikes when we arrived at the home and ran out into the field for a pick-up game of soccer with the local kids. I sat on the sideline talking with an older boy.

"I was in the USA," seventeen-year-old Manuel told me, "but one day immigration caught me and deported me back here."

"How was it in the USA?" I asked.

"I liked it there. One day I hope to go back — the work is a lot easier there than here. In the US, I just had to wash dishes and mow lawns. Here in Honduras, I have to carry bricks and other heavy stuff all day. It's a lot harder."

"How did you go there?" I asked.

"In bus and train," he told me. "I saved up about 2500 *lempira* to pay for the fares to get to Tijuana. Once I got there, I set out walking through the mountains to get into the USA. I walked all night — ALL night. By the time I reached the highway in the USA my feet were bleeding and I was crying. I met a woman and begged her to help me. She helped me find work. I wanted to stay there, but then immigration came and sent me back. Someday I'll go back. I'm trying to save money for the journey now."

Horizontes al Futuro was a home for street kids that came from families too poor to support them. They were not orphans, but their parents had approached the center and asked for help. Some of the kids had simply been approached on the street by staff at the center. They were allowed to live at the center for as long as they needed to — provided their behavior was in line.

"My mother brought me here when I was nine," seventeen year old Hugo told me. "I had never gone to school until then, so I started first grade when I was ten years old. I stayed here two years, but then my behavior went down the drain so they kicked me out. I went back to La Ceiba and spent two years there."

"What did you do in La Ceiba?"

"Nothing," came the reply. "I lived in the streets again and went right back to my old ways — smoking marijuana and stealing. Then I decided I didn't want that, so I came back. Now I'm in school, but I still have many, many years to go."

Each of the forty-two kids in the center had their own unique story, and I was fascinated to learn some of them.

When dinnertime came, we were invited into the dining room to eat with the kids. I found myself at a table with five kids under the age of ten. Four of them handed their stack of tortillas to one boy who surreptitiously snuck them into his pocket.

"What are you going to do with all those tortillas?" I asked him.

"I have cheese in my room!" he told me with a mischievous smile. "We'll eat tortillas and cheese tonight."

He had spent the day with his mother, and she had bought him a bit of cheese.

"I've got a mountain of cheese!" he declared. "It'll be really good tonight!"

It was such a different life from what my boys had lived. My sons had never gone hungry or needed to fend for themselves. As far as they were concerned, these were simply other kids to play with; their disadvantaged background didn't matter at all.

It was always such a treat to see Davy and Daryl jump right in with other kids. They didn't care what color their skin was or what language they spoke. What god they worshipped or what currency they spent made no difference whatsoever. The boys were able to strip away all those wrappers and see the people for who they were. And they accepted each one as an equal and a friend.

I couldn't help but think the world would be a better place if adults could do the same.

DAY
331

"Do you remember our camping trip to La Tigre?" Claudia asked. "Want to go back up there?"

I didn't have the foggiest idea what she was talking about. A camping trip? With Claudia?

We had arrived into Tegucigalpa a few hours earlier, and I was reunited with the daughter of the family I lived with as a Peace Corps Volunteer twenty-two years earlier. Claudia invited us to her home and, while John and the boys showered and talked with Claudia's daughters, my Peace Corps sister and I chatted and giggled like long lost girlfriends.

At my blank look, she continued. "Remember when we went camping up in La Tigre one night? It was going to be just you and me, but my brother wanted to come at the last minute, so he came too. We didn't have a sleeping bag for him, so he and I shared the one. Remember? It was just us three — that's the only time I've been camping in my life!"

It was amazing. I was back with my family again after all these years. I had dreamed of this day for years. Now I was there with my husband and children. Now, finally, they would understand what I meant when I talked about my Peace Corps days.

"Remember the fish soup?"

"The fish?"

"Yeah, Mom says she'll have lots of fish soup ready for you when you get to Choluteca!"

How could I have forgotten the fish?

I used to leave my village every weekend. Every single Friday I was on the 3:00 bus out of town. My backpack was packed and all I had to do was leave school, drop by the house to get my backpack, and I was off! Except during Lent. Then I left on the 11:00 bus.

I discovered very quickly that Gloria, Claudia's mother and my roommate in Honduras, made the most disgusting, absolutely vile, soup every Friday during Lent. Using some dried fish cakes or some such thing, she made soup for lunch. I hated it. I quickly figured out that I could escape eating it if I took the 11:00 bus out of town. Any excuse was good enough.

"I need to visit the Peace Corps nurse," I would say. "I'll have to leave school early."

"I've got a package waiting for me in Teguc. I've got to leave early to get up there to get it out."

"I need to get to Teguc early to buy toilet paper," I might say. "I need to leave school early."

Each and every Friday during Lent I made up excuses in order to get out of eating Gloria's vile fish soup, but I couldn't tell her I didn't like it.

And so it went for two years. Just before I left the country in 1987, I told Gloria about my dislike for the soup.

"Why didn't you tell me?" she exclaimed. "I can't believe you didn't say anything!"

I could envision the sparkle in her eye as she threatened to make fish soup for me twenty-two years later.

"Goodbye!" we called as the Verhage family pedaled away on their tandems. "Have a good trip! We'll see you sometime!"

We had known all along that the day would come when we needed to part ways, but that didn't make it any easier. We had been traveling together for over a month and it had been a very special time. We wanted to spend time with Claudia in Tegucigalpa, and even more time with her mother in my Peace Corps village, and there was nothing for the Verhages.

We planned to meet up again someday, but we had no idea when that day would be nor where. All we knew was that it would happen — some day, some place. We would make it so.

One part of our hearts rode away with the Verhages, but another part of our hearts couldn't be happier with where we were. We hung out with Claudia and her family for a few days. They took us to small villages surrounding the capital city. We spoke at the girls' school. I visited the Peace Corps office. It was wonderful to be back in my old stomping grounds.

As wonderful as it was to see Claudia, I wasn't home yet. My feet were itching and my heart was aching — I wanted to get back to Choluteca, my *pueblo*, and see Gloria once again. And I wanted to be there on Mother's Day.

Our initial plan was to ride down in the car with Claudia and her family for lunch, then return to Tegucigalpa the same day, but somehow I wanted to pedal to Choluteca. I wanted to arrive in my pueblo on my bike on Mother's Day. And so it was that I hatched the plan to send all our weight down with Claudia in the pickup and we would ride empty. Eighty-six miles — our longest day by far — but with no weight we felt we could make it.

At the crack of dawn, just as the first rays of the sun peeked over the surrounding mountains, we were off — finally heading to my village! It was a tough day, with an enormously long climb to get out of Tegucigalpa, and plenty of other steep climbs scattered throughout the day, but we finally pulled into Choluteca. We made it! We made it back home.

Adrenaline flowed as I pumped those final few miles to Gloria's house. My house. Where I lived some of the most special years of my life. Nothing mattered to me at that moment except that I was home. I fell into Gloria's arms and tears flowed freely. I was home.

There's something about the Peace Corps and the friendships we make while living in those villages that can't be replicated, and John and the boys stood off to the side and knew that this was my moment. It was special to them in that they had heard my stories for years, but we all knew that moment was mine.

We spent the next three weeks enjoying being part of my great big ex-

Gloria and I. It was such a treat to see the woman I lived with when I served as a Peace Corps Volunteer many years ago.

tended Peace Corps family. We slept in the same room I had stayed in all those years ago. Davy and Daryl attended classes at the same school I taught at twenty-two years earlier. We went to birthday parties and to the beach. We made traditional *mondongo* (tripe) soup. It was a wonderful vacation from our bike trip and we all rested and relaxed and enjoyed our time together.

The day finally came when it was time to move on. Nicaragua was only a few miles away and we needed to continue on our journey. With heavy hearts we packed our bikes and headed out to the road. The whole village came to see us off. As much as I knew we needed to leave, I left yet another part of my heart in Choluteca. With tears slowly rolling down my cheeks, I turned around for one last glimpse of the family I loved so dearly, then looked ahead to adventures in yet another country.

Chapter 10

A Step Back to a Simpler Time

NICARAGUA

Our plan was great. We would get up at 3:30 in the morning in order to hit the road in the predawn darkness to take advantage of the morning cool. By ten in the morning it was already blazing and forward progress slowed dramatically.

We vowed to wake up early every morning and ride hard for three or four hours. With any luck, we would be at the next hotel by then. We had long since given up hope of sleeping in our tent as it was nothing but a sweat-fest all night, and we were exhausted by morning. Seeing as how cheap hotels were available in most towns, we made the decision to hop from one to the next rather than attempt camping.

True to our word, we awoke in the middle of the night to get packed. Even so, sweat dripped off my nose and trickled down my legs as I stashed everything on the bikes. It was still dark when we climbed on our bikes and headed out.

In the predawn darkness, we made our way through a town slowly coming to life. Oxen pulling a cart plodded through a river beneath a bridge as the vivid sunrise lit the sky behind them. School kids dressed in uniforms sat in the seats of bicycle rickshaws as their drivers transported them to

classes. Mothers balanced plastic buckets of corn on their heads as they walked to the mill. Old men sat in the shade of trees chatting with others. Young men wielded machetes with precision as they cleared grasses out of drainage ditches.

It was life in rural Nicaragua. Everyone

Throughout Central America, we got up a 3:30 AM in an attempt to beat the heat. We were on the road just as the sun started to peek over the horizon. By eight in the morning, the heat was stifling.

rose early to take advantage of those few morning hours before the heat drove them to their hammocks.

As I cycled through those small towns, I couldn't help but think back to my time in India. The first time I visited the country, I traveled by train and distinctly remembered gazing out the train window at all those small villages and the multitude of daily activities that whizzed past before my eyes. I got a split second glimpse of rural life, but when the train finally stopped in the city and I got off, life was very different. That was when I made the decision to go back with a bicycle. Seven years later John and I cycled Pakistan and India and I got to see those villages in a way I never could while traveling at a faster pace.

My love affair with life in rural villages around the globe never faded, and I loved watching life unfold in front of my eyes. I loved slowly pedaling through remote towns and seeing people go through their daily routines. It reminded me of a simple life not dependent on all the trappings of modern society. Even though life was hard in the villages, there was a simple joy there that I didn't see in the cities.

A few hundred miles into Nicaragua, we awoke to pouring rain and made the decision to hang out for the day. The boys and I headed into town

School kids take a "taxi" to school.

to wander around and I watched them navigate around the foreign city.

One would think that eleven-year-old boys would be a bit intimidated at the thought of wandering around a city where they didn't have the foggiest idea where they were and didn't speak the language fluently, but Davy and Daryl were fearless. They headed into the thick of the busiest market with absolutely no fear of getting lost.

What blew me away was that they never got lost. Ever. The only explanation I could find was that my boys had developed some sort of homing device that always led them back to our hotel. Through their travels, they somehow developed an instinct to be able to find their way back no matter how many twists and turns they took.

As we meandered through the market, I thought back upon our year on the road and was filled with wonder. Wonder at how much my boys had changed and at how they had grown. It seemed like such a short time ago they were babies; now they were young men. They were intelligent, confident men who were capable of taking on the world — and succeeding.

DAY 354 "I'm getting worried," John said a few days later. "Davy's still not back." He had left twenty minutes earlier to buy some soda, and we hadn't seen him since.

"Do you know where a store is?" John had asked him.

"Yep! Sure do!" Davy replied.

We figured he would go to the small shop around the corner from the hotel, buy some Pepsi, and be back in a couple minutes. When he wasn't back twenty minutes later, we started to worry. What if he got lost? Did he even know the name of our hotel? How would he ask for help without speaking Spanish?

John and I dashed out the door to start the search.

"I wonder if he might have gone to the supermarket," I said. "It's a fair distance, but I think he knew the way there. I'll head that way and see if I can find him."

"I'll go the other way," John said — and we parted ways.

I found some artisans in the park who were just packing up their wares for the night. "Have you seen my son? With blond hair?"

"He passed by here about fifteen minutes ago. He was going that way." They pointed toward the supermarket. He was headed for the supermarket after all!

But when I got there — no Davy. Not a trace. I panicked.

I raced out of the supermarket and dashed back toward the hotel. If he wasn't there, I'd call the police... I'd round up a search party... I'd... I had no idea what I'd do.

As I passed through the park again, one of the artisans called out to me. "He just came by here! We told him you were looking for him at the supermarket."

I turned around and raced back and found Davy waiting for me in the parking lot of the supermarket.

Why did I doubt him in the first place? He knew perfectly well where he was going. He knew how to get back to the hotel. Would I ever learn to trust his abilities?

Poor John hadn't been so lucky. He wandered the pitch-black streets in growing panic. Davy and I returned to the hotel, and I had no idea where to begin looking for Daddy. The kids and I waited.

Ten minutes went by and I knew John was panicking. Fifteen minutes. I could picture John wandering the streets of the Nicaraguan city frantically looking for his son. A full thirty minutes after Davy and I got back, John finally returned and his heart could — at last — slow down.

The takeaway? The kids knew where they were going. John and I needed to trust them.

We had battled a killer headwind for sixty miles to arrive into Managua. We had been invited to a university to talk with the students so made our way there first. Late in the afternoon we were ready to head to a hotel.

"There aren't any hotels around here," our university host said. "This isn't the part of town with hotels, but I know of one about five miles away."

It was rush hour and, after eating something that didn't sit well, my stomach was doing acrobatics. As we readied to take off, I began to feel

Aldolfo and his sister Maribel, who were such a great help to us, continued their inspiration by seeing us off as we headed south out of Managua.

more and more nauseous, and started to wonder how in the heck I was going to manage to get my bike and me to a hotel.

"I think I'm going to throw up," I mumbled as I climbed onto my bike.

We headed into the fray with John and Daryl leading, followed by Davy, and I took up the rear.

"Hey John!" I shouted to be heard above the roar of rush-hour traffic a mile later. "What do you think about asking here at the church — we may be able to set up our tent."

"Hurry!" he replied. "The sun is setting fast and, if this doesn't work out, we'll still need to get to the hotel."

I raced into the church and explained our predicament to Adolfo, the youth pastor at the church.

"I don't have any problems with you using a Sunday School room for the night," he said, "but I don't have the authority to make the decision. I'll call the head pastor."

But the head pastor was preaching in some other church and couldn't be reached.

"I'll try the administrator," Adolfo told me. "Just wait."

With each passing minute, the sun fell a couple more inches and it was getting dangerously close to the horizon. My stomach was doing flip flops.

124

John had left the boys in charge of the bikes outside and come in to find out what was happening.

"Don't worry," Adolfo assured us. "We'll figure out something, but right now, I have to go record my TV show. Just wait."

We waited. Darkness fell and reaching the hotel was out of the question. My stomach did cartwheels and I was shaking like crazy. I lay down on the floor of the church while John went out in search of food for the kids.

Still we waited.

At 7:30, Adolfo finally finished with his show. I was passed out on the floor. John couldn't speak Spanish and had no clue what was being said. I dragged myself off the floor — and made a mad dash to the bathroom to throw up.

True to his word, Adolfo figured out something. John and the boys took all three bikes to the retreat center, while I rode in Adolfo's car. At 8:30 pm, we arrived at the center and — despite a few more mad dashes to the bathroom to throw up — we were checked in.

For the next week Adolfo took care of us. He play tour guide and showed us Managua. He served as our ambulance driver when John sprained his thumb and needed to get x-rays in case it was broken. Adolfo quickly became a friend and we were honored to get to know him.

Granada was a mere thirty miles away, but we managed to fritter away the whole day getting there. We passed a spot on the side of the road where people were bringing their fruit to a truck to sell and we stopped to talk with the driver. We found a bus stop with a supermarket right across the street so we ran over to buy a rotisserie chicken, a bunch of bananas, and chocolate milk before hanging out at the bus stop eating. We stopped at an American-owned bike store on the side of the road and talked with the owner who came to Nicaragua in the 80's to help out the Sandinistas and never left. While at that bike store, we met up with another long-distance cyclist and spent hours talking with him.

Most cyclists couldn't figure out how we traveled so slowly, but we rather enjoyed our slow pace. We enjoyed taking time to see what was out there rather than racing to reach the hotel and then locking ourselves in for the remainder of the day. Our way of travel didn't work for other cyclists, but it worked just dandy for us.

We celebrated one year on the road our final day in Nicaragua, with temperatures well over one hundred degrees. It was hot. Bloody hot. All four of us struggled in the heat. No matter how long we cycled in the heat, we never got used to it. It sapped our energy like an SUV guzzled gas.

I became convinced it wasn't possible to drink enough water to stay hydrated in that heat. Between the four of us, we carried three gallons of water on our bikes and when it was really hot, we filled them at least twice during the day. In addition to the many gallons of water we consumed that day, we managed to go through two liters of orange juice, 1.5 liters of milk, two liters of Squirt, two liters of Pepsi, and another soda with dinner!

I started thinking I should just hook myself up to some kind of automatic funnel — pour water in and have it come right back out through my sweat pores. Why even bother with the stomach?

We realized we needed to take extra precautions in the extreme heat. As we sweat, we lost not only water but precious salts as well and those needed to be replaced. I asked around and discovered that local pharmacies sold packets of rehydration salts designed for babies with diarrhea. I bought a bunch of them and we carried them in our panniers. On really hot days when we were in serious danger of dehydration, we added a packet to our water bottles and felt much better. They tasted vile, but it was worth it to keep our bodies functioning well.

We knew we still had many miles of heat through the rest of Central America before we would get up in the Andes and it would cool off.

Chapter 11

A Border is Just a Line on a Map

COSTA RICA

"Congratulations Daryl," I said. "You've just entered your eighth country."

My son turned to me and said, "What difference does it make, Mom? Crossing a border doesn't change anything. A border is just a line on a map."

As I passed through the border formalities, I thought about Daryl's words. He was right. We were still in the Central American jungle. People in Costa Rica looked exactly like those in Nicaragua. They spoke the same language and worshipped the same god. Nothing changed as we crossed that border except that we spent a different currency.

After spending so many years of my life poring over maps and dreaming of visiting far-flung places, I guess I had developed a bit of a "map syndrome." I saw a very distinct, physical line at that border. I saw a new country with a new government. In my mind, each country was a separate, unique entity and, of course, the people belonging to that country were unique and different from those from neighboring countries.

Daryl's words brought me back to reality. There was no line at the border. The people who lived on one side of the border were no different from those who lived on the other. My sons, at age eleven, understood that. I, at 48, was still working on it.

I was pedaling along the Costa Rican road and was quite bored. It was just another day

127

in paradise. Nothing in particular to look at. No villages to keep me entertained. Just mile after mile of lush green jungle.

Then I thought, "This is crazy! You're in Costa Rica and you're bored? Costa Rica is paradise on earth! It's a traveler's utopia! Costa Rica is one of the premier vacation destinations in the world. And you're bored?"

I feared I had become jaded. I was so accustomed to fabulous scenery and people that I zoned out when I only had tropical jungle to look at. We were pedaling through a lovely area, and I wanted to fall in love with the jungle and the monkeys swinging in the trees.

Yet I wasn't quite there. I was so focused on getting out of the blasted heat that I wasn't paying attention to the small details surrounding me like I generally did. My mind was so centered on getting to the next town and away from the interminable heat that I missed everything else.

For the first time, I started to wonder if it was all worth it. Cycling through the jungle was miserable; there's no other word for it. We awoke in the middle of the night and packed up as sweat poured out of our bodies. By first light we were on the road, but it was still blazing hot and the humidity level made it hard to breathe.

I mentally drew a map in my head and figured we still had eight hundred miles of jungle. Eight hundred miles of being covered with layer upon layer of sweat, sunscreen, and road grime. Eight hundred miles of nothing but lush green jungle on either side of the road. Was it worth it?

I wasn't quite ready to give up yet — that would come later — but I knew I wasn't enjoying the journey.

The following day I sank even lower. We had been amply warned by other cyclists about two things: the hills and the truck drivers in Costa Rica. By all account the hills were the steepest in Central America and the drivers were the worst. In our short time in the country, I had to agree.

We slowly ground up hill after hill while sweat fell like a river from beneath our helmets. At one point, John even took his helmet off and strapped it onto his trailer — he figured he was safer without the helmet than blinded by sweat.

And the truck drivers did their thing. Their Costa Rican thing. Regardless of whether the far lane was open or not, each and every truck driver that passed us held his ground and refused to budge an inch. It seemed like the attitude was that the lane belonged to them and four crazy cyclists hugging the edge of the road were nothing more than pests.

The third time a truck cut me so close my knuckles actually scraped the side as it whizzed past, I lost it. "What the hell is with this country?" I screamed to nobody in particular. John and Davy were too intent on controlling their own bikes on the narrow road to pay any attention.

"This is crazy!" I hollered into the jungle.

All I wanted was to get safely through the country and out the tail end. Was that too much to ask?

When we finally arrived at a hotel — shell shocked and frazzled — we knew we had to make a decision. There was no way we could stay on the main road; we weren't prepared to sacrifice our lives for our dream.

According to the map, we had one option — a small road that hugged the coast all the way to Panama. We would rejoin the main highway just a few miles before crossing the border. Our map indicated a 45-mile stretch of dirt road and, seeing as how it was rainy season, it could be terrible. We decided to take our chances and know we might have to push our bikes through knee-deep mud farther south but that would be better than facing certain death from Costa Rican truck drivers.

DAY 376 We set out the next day with the goal to make it as far as we could; we were on a mission to get out of Costa Rica. By early afternoon we could see the black roiling clouds moving our way and, with a massive downpour imminent, we pulled off the road into a small village to find a hotel. Strangely, hotel rooms with four beds were terribly difficult to find in the country. We settled for three beds, and Daryl and I resigned ourselves to sharing a small single bed once again.

Just as we tucked our bikes away under an overhang, the rain came. In the tropics, rain moved in fast and furious. In a matter of minutes it can go from bright blue sunny skies to pouring, pounding, frenetic rain. And it could pass just as quickly.

The rain came down by the truckload. Huge, heavy drops poured onto the corrugated tin roof above us and it sounded like we were standing inches from a train track as a train whizzed by. We shouted to be heard, but even then the deafening sound drowned out our voices. Waterfalls cascaded off the roof and splashed to the ground in massive puddles.

Davy and Daryl couldn't pass it up. "It's raining!" they shouted. "Can we play in it, Mom?"

Both kids dashed out into the pouring rain and delighted in getting drenched to the core in the downpour. They screamed. They shouted. They danced and twirled as raindrops quickly saturated their clothing.

"Can we jump in the pool, Mom?"

"You might as well — you're already as wet as you can get."

"Woo hoo!" came their shouts as they charged to the pool in the pouring rain.

We got to our hotel just before a torrential rain started. Davy and Daryl loved playing in the hotel courtyard.

I cycled along the road on Day 381 watching bright red macaws flying wild in the tropical jungle surrounding us. During our breaks, I watched leaf cutter ants making trails through the dense forest undergrowth. It was another day of listening to the loud raucous 'caws' and light dainty 'cheeps' of birds mingling with the raw, abrupt 'whoops' of toads.

We had just stopped to check into a hotel when a big black SUV pulled up in the parking lot next to us and a woman popped out. "LouAnn is my neighbor!" she told me. "She just told me about you guys via email this morning and now we find you on the road! What a small world!"

One of my dearest friends in Boise just happened to be this woman's neighbor? And she just happened to be here in Costa Rica? And we just happened to check in to a hotel right around the corner from her vacation rental? Can the world get any smaller?

Tonya invited us to her house for dinner and we spent a delightful evening eating hamburgers and swimming in the pool with her kids, but I spent the whole time puzzling about the serendipity of it all.

It is 25,000 miles around the world at the equator. There are seven billion people on our planet. And in the middle of nowhere in the Costa Rican jungle, we met another family from Boise. And not just any family, but the neighbors of our friends. I couldn't help but think, all over again, that our world wasn't nearly as big as we tended to think.

"I just took a hot shower!" Davy declared with a dreamy grin on his face. "It felt so good!"

For the first time in ages, our hotel had hot water and we spent the afternoon basking in the luxuriousness of it. As near as we could remember, the last time we felt the decadent sensation of warm water flowing over our bodies was back in San Pedro Sula in northern Honduras. It had been so hot for so long that we didn't need hot water, but it felt lovely anyway.

Our simple lifestyle had become normal for us and we only realized what we were missing when there was some kind of reminder like hot water. The only belongings we owned were those we carried on our bikes. We each had two sets of clothing and wore the same set until we could wash it, then we changed into our clean clothes. The boys had a handful of toys; I had a small container of beads. We didn't need much.

It wasn't all that long ago that we had lived in our large home in the suburbs. We had two cars in the driveway, one of which was rarely used. The boys had buckets overflowing with toys of every imaginable variety, yet most were sorely neglected. We had an entire closet full of towels and four times as many sheets as we had beds. Amazingly, we didn't miss any of it.

I wondered how long it would take for us to fall into our old patterns once we got home.

We were getting tired of crowds of tourists everywhere. It seemed that ever since we arrived into Costa Rica we had dealt with hordes of tourists everywhere. We couldn't even get away from it when we were cycling in what appeared to be remote areas — in the middle of nowhere we saw signs for ziplines or ecotours. There was no way to escape, no way to immerse ourselves in the "real" Costa Rica — I feared "real" Costa Rica no longer existed.

As eager as we were to get off the tourist route, we had heard so much about Manuel Antonio National Park that we couldn't pass it by. And true to its promises, we saw lots of wildlife — a couple of three-toed sloths way up high in towering trees, a whole messload of monkeys, iguanas scurrying here and there, woodpeckers drilling holes in trees, and bats hanging upside down. The boys spent hours and hours playing in the waves and running through the rainforest.

Heading south out of Jaco we hit road construction, and they only had one lane available for traffic. Unfortunately, they crammed two lanes-full of traffic into that one lane! I didn't think these big trucks would make it, but they managed to squeeze through.

What was not impressive, however, were the crowds. The pathway through the rainforest was little more than a four-lane divided highway filled with two-legged traffic. Enormous groups with guides blocked the path as their guide explained this or that. Telescopes were set up in the middle of the path to better see the animals.

Although I understood the need for tourist dollars, I couldn't help but wonder about the long-term effects of droves of tourists. We were there in the off season, yet the country was swarmed by people from all over the world. I wondered how long they would be able to sustain that level of tourism before it collapsed. People came to Costa Rica for the native culture, but how long could it last with this level of outside influence? Was this whole tourism thing a good thing in the long run? I had only questions, but wished for answers.

As we continued south along the coast, the entire road was lined with condos and development offices and great big tourist traps. The beach was lovely, but all the junk that came with it was awful. Trash littered the side of the road, traffic was crazy, big shops sold souvenirs, and tourists bought it all. We couldn't wait to get off the beaten path and back to normal Central American life.

For weeks we had been fretting about the 45-mile stretch of dirt road our map indicated. Since it was rainy season, we had feared it would be one big mud-fest and we would be slipping and sliding the whole way.

We set off bright and early, just in case those forty-five miles took us all day. It was easy! In fact, the first half of the dirt road had such a good surface we could maintain our regular speed. The road did deteriorate toward the end, but not too badly.

In the end, our biggest enemy ended up being dust on the road rather than mud. We reached the end totally covered with filth. Our bodies were slathered with dust mixed with copious amounts of sweat. At least we found a hotel with a shower at the other end.

We were on the road by 5:30 in the morning on our last day in Costa Rica. Three hours later we arrived at the border with Panama — the border! We could have crossed the border and made it another fourteen miles to a small town, but opted to take the day off.

"You want a room all the way until tomorrow morning?" the clerk puzzled when we checked in at 8:30 in the morning. I'm relatively certain they don't get people wanting to spend the day in the border town.

We found a wonderful hotel with enough beds for all of us and air conditioning. It was actually considerably cheaper than many of the other places we had stayed in the country. "Today we got to the border of Panama," Davy wrote. "We are staying at a GREAT hotel. It has one fan, 3 single beds, one double bed, two chairs, one table, one toilet, one sink, and one shower with a glass panel to stop the water. It even has air conditioning!"

We enjoyed the day relaxing in the cool air-conditioned room, watching TV, reading books, and drinking Pepsi. I wandered around, enjoying the hectic delights of the duty-free market.

If only all of Costa Rica had been as delightful as the border town, it would have been one of our favorite countries. We could only hope Panama would be better.

Chapter 12

Crossing Over

PANAMA

It was love at first sight. I had totally expected to love Costa Rica and hate Panama, based on what we had heard about the countries. It didn't take long to change that. Within thirty miles, I was in love with Panama.

Panama had good roads with two lanes for each direction so cars could go out and around us rather than screaming past a couple feet from our sides. Although the heat hadn't abated, it didn't seem nearly as bad when we were able to cycle without fearing for our lives every time a truck screamed past.

When we arrived into David, we found a hotel room with *four* beds (such luxury!) and air conditioning and a private bathroom for half the price of itsy-bitsy, teeny-tiny rooms in Costa Rica. I found a supermarket a few blocks away with lots of food, including American food at better prices than we paid in the USA. The hotel had fast internet and friendly people. Such a contrast to what we had found in Costa Rica!

The one thing that hadn't changed was the rain.

We had noticed dark clouds amassing ahead of us for a while as we pedaled toward the end of Central America. We knew rain was imminent — the only question was how long it would hold off before dumping. We pedaled harder to make it to the next town before the skies opened up.

Three miles from town, we began to feel the first drops. It was starting; within minutes it would be pouring. All four of us kicked it into high gear and pedaled furiously. Maybe, just maybe, we could make it before the massive downpour started.

Unfortunately, we didn't.

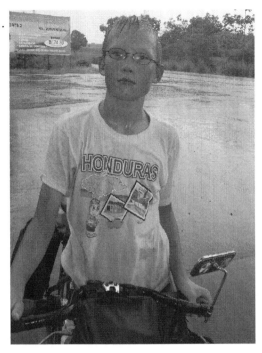

Throughout Central America, we were fortunate in that we always managed to find a place to wait out the rain. This day in Panama, we didn't make it. It started to rain about three miles from our destination. With less than a mile to go, Davy got a flat tire and had to walk in the rain.

We were less than a mile from town and shelter, with rain pouring down and creating rivers in the road, when Davy stopped.

"I've got a flat tire!" he called ahead to John.

"I can't fix it now!" John yelled back. By now the rain was coming down in waves. "You'll have to walk into town."

Davy walked his bike while I pedaled slowly to stay with him as water poured from the sky. By the time we pulled into a gas station and took shelter, we were drenched — soaked to the core. John sat down under the awning and took Davy's wheel apart.

I watched my husband fixing Davy's wheel and thought about how lucky we had been. "You know, John," I mused. "This is the very first time we've been caught in the rain on the road."

Rainy season had started when we were in Honduras, but somehow we had managed to evade the rains. There had been many times when the clouds dumped their loads immediately after we had checked in to a hotel, or when we were sitting in a restaurant eating, or just as we passed under a bridge so we could wait it out. Somehow we always avoided the rain. Until today.

In all honesty, it wasn't all that bad. In fact, it cooled us off and felt quite good. I knew that would change quickly once we got up in the Andes though.

DAY 394 We headed out just as light began to illuminate the road and climbed hill after hill through northern Panama. Amazingly, the kids actually wore long-sleeved shirts for a little while in the morning. We had climbed enough the day before that it was actually quite cool at daybreak.

It wasn't long before the boys peeled off those shirts and the sweat-fest began. Mile after mile we ground up long, agonizing climbs and plunged down the other side through dense tropical forest as the sun beat relentlessly.

But all too soon — and a bit too far away from Santiago — the sky began to darken and we knew it was just a matter of time before the skies would open for their regular afternoon purging.

We raced up the hill trying to reach shelter before the rain came. Just as the rains started we reached a little roadside stop with a couple of small restaurants, a bar, and a small store. We ordered lunch and waited for the rain to pass.

But it never did.

In time, it became apparent that our choices were to ride in the pouring rain or pitch our tent in the vast, covered area of the bar. We opted for the tent.

It didn't take the boys long to get involved in a soccer game with local kids, and John and I spent a quiet afternoon watching the rain create more puddles in the parking lot.

The bar, which had been very quiet all day, was quite the rocking place later that evening. A small crowd hung around, getting drunker by the moment, and we began to question the wisdom of setting up our tent in the middle of it all. I sought out the owner of an empty restaurant next door and asked permission to sleep in there.

It looked perfect — totally sheltered from the rain and plenty big enough for all of us and our bikes. The trouble was that it was hot. I mean hot. The second we walked through the door, the heat hit us like a wall.

"I say we don't bother with the tent," I told John. "Let's just put the tarp down and lay out the mats. We don't have to worry about rain since we're inside, and it'll be a lot cooler without the tent."

What we hadn't counted on was the bugs. Thousands of them. Maybe millions. They bit hard and fast and itched like crazy. Bug spray was totally ineffective against them. We pulled out our sleeping bags to protect us from the bugs, but then we sweated like overheated pigs.

We lathered more bug spray on in the hopes that the next layer — unlike the previous umpteen layers — would somehow be the magic bullet and provide some relief. It didn't.

Bright and early we were up and packed; we weren't sleeping anyway. In an extreme sleep-deprived state, we managed the eighteen miles into town on autopilot and started the search for a hotel.

We narrowed our choices to two hotels — a slightly more expensive one with a swimming pool, or a cheaper one with a room big enough for the bikes to fit in that was right next to the public pool. In the end, we opted for the cheaper one, piled the bikes in, showered, and headed out to Domino's for pizza.

But when we came back — half asleep and dreaming of naps — the room was blazing hot. Hotter than the oven they had cooked our pizza in. The air conditioner was busted.

We packed everything up and moved across the hall.

"Get your swimsuits on!" I told the boys. "We'll head over to the pool."

Daryl went in the bathroom to change — and came out a few minutes later. "The toilet won't flush. There's no water in it." Sure enough, there was no water in the sink or toilet.

I marched back up to the desk. "Would you get someone to fix the water? We don't have water in the bathroom."

A few minutes later, we were at the pool. "We are closing right now," the guard told us. "We close at three, and it is now only four minutes til."

Could anything else go wrong?

By the time we went to sleep that night, it had all worked out. We got the water turned on in our room, the air conditioner worked so well we had to pull out our sleeping bags, and we were able to spend the afternoon in the pool at the hotel we almost stayed at. As always seemed to happen, things worked themselves out and all was well.

What didn't work itself out so well were Davy's toes. Three weeks earlier Davy told me his toe was hurting. I figured it was an ingrown toenail and cut the nail way back. I figured that was that.

A few days later, he complained about it still hurting. We started cleaning it every morning and night with alcohol and bandaging it up real well with antibiotic ointment, but the infection was deep within and the medicine wasn't doing a whole lot of anything.

It took a couple of weeks for it to finally open up and drain. We were happy to see that and hoped we could get it cleaned up for good.

A few days later, it closed up again.

When we got to Santiago, we trotted off to see the doctor.

"It's ingrown," the doctor told me. "But it's ingrown way down next to the base. The only way to get to it is to remove the nail."

I translated for Davy. "He's going to pull out my toenail?" he grinned. "How cool! I wanna watch."

Davy sat on the table and watched as the doctor cleaned his toe, then injected the painkiller. Davy gritted his teeth and clung to my hand as the medicine slowly went into his toe. "That hurts," he mumbled. "It really, really hurts."

Once his toe was deadened, however, Davy was fascinated. The doctor grabbed a pair of clippers and cut straight down into the nail, then pulled half of it out using some sort of needle-nosed pliers. Blood oozed as the doctor dug down into Davy's skin to find the piece of nail that had embedded itself inside.

"That's so cool," Davy said as Doc poked and prodded and groped. He was fascinated by the whole process. "Look what he's doing!"

After what seemed like forever, the doctor finally held up his bloody pliers with a piece of toenail about ¼" across in the jaws. "This is what was causing the problems," he told Davy as he gently placed the piece in Davy's hand.

"Look at this!" Davy exclaimed as he held out the chunk of nail for me. "Look at what was in my toe."

We put our son on painkillers and antibiotics and resigned ourselves to hanging out for at least a week before he could ride again.

That afternoon I went out to buy food and as I walked into the lobby of our hotel I happened to glance up at the wall — and found myself staring smack dab into a map of the Americas. My eye immediately went to Panama and then it traveled up to Prudhoe Bay. Wow! It was a long way up!

Then my eye traveled down — way down to the tip of South America. The most amazing part of it was that the way up was significantly longer than the way down. I understood that a lot of that phenomenon had to do with the distortion in the map and all that, but so what? The map told me we were over halfway to Ushuaia!

I had spent hours poring over maps and studying them carefully, but they were all regional or specific country maps. There was a definite sense of accomplishment watching us move slowly across the map of British Columbia or Mexico or Costa Rica, and I knew those were small areas and it wasn't all that big of a deal to get across them. I hadn't seen our journey plotted out in its entirety since we left Alaska and was amazed to see how all those little maps added up. All those itty bitty steps, every single one of those four hundred days, had merged to create a great big line on the map.

I loved our maps; they were wondrous things. They showed where we would find cities and towns. They told us where the rivers were. By using our map, we could calculate how far we needed to go and how much food and water we needed to stock up on. Our maps were wonderful things indeed.

But there were some things maps didn't tell us — and it was the things unsaid that could sometimes cause problems. Maps, for example, didn't tell us when we were arriving at a major tourist trap resort town, and that could be a problem.

When we finally got back on the road, we pulled into a town called Santa Clara and tried to find a hotel. Unfortunately, in major tourist resort towns hotels were expensive — very expensive. We were in trouble.

We traipsed from one hotel to another hoping that somehow one of them would be reasonably priced. Nothing. Nada. There was no way we could find anything even remotely resembling a figure in our price range.

"Why don't you camp on the beach?" an American retiree from Indiana asked. "I've got my RV parked here and they are only charging me $5/ night. Surely they'll let you camp here for a reasonable price."

We had been reluctant to camp because of the heat — cramming four hot, sweaty bodies into our itty-bitty tent made for an uncomfortable, sleepless night. Camping on the beach, with the sea breeze blowing, sounded delightful.

We pitched our tent in the soft sand and looked forward to a night listening to the waves crashing onto the beach. Unfortunately, the cool sea breeze died out just about the time we crawled into the tent.

The night was utterly still with not even a hint of a whisper of wind and the tent was stifling. High temps and humidity levels through the roof didn't lead to comfort in a tent. I fell asleep about thirty minutes before John woke me up in the morning. I was exhausted.

We packed up and climbed on our bikes. Within the first hour, my stomach started hurting and it periodically cramped up, feeling like someone took a staple gun to my gut. I had gotten dehydrated the day before and was still feeling the effects of that. My head was spinning and I wasn't quite sure which way was up. And I was tired.

I was pedaling up steep hills on one of the hottest days ever, already dehydrated and getting more so by the minute, sick to my stomach, dizzy, and tired. I wasn't sure I would make it to town.

Eleven-year-old Davy, knowing I was feeling lousy, fell into position right behind me. All day he stayed right on my tail — never dropping back, never pushing on ahead. Escorting me.

Throughout the day I glanced in my rear-view mirror at the young man behind me. "I'm so glad he's there," I thought. "If I collapse and tumble down, Davy will be able to help. He'll know what to do." I was very comforted by that thought.

I suppose there comes a time in every parent's life when they realize the tides are turning — when they realize their children are, all of a sudden, able to take care of their parents rather than being cared for — but I never expected that day to come so soon.

There was a part of me who would willingly collapse into my son's arms, knowing he was a young confident man capable of rising to whatever challenge lay before him. There was another part of me, however, that rebelled at the idea. I was Mom. I was the provider. I was the strong person in this relationship. Davy was my son, my baby. My little one whom I cradled in my arms and kissed his boo-boos. It wasn't time for him to grow up. I wasn't quite ready for that to happen.

And yet I couldn't turn back the hands of time. My boys were becoming young men.

I realized I had been taking my boys for granted. When we first started our journey over a year earlier, I was bursting with pride seeing the boys rise to whatever challenges we put in front of them, but lately I had been taking them for granted. There was no longer any doubt that the boys could ride their bikes to Argentina, so I forgot how remarkable they were. I was reminded that day just how much I had come to rely on them.

DAY 405 It had taken us two weeks to travel through Panama until we reached the Panama Canal. The Bridge of the Americas was a daunting sight: a huge structure of gleaming metal rising up out of nowhere, a long expanse of narrow roadway with no shoulder whatsoever. But in the end, our little family went up and over. As I pedaled over the bridge separating the Americas, I quickly peeled my eyes away from the road for a quick second. Below us dozens of boats floated in the water waiting to pass through the canal. Fortunately, the traffic wasn't bad since it was Sunday.

We reached the other side and were funneled onto a major highway into the city. Not wanting to battle traffic for miles, we took the first exit, figuring we would wind our way through the back streets toward the center of town.

A woman flagged us down as she pushed her baby in a stroller. "You guys aren't planning on going through up there, are you?" She pointed ahead, exactly where we figured we would go. "They'll rob you blind if you try to go through that neighborhood."

We were headed right for it.

Davy and Daryl watch a hospital boat go through a lock at the Panama Canal.

We flagged down a passing police car. "Would you please escort us through the neighborhood up there?" we asked. "We've heard it's nasty." With a police escort we slowly made our way through town.

It wasn't until we were checked into a hotel and had everything unpacked and up to the room and the bikes safely stored away in the garage that it hit me — WE CROSSED THE PANAMA CANAL! That was huge. Enormous! We had traversed the entire continent of North America by our own muscle power!

And Daryl? Mr. Literal, himself? "We didn't pedal it all," he reminded me when I congratulated him on his accomplishment. "We took a ferry across that river in Belize and we had to ride in the pilot car through that construction zone in Canada. Remember?"

But gosh darn — I was proud of my husband and boys. They had hung in there every inch of the way. They dealt with freezing cold and blistering heat. They ground up hills and battled headwinds and swatted more mosquitoes than I could count. And they did it all with smiles on their faces. Well, maybe they weren't actually smiling, but close enough.

And I was proud of me, too. I had come a long way since those days in Idaho when I questioned my abilities. I had pedaled 9100 miles through nine countries. I had mastered the fine art of rounding up food for my family. I had made it up massive climbs and survived bitter cold. I was strong and healthy and more proud than I ever thought I could be.

We were south of the Panama Canal, and that was pretty darn cool.

Photo Section

All our possessions for the next three years were in these boxes. Everything was checked and double-checked to make sure we were adequately prepared.

John and Daryl edge closer to the Brooks Range.

Davy and I ride toward the Brooks Range on the Dalton Highway.

Davy climbs up Atigun Pass (4,738 feet). This was our first pass and, although it was relatively small, was a huge success.

Davy & Daryl

The Yukon. As the morning clouds burned off, a warm sunshiny day was revealed to us.

Enjoying a gorgeous day on the Alaska Highway in the Yukon.

143

Enjoying the Canadian Rockies in one of the few precious hours without rain in Jasper Provincial Park.

It was always a treat to see elk on the highway.

The summit of Saddleback Pass. On our one non-rainy days on the Icefields Parkway, John and the boys went for a hike. I stayed in the campground near the wood stove.

Grand Teton National Park. Although the Tetons dwarfed us, we were riding on a valley floor so it was relatively flat.

Riding through the Bitteroot Valley in Montana.

Davy rock climbs under a giant arch in Arches National Park.

Not only was it cold and windy as we rode through Texas, there were also many hills to climb.

Spider Rock in Canyon de Chelly. According to Navajo legend, Spider Woman climbed up to earth on Spider Rock. She taught the Navajo people how to weave.

John and Daryl ride past the famous red rock mesas of New Mexico.

The northern Mexico countryside consisted of mostly shrubs and a few trees.

We spent the day at the La Venta Museum in Villahermosa. It was a huge, mostly outdoor museum in the middle of the huge city where they allowed the jungle to grow. A bunch of huge artifacts from the

Olmecan civilization were moved there from La Venta. Davy later recognized the carvings in Belize as being the same style.

Mayan city of Palenque.

The Mayan city of El TajÌn flourished from 600 to 1200 AD.

147

Cycling on the southern coast of the Gulf of Mexico in the Yucatan.

Everyone in Belize was very friendly and we saw lots of smiles and waves.

A squirrel monkey in Manuel Antonio National Park, Costa Rica.

We saw more ox and donkey carts in Nicaragua than any other country.

A small town in Honduras.

The sight of civilization and the big city of Cartagena definitely brought a smile to my face. I had been miserable on the five-day boat trip to Colombia, but the adventure of the open sea was worth it.

The San Blas Islands between Panama and Colombia. The Kuna people travel from island to island in small dugout canoes. If the wind was favorable, they put up a sail to help them out.

149

It was late and getting dark when we arrived in Medellin. On top of that we were exhausted. Consequently we didn't have much energy or time to pick a hotel. We ended up in the red light district with bars, prostitutes, and homeless people everywhere we looked.

The Central Hotel in some small town in southern Colombia where we stayed for the night.

While staying in Pimampiro we participated in a holiday that celebrated the miraculous appearance of a beautifully painted virgin in a cave in a village in the mountains. More than 500 people walked the twelve miles up to the village where it appeared.

Davy checks out some Galapagos sea lions and vice versa.

John's mother met us in Quito. We headed to Otavalo for the Saturday market - the largest market in all of South America.

As we descended from the paramo to the Amazon basin, the vegetation gradually changed from drab grassland to dense jungle.

The Peruvian desert changed every day. It was really rocky and hilly one day, but we never knew what tomorrow would bring.

After riding over 180 miles on the steep mountain roads, we finally hit the Altiplano in Peru where it was flat.

Hiking around Pisac, Peru near Machu Picchu. We were very winded as the altitude was near 11,000 feet.

The Floating Islands of Lake Titicaca.

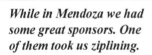

While in Mendoza we had some great sponsors. One of them took us ziplining.

We loved camping out when it wasn't bitter cold! We could read or play cards in the tents then, but when it was cold we had to crawl into our sleeping bags very early.

A rancher and his alpaca check us out.

Mile after mile of grasslands, better known as the Argentinian pampas.

Tierra del Fuego. It was cold out but we had waited out the wind the day before and didn't want to wait longer. Seeing as how the wind was not quite so strong, we bundled up and took off.

Aguilar the gaucho was a wonderful man — with a fierce storm imminent, he let us sleep in his shed.

We visited a colony of 120,000 Magellanic Penguins who live on an island near San Julian in southern Argentina.

154

*The end of the road and the end to a
way of life which we will always cherish.*

*A Vietnam vet wanted Davy
and Daryl to take a picture
of themselves with this flag
in Ushuaia.*

*It really meant a lot to us that people cheered us on and welcomed us back in Boise.
It made the trip much more meaningful and worthwhile when we knew we shared it
with such enthusiastic supporters.*

155

Chapter 13

Sometimes You Can't Stop and Smell the Roses

COLOMBIA

South America! I could see the faint outline of something solid off in the distance and knew it could only be a brand new continent. I couldn't wait to get there — in more ways than one.

In order to get through the Darien Gap, a 75-mile stretch of swamp between Panama and Colombia, we had taken a boat. Guinness World Records had given us the choice of flying or taking a boat and the boat sounded like the better idea. We would spend a lovely five days at sea and visit the pristine San Blas Islands on the way.

What we hadn't expected was rough seas. Within minutes of boarding the boat, thirteen out of the fifteen people on board were puking over the edge, including three of us. The two days we spent in the protected waters of the islands were wonderful, but I was more than happy to see Cartagena, Colombia, come into view.

I was also excited at the idea that we would finally step foot on South America. North and Central America were behind us. Colombia would be the start of yet another chapter in our journey.

Every cyclist we knew who had passed through Colombia ranked it as one of the best countries ever. Everyone we knew who had never been there said we were crazy to go. "It's way too dangerous," they said. "You'll be caught up in the drug cartel violence for sure." We opted to believe the cy-

Ranchers used mules to haul their milk to the road where they delivered it to trucks.

clists and were looking forward to exploring the country.

What we looked forward to more than anything else was the Andes — specifically, the high altitudes of the Andes and the cooler temperatures. We were tired of the sweltering heat of Central America and ready for a change. We knew the change would come with tough climbs into one of the steepest mountain ranges in the world, but we were ready. We were more than ready; we couldn't wait.

In order to reach the mountains, however, we had to slog through three hundred miles of coastal lowlands.

We cycled out of Cartagena on a Sunday morning and immediately after leaving the city began pedaling up a gentle climb. I couldn't figure out why, but I died. I didn't have any energy at all. The hill wasn't a bad one, as hills go, but I was struggling big time. I seemed to be panting like crazy and felt weaker than a rag doll.

So when we pulled into Turbaco twelve miles from Cartagena, we looked for a hotel. Unfortunately, the only one in town wouldn't accept kids. We sat on the side of the road trying to figure out our next step.

Right about then, a cyclist pulled up and started asking the normal questions — where were we from? Where had we cycled from? How long had we been on the road?

When he found out we were looking for a place to stay, he asked, "Why don't you stay in my house? I have an empty house just a block from here.

Five sloths lived in a big tree in the central park of Tolu. Most of the time, the sloths were way up high in the branches and were totally still. One day, this sloth was only about fifteen feet off the ground.

There used to be renters in it, but they recently moved out and it is now sitting empty. There are no beds, so you'll have to sleep on the floor. What do you say?"

And so it was that we met Tony. Tony brought us to his church service — a small home service with about fifteen people. And the pastor of the church happened to have a house that wasn't rented at the moment either — with four beds. Why didn't we stay there?

John and I spent a delightful afternoon with Tony and the pastor while the boys played with the kids from church. Colombia was off to a very nice start.

We played leapfrog with a milk truck as we cycled along the rural Colombian road. Early in the morning, local ranchers brought milk jugs to the highway on horses, mules, or bicycles. As we pedaled by, we watched the ranchers standing on the side of the road with one or more milk jugs. Eventually, the milk truck arrived and the rancher helped the driver empty the jugs into the big vat in the bed of the truck. As the truck drove away, the rancher hooked the jugs back on the horse for the trip home.

We had spent the morning cycling through the flat coastal lowlands, playing leapfrog with the milk truck for much of it, when we arrived at the junction for a small town.

We turned off the road to head into town. I left John and the boys at the park while I headed out to find a hotel.

A few minutes later I arrived back at the park to find my three boys standing with their necks craned backwards, gazing up into the tree. "Nancy, look!" John said as he pointed up amid the branches. "There's some kind of animal up there!"

Sure enough, curled up in the middle of the leaves was a furry animal. I turned to the man who had pointed it out to the boys. "What kind of animal is it?"

"A sloth," he told me. "There are a bunch of them who live in this tree. Look! There's another!"

The four of us stood gazing upward at the slow-moving animals for a while before slowly making our way to the hotel.

Later in the afternoon, after a nap and a shower and a movie on HBO, I headed out for a wander around town. I smiled at the man with the beautiful smile who sold me corn on the cob on a stick, chatted with the fruit vendor selling watermelon and tangerines, and gossiped a bit with the man in central park who made me a delicious glass of fresh-squeezed orange juice.

There was something about those small villages that I loved. That was why I enjoyed traveling on bikes — even when it was blazing hot. The bikes allowed us to get a glimpse of life that most travelers missed.

We were getting closer to the Andes. As we cycled through the flat, boring, green countryside, I couldn't help but think about the massive mountains just ahead of us. As excited as I was to BE in the mountains with cool temperatures, I was getting cold feet about getting there. How bad would the climbs be? Was I strong enough to handle them?

I knew John and the boys could make it, but could I? Our very first climb would be a whopping six thousand vertical feet in just twenty-three miles. All four of us were seriously scared of the climb. We knew it would be, by far, the worst we had encountered yet. In my mind, I built it into some kind of monster to conquer — a monster bent on destroying us. I feared it would do exactly that.

We had left the broad open plains behind and snaked our way up into an ever-narrowing river valley. Rather than the broad views of open fields we had seen since we arrived in Colombia, we saw only lush green hillsides on either side. All day the hills grew in magnitude as we penetrated deeper and deeper into the valley.

As the hills grew, so too did the water sources. For miles on end we pedaled past springs gushing from the hillsides, and there were many streams and waterfalls. "Can we, Mom?" Daryl asked.

"You bet! Jump in and enjoy!"

John and I sat dangling our feet in the cool water and chatted. "You know what amazes me?" John asked. "Davy and Daryl are incredible. They never complain about anything, no matter how hard it gets. I've heard it said that life is 10% what happens to you and 90% how you react to it and our kids are living examples of that. Our journey has been hard for months now — this heat is excruciating. But the boys just take it as it comes and never complain."

"What I love about them is how much they appreciate simple things," I said. "Did you read Daryl's journal entry a few days ago? He said, 'A girl gave us free water today. I suppose that's not a big deal in the US, but here where most people are poor it's a lot.' That kid — he has a good heart."

We finally arrived in Puerto Valdivia, at the base of the climb. We had been warned by other cyclists that the climb started immediately after crossing the bridge just out of town and didn't end for twenty-three miles. I sat on the balcony of our hotel and gazed up at the mountainside we would climb the next day. It was a daunting sight watching the headlights far above me knowing that my legs would somehow have to propel me up there.

As much as I had enjoyed the transition in countryside, the transition I was looking forward to the most was a change in climate. The very next day we would leave the heat of the lowlands behind when we climbed into the Andes. I was excited to pull out my long-sleeve shirt again. I wouldn't even have minded having to dig my winter jacket out from the depths of my pannier.

What I was not looking forward to was the climb itself. Although I knew we would face many more climbs in the months to come, this one was the most significant. The Andes had arrived.

 We packed up in the morning not quite sure exactly what was coming, but knowing it would start immediately after the bridge fifty meters from our hotel. I jumped on my bike and set off...

...and my chain just rattled around. Somehow, who knows how, my derailleur had broken.

All my pent-up nerves bubbled over and tears started falling. "What can I do?" I babbled. "I can't ride the bike if I can't shift."

"It'll work," John assured me calmly. "I'll just take a few links out of the chain and set it on your biggest chain ring. From what I hear, you'll be in your lowest gear all day anyway."

Fifteen minutes later we were on our way. I had only one gear, but it didn't matter much anyway. Just as promised, the climb started immediately past the bridge and it was just as bad as we suspected. As a family, we decided we would make it three miles before taking a break. Those three miles nearly broke us, but we made it.

After a quick break, we set off again. Once again, we set our sights on three miles. Less than half a mile later, we were walking our bikes with our sights set on fifty steps before stopping to catch our breath. We plodded along counting steps. "13 ... 14 ... 15 ..." We huffed and puffed as we counted together out loud. "... 48 ... 49 ... 50"

After each break, we decided on a new goal: fifty steps, then thirty, occasionally seventy-five.

Fortunately, it was only really steep for a little while before leveling out somewhat and allowing us to pedal once again.

Sweat poured off our bodies as we struggled up the monster. Slowly, ever so slowly, we made headway. And then, we found a swimming pool — a waterfall-fed swimming pool, no less. "Can we, Mom?" The boys jumped off their bikes, changed into their swim suits and dove into the frigid water. John and I sat beside the pool and relaxed.

Finally, after climbing 2700 vertical feet, we arrived into Valdivia and faced the climb to end all climbs. The hill into the center of town was crazy steep and we didn't even attempt pedaling, but just started pushing. It wasn't long before helpful locals came and helped. With three kids pushing each bike, we arrived into the plaza and began the next phase of our day.

Our day, as long as it had been, was not over. We still had to unload the bikes, carry all our gear up to our third-floor hotel room, and then haul the bikes and trailers up. Only then could we think about showers and food.

But we were in the Andes! Our climb had resulted in a delightful change in climate and it felt great. We still had half the climb in front of us, and a broken bike to deal with, but we were thrilled with where we were.

Early in the morning I kissed John goodbye and headed out to the bus stop. It was a four-hour ride into Medellin, where I hoped I could find a derailleur to replace my broken one. I had spent a few hours the previous evening researching bike shops and could only hope I'd be able to find something. My derailleur was a standard part and, given Colombia's dedication to cycling as a national sport, I was hopeful but still expected a difficult day.

As it turned out, it couldn't have been easier. I got off the bus two blocks from an excellent bike store, bought the part I needed, ate lunch at a nearby restaurant, then climbed back on the bus to return to my family. My broken derailleur cost us a day, but was a pretty easy fix.

It was a long grind up the rest of the hill. We still needed to climb another 3300 feet before reaching the top. We pedaled up switchbacks and through dense fog. Small houses covered with bright flowers were scattered along the side of the road. Local cyclists took the easy way up by holding on to the backs of trucks as they slowly made their way to the top. We did it the hard way.

Late in the evening, just as the sun set behind the mountains, we saw the twinkling lights of Yarumal and rejoiced in the completion of our first major climb. The Andes hadn't defeated us yet.

I had never really thought about how controlled OUR society is. For ages we had been cycling through hot lowlands. I never thought about how that affected the way people lived and just took it for granted that everything would shut down and the streets would be deserted in the middle of the day. The transition, starting in Mexico, had come gradually and the changes were a natural part of it.

All of a sudden we arrived up in the mountains and, in the blink of an eye, everything changed. I walked out of our hotel room in the middle of the day to find something to eat, and found a teeming mass of humanity. Old men stood on the sidewalks chatting, young men hung out in a restaurant drinking beer, a bunch of pool players cheered and shouted. I had forgotten that life goes on in the middle of the day sometimes.

For us, the change meant a whole different set of clothes. We rummaged around in our panniers to find clothes we hadn't seen since Texas. We started wondering if we might even end up having to wait a bit in the morning before getting on the road so it could warm up a little bit.

It was my 49th birthday and John's and my 18th anniversary and we planned an easy day and great celebration in Medellin that evening. It was a fabulous day with awesome weather, bright blue skies, and cool mountain temps. The terrain was a bunch of rolling hills along with some pretty amazing downhill runs.

It was late afternoon when we entered the city and asked directions for the center of town from a motorcyclist. "I'll take you there!" he said. We took off after him.

At the next stoplight, our escort started talking with another motorcyclist who was stopped next to us. "I'll join you!" he said.

As we penetrated deeper into town, we picked up another escort at each stoplight. They were happy to lend a helping hand, and we were thrilled to have the escorts.

By the time we finally made it to the center, we had only one hour of daylight left. We thanked our escorts, and I left John and the boys with the bikes while I took off in search of a place of stay.

Hotel after hotel turned me down as they didn't allow kids. One looked good, except we would have to haul everything up to the fourth floor. It would have to do, so I headed back to grab my family.

The four of us made our way through the crowds to the hotel. "Someone just took the room you looked at," the receptionist said as we traipsed through the door with our fully-loaded bikes. "We don't have another one that will fit you."

Pushing our bikes, we headed out into the fray. By now, the sun had bid us goodnight and complete darkness would be upon us within minutes. We stopped at one hotel — the halls were too narrow to get the tandem through. Another one was too small for the bikes. We raced from hotel to hotel, hurriedly checking out each one.

At last we found a place and hurriedly ferried stuff up the stairs. Panniers, handlebar bags, drybags, Davy's bike, my bike and trailer....

"You can't put all that in your room!" the woman said. "There is no way it'll all go in there."

"It'll fit," I told her. "Trust me, we've had all this stuff in much smaller hotel rooms before."

"But it's too much!" she insisted. "If they come for an inspection and find all that stuff, I'll be in big trouble. You will need to get another room and put your bikes in there."

In the end, we managed to convince her it would all fit in one room. I suspect the fact that we were all bone tired and it was completely dark outside helped. Could she really make two little kids haul everything back downstairs and head out into the darkness?

We stashed our gear, washed our hands, walked to the nearest restaurant for a chicken dinner, took ice cold showers, and collapsed into bed. The birthday/anniversary celebration could wait.

We spent a delightful week in Medellin exploring hands-on science museums, playing at water parks, and eating chocolate cake before heading out once again.

Shortly after leaving Medellin, we pulled into a small town at eight in the morning after a massive 5000-foot descent. As we entered town, we saw signs advertising a water park. "Can we stay here?" Davy pleaded. "Please!"

"It's a long way to the next town," Daryl reasoned. "It might be hard to make it there. Maybe we should stay here."

And so we checked into a hotel before many people were even out of bed and headed over to the water park for the day. Sometimes you just gotta do it, if you know what I mean.

DAY 451 We were close, but oh-so-far away. Manizales, where some readers of our blog had offered us the use of their vacant home, was only fifty-five miles away. We were excited about taking an extended break from our bikes and about the idea of having a house to stay in. The house was empty so we would sleep on the floor, but that was okay — it wasn't a hotel. Now we just needed to get there.

The trouble was two-fold: Manizales lay about 7000 feet higher than where we were and my knee had started to hurt. A major climb with a bum knee didn't sound like a great idea.

To solve the problem we came up with a brilliant plan, or at least it sounded brilliant at the time. We would completely unload the bikes down below and put everything in a taxi. I would then go up in the taxi and stash everything in the house, then taxi back down. The next day, with only toothbrushes and water bottles, we would do the climb. We figured we could do it in one day without weight.

Surprisingly, our plan was executed without a hitch. Our gear was up above and we only had to pedal to the sky. After driving up, I had an inkling of what was to come, but somehow perceptions are different in a car than on a bike.

The first thirty miles of the day were easy — eight miles screaming down the 1500 feet we had climbed a couple days ago, then following a river for a while. We were all feeling quite confident about getting to the house — only another twenty-five miles to go. How bad could that be?

How bad? Real bad. As soon as we hit the steep climb, we also hit road construction. For five miles we battled bumpy roads and dust so thick there were times I couldn't see Davy a few feet ahead of me. Within minutes, the dust had mingled with copious amounts of sweat on our bodies and rivulets of sweat ran through it creating white streaks down our legs. "How much more of this construction do we have?" Davy called back to me. "I don't think I can handle much more of it!"

In time, we passed through and hit pavement again. *Manizales 19* the sign read. Nineteen kilometers to Manizales — then we had to get over to La Enea, the small community the house was. We figured we still had about eighteen miles to go. And then it turned steep.

One thing we had learned about the Colombian Andes was that Colombians didn't seem to understand about grades. Anything over about 7% grade is tough on a bicycle. Really tough. We ground our way up the 10 – 12% grades feeling more and more grateful that we had ditched our weight. We were in our bottom gears as we slowly snaked our way up the mountainside.

Finally, we saw the cut about four miles up. "That's got to be it!" John said. "You can see where the road cuts through up there. That should be the top and then it'll (hopefully) level off. It'll take us an hour to get there though." We only had two hours of daylight left.

We made it to the cut, came around the corner and saw the road zigzagging up one side of the ridge, then doubling back on the other side. At the top, there was yet another cut. "Maybe that's it!" We pushed on.

About that time, my knee started twinging again. Every once in a while my right knee sent out sharp stabbing pains that nearly crippled me. I pedaled with my left leg for a while — which is nothing but difficult when you are climbing a 10% grade. Gradually, I brought my right leg back into play, terrified of when the twinges would come again.

With about twenty minutes of daylight left, we pulled up to the bus station in Manizales. "Do you know where a hotel is around here?" I asked a guard. "We had hoped to make it to La Enea today, but it'll be dark soon and there is no way we can make it."

"La Enea is only two or three miles from here," he said. "You should be able to make it."

We debated. Go for it? Or find a hotel? We were so close — so close we could taste it! And yet, we were beat. Fried like an egg. Tired beyond belief. We had no idea what the terrain was like, except I knew the last mile or two were up, and I knew it was farther than two or three miles. Other than that, I remembered nothing from my visit the day before.

In the end, we opted to go for it, and set off into the growing darkness. I happened to have a couple of small blinky lights with me so I dug them out and we strapped them on our bikes.

The four of us pedaled like mad in an effort to get off the Pan-American Highway with all its traffic. Fortunately, we had a decent shoulder to ride on, but it was still scary. We didn't like riding at night with inadequate lighting.

It was totally black by the time we saw the first sign for La Enea. We pulled off the road and asked a group of men how to get to the house. "Fol-

We took a rain day in Rosa. Good thing we did!

low the main road another mile or so and get off at the next exit. Then go up all the way up to the end of the road."

Did I mention that it was up? One more mile of climbing on the main highway, then another mile of climbing into town. Up, up, and more up.

We stopped in town to pick up some chicken and fruit, and then continued up to the house.

The house! We made it! It was just a small, simple house, but it was a place to call home for a while. We were thrilled to be there.

For six weeks we hung out in Manizales and did a whole lot of nothing. We managed to get the essentials done, but mostly we just relaxed. John rebuilt the bikes and replaced all the worn out parts, Davy had his big toe on his other foot operated on to remove another nasty ingrown toenail. We took advantage of the time down time to work on the boys' math lessons. I wrote and played with my beads and enjoyed cooking with a real stove. The boys discovered gaming places where all the local kids hung out playing video games. It was just what we needed after sixteen months on the road.

As wonderful as our time in Manizales was, we knew the time was coming that we would need to move. Our quest for the end of the world was still on. We set a date and began to prepare ourselves to leave our new home.

"Mom," Davy said the day before we were scheduled to head out. "My toe hurts."

Davy took off his shoe and peeled off his sock. His toe, the one that had been operated on in Panama, was bright red and infected. The toenail had started growing back in, but was embedding itself in the skin again. He would need it removed.

We spent a couple of days trying to figure out what to do. Should we stay in Manizales for three more weeks? Or find another village in Colombia? Or push on to Ecuador? Unfortunately, our visas were due to expire so we couldn't remain in Colombia long enough for our son to heal from surgery. We had no choice but to push on.

The race was on.

It was a race against time as we cycled through southern Colombia. With each day, each mile, each pedal stroke, the clock was ticking.

Each night I managed to round up hot water from the hotel staff or a nearby restaurant to soak Davy's toe with epsom salts. Each morning I bandaged the toe with antibiotic ointment knowing very well it was only a matter of time before infection set in. How long could we keep it at bay?

All went well for the first few days. We made decent mileage and had no unforeseen detours or detentions. The only detour we made was to head into Cali to pick up Kindles for the kids; we had discovered that reading material in English was too hard to find. Now, with their new electronic books, they had as many books as they wanted to read.

We were feeling good as we pulled into Popayán, knowing we only had another 250 miles to go — 250 miles of soaking and bandaging and praying the microbes would hold off a few more days. But shortly thereafter, our plan began to unravel.

We awoke to pouring rain in Rosas and delayed our departure until it stopped. It wouldn't be a hard day anyway, so a 10:00 departure would be fine. But then came the dreaded words: "I don't feel good." Davy made a nose dive back into bed, which led to our first unexpected day off. Tick, tock, tick, tock...

By the next morning, the rain had stopped and Davy was better, so we pushed on. That night in Estrecho, however, was a nightmare. I awoke in the middle of the night with the most intense back pain I had experienced in years. I was in agony. I slithered out of bed onto the floor and crawled on my belly to the drybag with our sleeping mats. Somehow I got the mats out and under me, where I slept the remainder of the night.

Carlos, our host in Pasto, cycled with us to Pilcuan where we spent the night with his family. As it turned out, Davy and I left our bikes there for a few weeks in order to race to Ecuador.

But then morning came, and we faced a dilemma. Push on? Or wait it out? Tick, tock, tick, tock. Davy needed surgery and we didn't know how long we could wait.

John and the boys helped me pack my bike and we set out. I could pedal relatively pain free, but getting on the bike was torture. Getting off was even worse. I hobbled into restaurants like some crippled, bent over old woman. My walk was one of those crooked Hunchback-of-Notre-Dame shuffles, but each mile closer to Ecuador was one mile closer to Davy's surgery.

"Today was very hard," Davy wrote that evening. "We went over lots of hard hills in the heat. It was very, very hot. I drank both my water bottles even after one was refilled and I was still very thirsty. Finally, after hours and hours of riding, we got to a small town. Mom's back was hurting a lot."

DAY 494 By the time we pulled into Remolino, I was hurting. Each pedal stroke sent bolts of pain radiating throughout my lower back. We knew decision time had come. I had pedaled each and every one of the 10,000 miles we had traveled up to that day, but I couldn't go on.

The next day I loaded my bike and all our gear into a pickup truck and headed up to Pasto the easy way. The boys would leave the following day to climb the seven thousand feet to the city. We had no idea what our plans were beyond that, but knew we somehow — by hook or by crook — had to get to Pimampiro in Ecuador where some readers of our blog had an apartment waiting for us.

John and the boys took two days to do the climb, and straggled into our host's house exhausted. "My legs are jelly," John told me. "There is no way I can push on tomorrow." But that clock was ticking. Hot water, epsom salts, and antibiotic ointment only go so far.

By then my back had recovered enough that I could ride, so we set out. John and the boys were exhausted, I wasn't quite sure my back would hold, but we packed up and headed out anyway. Only ninety miles to go.

Somehow fate intervened and we ended up with one more night in Pasto, and we made a quick trip to a doctor to check out Davy's toe. Although the doc assured us all was well and we could make it to Pimampiro before having the surgery done, Eduardo's story scared the living bejeezus out of me.

"A mosquito bite on my ankle got infected a few years ago," the local cyclist and new friend told me on our way back to our bikes after the visit to the hospital. "I didn't think anything of it, but all of a sudden it turned into gangrene. They thought they would have to amputate my leg at the hip, but in the end they saved it after sixteen surgeries." I was more worried about Davy's toe than ever.

The next day we managed to make it to a small village where the cousin of our host in Pasto lived, but the following morning, the dreaded words came again. "I don't feel good."

Sometimes you've had enough. Sometimes you reach the end of your rope and can fight no longer. There comes a point when you realize you've given it a valiant effort and you've fought a good fight, but the forces of nature are simply too much. We reached that point that morning in Pilcuan. We had given it our all. We had tried to make it to Ecuador, but realized we just couldn't do it.

Davy and I left our bikes in Pilcuan and jumped on a bus. Daryl and John continued on by bike. At some point, when Davy's toes were better and we weren't racing against Mother Nature, Davy and I would take the bus back to Colombia to retrieve the bikes.

In the end, we won the battle against the clock. We arrived into Pimampiro. The toenails on both Davy's big toes were removed. We had an apartment to hang out in while he recovered. The local store carried pancake mix.

Life was good.

Chapter 14

More Than Halfway to a Dream

ECUADOR

There were advantages beyond just letting toes heal to being stationary in a small village. One of the best ones was being able to participate in local festivals.

The story of the Shanshipamba festival was that twenty-seven years earlier a seven-year-old girl saw a bright flash of light as she wandered through the mountains. When she went to explore it, she saw that the rocks in a nearby cave had broken apart and a brightly colored Virgin had been painted on one of the rocks. That rock is now the centerpiece of the church in Shanshipamba, and every year hundreds of people make the trek up to venerate it.

Early in the morning the streets of Pimampiro were filled with worshippers making their way up to Shanshipamba. The procession was led by a group of dancing kids dressed in traditional costumes. After the kids came a marching band playing Andean music followed by a bunch of floats decorated with images of the Virgin and filled with kids dressed as angels. All around them were walkers.

The group slowly made their way twelve miles up into the mountains, most of them walking the whole way. Davy, Daryl, and I, having heard

of the festival only that morning, took off on a bus a few hours late to join the group en route. When the bus caught up, we jumped off and started walking. After about five minutes of walking in the intense equatorial sun, Daryl was ready to call it quits. "Can we jump on one of these trucks, Mom?"

A minute later, he ran up to a jam-packed truck and jumped onto the bumper. "See ya later!" he shouted.

Davy and I figured he would ride a little ways, then get off and wait for us, so we kept walking. A while later, still no Daryl. We jumped on a truck and hoped to catch up. Still nothing.

I was way up in the Andes with a missing kid, and that "mom" part of me took over. What if? What if the truck Daryl climbed on was going to some other village and he ended up way over the mountains in the Amazon basin? What if he got lost? What if?

Even though I knew there was no way out of the mountains except through Pimampiro, and I knew that Daryl would be able to find a way back down somehow, and I knew that the kid was perfectly capable of taking care of himself, I still had that niggling little doubt in the back of my mind. What if?

Eventually I came to the conclusion there was nothing I could do anyway, so Davy and I hopped off the truck and walked the rest of the way to Shanshipamba. And sure enough, when we arrived Daryl came running up with a huge grin on his face. "I beat you BAD," he declared.

Later in the evening, as I looked back on the day, I was convinced I was the luckiest mom on earth. I had two boys who loved going out to explore the world, and we had the time and opportunity to do exactly that. We were in a situation where the boys could take off and jump on trucks headed up in the mountains and I knew they would be okay. They were confident, capable, and intelligent. What more could any mother ask?

A few days later, I was walking around the market in Pimampiro with Davy. Carrying our large basket of fruits and veggies, he turned to me and said, "Mom, why are Americans so afraid to travel?"

"What do you mean?" I asked.

"So many Americans are afraid to leave America. They think that as soon as they leave the country they'll be beaten up or robbed or hurt, but I look around and all I see are nice people. All these people selling oranges and green beans aren't here to hurt us. Why are so many people afraid of them?"

As we continued walking through the market, I pondered Davy's words. He was a young child, but had more wisdom than many adults I knew. He understood that people around the world were simply trying to live, just like we do in the United States. They are no different from us and they are not to be feared. I was thankful, once again, that we had the opportunity to show our sons the world.

DAY 541 I like Pimampiro," Davy wrote in his journal. "It has wonderful views, wonderful people, and wonderful food — even though there is only one place in town that you can get ice for your soda. That place has great ice cream! I had a lot of fun here. I helped make a new roof for a poor person, and the school has some great games. You can also go out to the 22 other villages around here up in the mountains."

Our six weeks in Pimampiro had been wonderful, but finally the day came when we loaded up our bikes and headed out. We were all feeling the effects of being off the bikes so long as we inched our way up and over hill after hill after hill. Daily climbs in the Andes were equivalent to full-blown passes in the Rockies, and our bodies were ill-prepared for the demands.

After three days on the road, we set out early in the morning for the short ride to the equator. "It's not supposed to be this cold at the equator," Davy mumbled as huge fluffy clouds billowed out of his mouth. "It's supposed to be hot here!"

In the tropics, temperature is dependent on elevation, which led to chilly temperatures at 8000 feet in the mountains. We had all been taught in school that it was hot at the equator, but our experience was different. As we neared the equator I wondered what other "facts" about our world were wrong. How many times do we try and generalize something that can't be generalized? I was glad my sons were learning first-hand rather than relying upon school books.

After a massive downhill run and equally massive climb, we made it! The equator! A huge monument declaring we were at 0'00" rose dramatically from the middle of a large plaza. The boys immediately ditched their bikes and headed out running — playing as only kids can do.

We danced. We shouted. We rejoiced. We had done it! Way back in Alaska we rejoiced when we reached the Arctic Circle. In Mexico we celebrated crossing the Tropic of Cancer. And now — the equator! *Mitad del Mundo!* Half of the world! We had pedaled 10,267 miles and were feeling on top of the world.

Reluctantly, we pulled ourselves away from the monument and climbed back on our bikes to pedal into the southern hemisphere. Were we riding upside down?

After hanging out for so long, we were excited to be making headway, but then we reached Quito, where we fell into a black hole again. Our intention had been to continue south for the next month, find a place to stash our bikes, and return to Quito to hang out with John's mom when

At the equator - another huge milestone.

she arrived in Ecuador. Intentions were great things, but had this tendency to… well, remain intentions only.

Upon our arrival in the Quito area we headed to the house of some readers of our blog — Steve and Maria. Steve, who worked at the British School, arranged for us to give a presentation to their students. And, seeing as how we were there immediately before Christmas break, one of the teachers asked us to housesit for her while she went to Mexico.

And then a trip to the Galapagos Islands fell in our lap.

We quickly changed our plans, booked flights to the Galapagos for a four-day tour, then planned to housesit for a couple weeks. By then, John's mom should be in the country.

It was in the Galapagos that I realized the depth of the boys' education and that they were learning even while playing around.

One evening I decided to take advantage of the fact that we were in the Galapagos to help my boys learn Darwin's theory of natural selection. I had taught middle school science enough years to know that, for some reason, the theory was difficult for kids to learn. In order to truly understand it, you had to connect many dots — genetics, environment, change over time — and that was hard for most kids.

I rounded my sons up, made them turn off the movie they were watching in the lobby of the boat, and corralled them into our cabin. It was "school time."

173

"Today we're going to learn about Darwin's theories of evolution," I told my sons once we were properly situated on our beds and ready for school. "Can you tell me who made the Galapagos Islands famous?"

"Charles Darwin!" they cried out.

"Exactly," I replied. "And do you know why?"

"Because this is where he saw all the unique animals and came up with his ideas about evolution."

"You're good! What ideas are you talking about?"

"Natural selection, Mom. The survival of the fittest and all that. The animals that are best suited to live in an area are the ones who manage to pass down their genes so, over time, the whole species changes."

I was blown away. The whole time our guide had been explaining it, all I saw was the boys running around the islands oohing and aahing over the cute little sea lions. And yet they had learned after all, as though by osmosis.

"Lesson's over!" I told them. "Go back to your movie."

That evening Daryl wrote in his journal: "We went on a hike on an island. I saw a cute little sea lion. The sea lion was so cute when he walked, waddling from side to side. It was also cute when it scratched itself. The sea lion was in the middle of the path so eventually, to move it out of the way, the guide stepped over it. It let out a cute little shriek. Then another person stepped over it and it did the same shriek and stepped away. Then we went on the hike."

I had already discovered that I loved Ecuadorian festivals, and New Year's Eve was no exception. We wandered around all day and were amused by the *viejos,* stuffed dolls of varying sizes that represented the old year, guarding houses or tied to cars. They would be burned at midnight. There were also *viudas,* men dressed as women dancing in the street who were 'widows' of the old year. They kept us entertained for hours. It was a wild celebration and we danced and partied until the wee hours of the morning.

Eventually, Grandma arrived and we enjoyed celebrating Christmas with her in January. She brought all kinds of goodies for us all and the boys loved their new Star Wars action figures and Nintendo DS. With Grandma, we headed out to the Otavalo market, the equator, and to a restaurant renowned for its traditional Ecuadorian music and dancing.

And finally it was time to hit the road again. The day after celebrating Davy and Daryl's twelfth birthday, we climbed back on our bikes and headed out.

We should have known that tackling a 5300-foot climb right off the bat after a couple months off the saddle was not a good idea.

We headed out, struggling to reacquaint ourselves with the feel of our heavily-laden bikes, and headed straight up. We had been staying at around 8,000 feet in altitude and would crest a mountain pass at 13,300 feet before dropping down into the Amazon basin.

We climbed around 2000 feet before finding a small pueblo with a huge grassy field outside the church and school, and decided to call it a day.

"We left Quito today," Davy wrote as we snuggled together against the cold in our tent. "It felt good to be on the road again — for the first part anyway. After about nine kilometers we started on a huge hill. It took us an entire day to go fifteen kilometers. We are out of shape after so long off the bikes. After we set up camp in a school, Mom gave us each a Tootsie Pop. It gets cold up here."

We packed up the following morning as billowy clouds puffed out of our mouths with every breath and headed up to the pass. As I pushed my bike up the steep slopes of the mountainside, I stopped frequently to collapse over my saddle and catch my breath. John wasn't doing much better.

The boys were incredible. Daryl, who was walking so John could take the tandem up alone, helped push my bike the whole way. Davy walked right beside me, offering encouragement. At one point, Davy offered to take my bike so I could push his much-lighter bicycle. He quickly discovered just how heavy it was and we switched back.

As we climbed higher into the *paramo* (a high altitude desert ecosystem), the temperature dropped and a wicked-cold wind blasted us from above. We piled on more and more layers in an attempt to keep warm. By the time we finally crested the pass, all four of us were completely, unequivocally exhausted.

We had been warm enough on the ascent when we were working hard, but the descent was a different story. Our winter woolies were buried in the bottom of our panniers, so we decided to simply grin and bear it — it was, after all, only three miles to town. Or so we had been told.

With frozen fingers glued to our brake handles we dropped down three miles, then four. Then five. What happened to the town?

There were only twenty minutes of daylight left when, after racing down nine miles, we saw a sign indicating Papallacta was two miles off the road. What to do? Head to the town on the dirt road? Stay on the main road and hope like heck there was something there?

In the end, we turned onto the dirt road toward town. The road quickly

Leaving Quito, our destination was the Amazon Basin. To get there we had to climb up and over the Andes, then descend into the basin.

deteriorated to loose scree several inches deep, and we struggled to control our bikes on the steep downward slopes. At one point, I lost the battle and tumbled down, taking Davy down with me.

Just as darkness fell we arrived into town and checked ourselves into the first hotel we saw.

After all that, there was a silver lining to it all. Papallacta was famous for its hot springs and our hotel had a lovely little pool. We soaked our aches and pains away in the hot water after our way-too-strenuous day.

I rolled over and opened my eyes a crack — just enough to see Daryl and John fighting over the Nintendo DS Grandma had gotten the boys for Christmas. Suddenly Daryl reached over and yanked the card out of the machine.

"You ruined it," John said.

"No, I didn't," Daryl insisted. "I just took the card out."

"I bet it's ruined," John continued. "The system was running and you yanked it out." He took the card and gently reinserted it into the slot. All the data was corrupted. The boys' brand new Nintendo was worthless.

Davy, who had been sleeping soundly the whole time, burst into tears when he heard the news. His Nintendo, his present from Grandma, was destroyed.

"You might be able to get the card reformatted," John told him. "You'll have to get the system reinstalled. They can probably do that at the game places in some cities farther south. We'll check around when we get there."

"Can we go to Quito and get it fixed today?" Davy begged. "Please, Mom?"

"No way, sweetie," I told him. "Quito is three hours away over a mountain pass. It's crazy to go all that way just for a stupid Nintendo."

"Please!" he begged.

Sometimes I looked into those puppy-dog eyes and my heart melted. This was one of those times.

We were assured by people from Quito that all the shopping centers were open on Sunday. They closed early, but if we left right away we could get there in time. Davy and I hopped on a bus and headed into town to see if we could get the Nintendo fixed.

Hours later we arrived into Quito and took a taxi to the shopping center where we had bought the card a week earlier. It was closed. People milling around outside were puzzled; all the shopping centers in Quito were open, except Espiral. But, they told us, we could go to Caracol and find a video game shop there. We jumped in another taxi.

In the end, we found a shop that could maybe do it, but there were apparently many versions of the system and he didn't have the version that worked on our card. Disappointed, we walked away empty handed.

DAY 585 "Mom," Davy said as I sat in the hotel restaurant writing and drinking my morning coffee the next day. "Can Daryl and I go to Quito to get our Nintendo fixed?"

"What?" I exclaimed. "By yourselves? Are you crazy?"

"I know how to get there, Mom. We won't get lost."

To get to Quito they would have to leave our hotel and walk twenty minutes down the hill to the main road. They would wait there up to thirty minutes or so for a bus to take them over the pass and into the suburbs of Quito. Then they would need to change buses and head into the city proper. At that point, they would hop into a taxi to the shopping center. And reverse the process to get back out to Papallacta. All told, the entire process of simply getting there and back would take around six hours or more — plus they needed time to get their game fixed. And they wanted to do it *alone*?

"I went into town with you yesterday, Mom. I know how to do it."

I knew in my heart they would be fine. It was a fairly straight-forward ride over the mountain pass, and they had both gone into town many times from the suburb we housesat in where they would change buses. They knew the name of the shopping center and knew how to ask for help. What could go wrong?

Only about a million things.

I also knew that at some point I had to let them grow up. At some point I had to start to cut those apron strings and allow them to fly on their own.

All day, John and I sat around chewing our fingernails. What if? We had set up a contingency plan in case something went wrong, but would it work? What if they panicked? What if? All of those times in the past where my sons had proven their capabilities to me were lost in my mind; all I saw were two young, vulnerable boys exploring a foreign country on their own.

According to my calculations, the absolute earliest they would be back was 6:00. By 6:15 I was on the edge of panic.

"What are we worrying about?" John asked me. "They would only be back already if everything went like clockwork. One bus they had to wait for, or taking longer at the shop than calculated, and they would be later."

At 7:00 the boys walked in the door triumphant! They had succeeded in everything they set out to do — they made it to Quito, got their Nintendo DS fixed, bought pizza on the way back, and managed to get to the hotel safe and sound.

And me? Maybe I learned to let go a little. Just a little.

Four days in Papallacta in the cold and the rain was enough. We had hoped the rain would pass as the *paramo* was simply too beautiful to ride through in the dark and dreary cloud cover and rain. We wanted to see it in all its glory, but finally came to the conclusion it wasn't going to happen. We packed up and took off.

It didn't take long before we left the high grasslands behind and entered into dense rainforest. For thirty miles, we plunged downward gripping our brake handles to maintain control of our bikes. As we descended into the rainforest from the mountains, I was struck by the sheer vastness of it. I gazed out over the valley and all I could see was trees, trees, and more trees as far as my eyes could see.

Cycling through the rainforest, green was the color of the day. Dark green, light green, pale green, bright green. Big green trees and small green bushes. Green in the air, green on the ground. Green, green, green.

As we descended from the mountains, I had looked out over the vast expanse of rainforest and it looked homogenous. An enormous sea of green.

178

From down in the middle of it though, the rainforest took on a different perspective. Rather than one enormous mass of green, we now cycled past individual trees. Some had big leaves, others small. Some were tiny little things while others were gigantic.

But every once in a while we found a bright splash of color, as though angels occasionally dropped a bucket of red, orange, yellow, or purple paint from above. I was surprised at how much I looked forward to that occasional bright burst of something other than green. In the sea of green, those flowers stood out like neon lights on the Las Vegas strip.

After a few hundred miles in the jungle, it was time to climb up and over the Andes one more time. It would be about one hundred miles of pedaling to take us up to 13,000 feet and back down to the coast.

We had learned quickly that the Andes were radically different from the mountains we were used to. It was many miles to get from one side of the Rockies to the other in the USA with many peaks and valleys along the way.

The Andes were different. We would climb to the top in one massive climb, and then plummet down the other side. One very narrow, but incredibly high and steep, mountain range was all that separated the Amazon basin from the Pacific Ocean.

"Mom," Davy said as we ground up the hill side by side. "My toe hurts."

My heart took a nosedive and landed somewhere near my feet. I wanted to scream and shout and stamp my feet and curse the toe gods, but no matter how big a temper tantrum I threw, it wouldn't change the fact that Davy's toenail was ingrown. Again.

John and I were in complete agreement: we had to get it taken out, and we had to do it now. We had been there too many times; if we waited, it would get infected and then Davy would need to take antibiotics before they could operate and we would wait around forever. It looked clean — it was time to have it done.

"What's the doctor going to do, Mom?" Davy asked as we headed out the door of our hotel in Ambato for the hospital. "I don't want that shot again. Please."

We arrived at the emergency room and headed in. "Mom, I don't want a shot," Davy pleaded.

"I don't want the shot," he said as he took off his shoes.

But, of course, he needed the shot. He needed to have his toe deadened before they ripped out his toenail.

"I hate the shot!" he wailed as the doctor injected medicine into his toe. My heart broke and tears streamed down my face as I clung to my baby, wishing more than anything we could solve this problem once and for all.

We had been so optimistic when we pedaled away from Pimampiro. The curse had been lifted and Davy's toes would be fine. For three months we'd had a reprieve from the pain of ingrown toenails. But now, we were back to square one and we had no idea where to go from here. We could only hope and cross our fingers that his nail would grow in properly.

Stashing our bikes in Ambato, we headed back down the hill to Baños to hang out while Davy's toe healed. Baños sits nestled at the base of Volcan Tungurahua, an active volcano. After being dormant for many years, the rumblings started again in 1999. Now, eleven years later, it was still erupting.

We could hear the explosions echoing across the valley and saw the large plumes of smoke rise into the sky from the peak of Tungurahua. A couple of times we went high into the surrounding mountains in order to see the lava glowing red in the night, but clouds moved in each time so we missed it.

As I drank my morning coffee in the hotel restaurant, I struck up a conversation with Fabiola, a worker at the hotel. "We went out to see the volcano last night," I told her.

"I see it all the time," she replied. "Every single night I see it through my bedroom window."

As it turned out, Fabiola lived with her husband and nine-year-old daughter in a small village on the side of the mountain directly in the path of potential lava flows from Tungurahua. As we waited for Davy's toe to heal, I spent a lot of time talking with Fabiola and her husband, Pablo.

"Why don't you move away?" I asked. That sounded like a reasonable course of action to me as I certainly wouldn't want to deal with the high probability of being buried alive by a volcano some night.

Fabiola and Pablo had a house in the village of Puñapi. They had a small farm where they raised vegetables and had fruit trees. Puñapi was home.

It had been eleven years since Tungurahua started its eruption. Eleven years of dealing with the occasional burst of fireworks and rocks falling upon their house. Eleven years of living in constant fear and danger. One morning they woke up to find a volcanic rock the size of a football on their living room floor and a hole in the roof.

And yet, they couldn't move. They barely eked out a living as it was; there was no way they could afford a house in another town. There was no way they could afford to start over.

"We don't have the money to buy a house somewhere else," Pablo told me. "We can't sell this house because nobody will buy a house in danger of being buried. The bank won't lend us money because they don't trust what we have as collateral. We have no way out."

In 1999, when the volcano first rumbled to life, the family spent three months in a shelter in a neighboring village. For ninety days they slept in a classroom at the local school with nine other families. Mats were laid out side by side with barely space to turn over. There were only four toilets for the five hundred people taking refuge in the school. There were no showers. The families rotated through the one kitchen they shared.

Both Fabiola and Pablo loathed the idea of going back to that situation. They did it once, and hoped they wouldn't have to do it again. They opted to take their chances and hoped Tungurahua would give them a bit of warning before the big explosion so they could get out of town.

And if not — they would be buried alive in the house. It was a risk they accepted — a risk they had no choice but to accept.

"I feel badly for them," Daryl said when I explained what was happening with Fabiola and her family. "I'm so glad we can leave."

Our sons' education extended far beyond the standard academics.

Davy's toe was more or less better. It still hurt a bit if it wasn't wrapped, but as long as I kept it wrapped with gauze it was fine. We made the decision to push on to a small village on the other side of the Andes to wait out Carnival. We had been warned repeatedly about the drunk drivers who would fill the roads during the holiday, and decided we would rather not meet one on the road.

The plan was to get over the pass on the highest paved road in Ecuador and onto the coastal side of the country before the weekend came. That way, we would be poised for a quick and easy jaunt to Peru to get out of Ecuador before our visas expired.

John and I studied our map and chose a nice, small village to wait out Carnival. We would have liked to participate in the celebration, but were mostly just antsy to get on the road. We would lay low in a small hotel in Guaranda and take advantage of our down time to work with the kids on their mathematics. As soon as it was safe to hit the road, we'd be on our way to Peru.

Following a small river up a narrow valley, we meandered up the mountainside until we reached the *paramo*. It was a beautiful ride through the stark, windy grasslands of the *paramo* which we thoroughly enjoyed.

As we plunged toward the coast on the other side of the pass, I started thinking about that very fact — we were on the Pacific side of the Andes.

In only ninety miles we had climbed from the rainforest of the Amazon basin to the top of the Andes Range, 13,600 feet above sea level. We had pedaled from 1000 feet above sea level to the same height as the highest peaks in Colorado in those ninety miles. But now we were over the top and were looking forward to flat coastal desert riding.

DAY 611 As we entered the small town of Guaranda, where we hoped to wait out Carnival, we were puzzled. The streets were lined with vendors and there was a large stage set up in the plaza. Colorful banners strung over the roads announced various events.

"What's going on?" Davy asked as we rode into town. "This doesn't look like a quiet little town."

We were confused. We had heard about big Carnival celebrations in Ambato and a few other locations around the country, but hadn't expected anything in Guaranda. We couldn't have been more wrong.

"Water guns!" Daryl shouted as we circled the town looking for a hotel. "Can we get one, Mom?" A kid squirted us with the gun he was holding. "Please?"

Water poured down from above and we craned our necks to see what was happening. Kids on the roof of a building poured buckets of water over the edge onto us. "It's a water fight!" Davy shouted. "I wanna play!"

We found a hotel, safely stashed our bikes, then headed out to buy water guns for the boys. With huge grins splashed across their faces, they charged out the door to find some local kids to play with.

After talking with a few people, I figured out that not only were we wrong about Guaranda being a little sleepy town during Carnival, but it was *the* place to be for a rowdy celebration. Other cities were known as being tamer and gentler; Guaranda was the party capital of Ecuador.

For the next week we enjoyed eight-hour parades with fabulous costumes and high-energy dancing. The boys played with their water guns and came home soaking wet.

"Hey, Mom," they said as they traipsed in the door. "Can we get some *karaoki*?"

"Some what?"

"*Karaoki* — it's a type of spray stuff that people use here. It's a pressurized can of shaving cream-type stuff and it shoots about ten feet. They use it to shoot people. Can we get some?"

After that, the boys not only came home wet, but also covered with foam

Carnival. Davy loved fighting with his water gun and spray - what a blast! He didn't like it all that much when he got creamed though!

residue. I didn't mind as they had a blast and only stopped when they were far too exhausted to continue running.

"This feels weird," Davy said as we pedaled side-by-side along the pancake-flat road of the coastal plain. "I'm not used to riding on flat roads."

Davy and I talked about flat roads and, as far as we could remember, the last time we cycled a flat road was near Cali, Colombia, many months earlier. We had either been grinding up impossibly steep grades or plunging down the other side for ages. We figured we would get used to it very quickly. From what we had heard, it would be flat all the way to Lima over a thousand miles away.

Along with the flat coastal road came heat; we were back to the dreaded tropical temperatures again. I felt like all I did was complain. When we were in the mountains I complained about the steep climbs; now that we were in the lowlands I complained about the heat. There was no satisfying me. We pulled out the rehydration salts and pushed on.

There was no stopping us though. Our visas were due to expire soon and we were sprinting for the border. Day by day, we drew closer to Peru. Ecuador had been wonderful, but we were ready for a new country.

Chapter 15

The Impossible Dream Becomes a Nightmare

NORTHERN PERU

"Where's the Nintendo?" Davy asked as he held the unzipped lid of his handlebar bag.

"I put it back," Daryl replied.

But it was gone. Stolen right off Davy's bike while we were in the border office.

Davy and Daryl had one small bag for whatever they chose to carry. Their few toys were precious to them and were never far from their sides. Davy carried the Nintendo Grandma had given the boys a few short weeks before. He also carried their Star Wars figures and Transformers they had played with so lovingly and taken care of so carefully for the past months. Now the entire toy bag was gone, swiped in a small plaza at the border while I was handling our exit from Ecuador.

Daryl, always the practical one, simply shrugged his shoulders and muttered, "Well, it's gone. There's nothing we can do about it now."

Poor Davy didn't take it so well. His face crumpled up and tears started falling. I hugged my darling while cursing the bastards who stole his toys.

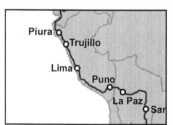

I kissed him on his forehead, and we pulled our bikes onto the road to head off to the Peruvian immigration office.

As we slowly made our way through the crowds, I heard Davy sobbing beside me. Out of the corner of my eye, I saw him wipe tears off his cheeks. "I don't have any toys to play with," he sobbed. "It's all gone. I don't have anything."

At one point, he stopped riding and slowly unzipped the small pocket on the front of his handlebar bag. He reached in and pulled out a small red Hotwheels car. He looked at me with bright red eyes and sobbed, "This is all I have!"

I was furious. Why would those SOBs steal my kid's toys? If they had to steal something, why not take something of mine? But my son's toys?

Toyless, we headed into Peru. Just as other cyclists had informed us, the landscape made a sudden, dramatic transition from the lush green country-side of Ecuador to barren desert.

Unfortunately, the drivers made a dramatic transition as well. I felt as though we had been magically transported back to Costa Rica where we dealt with lunatic drivers. We had ridden on plenty of narrow, shoulderless roads throughout our journey, and drivers were always polite and courte-ous, except in Costa Rica. Typically, drivers understood they needed to share the road with us — and pedestrians and donkey carts and the occa-sional goat herd that meandered down the road in search of greener pas-tures. They waited until they could pass safely before driving past.

But in Peru? The blasted moto-taxis thought they were king of the road and barreled on regardless of what might be in front of them. Truck drivers refused to budge an inch and blasted their horns angrily as they zoomed by within inches of our bikes.

Frazzled from the road, we arrived into the small beach town of Zorritos. Davy and Daryl had wanted to swim in the ocean since we dropped down out of the Andes, but we had needed to rush on to cross the border before our visas ran out. Now, we figured we had the luxury of time so could stop early for the day.

We traipsed from one hotel to the next, trying to find something within our price range. Unfortunately, the cheapest we could find was three times what we had been paying in Ecuador. Reluctantly, John told the boys we would need to push on and we started cycling out of town. Just on the edge of town, we passed one more hotel. It was a dive, but we could afford it.

After stashing our bikes, we made a beeline for the beach. All four of us relaxed and played and jumped waves. We screamed and shouted and thoroughly enjoyed the ocean again. The last time we had seen the water was when we first arrived in South America seven months earlier.

As it turned out, that romp in the waves was the only positive aspect we could find of Zorritos. At a local restaurant, we quite literally left our rot-ten meat and dried out rice on the plate and walked out. We weren't picky eaters by any stretch of the imagination, but when the food is that bad not even hungry cyclists will eat it.

And our hotel was dismal. It was hotter than blazes, and there was no air conditioning or fan. The room was infested with biting bugs but it was too hot to cover up. My bed consisted of metal poles spaced seven inches apart, much like a ladder covered by a two-inch layer of foam. I spent the night squirming around trying to position the metal bars on varying parts of my body when the others went numb.

Things were bad, but about to get worse. The next day we arrived into Mancora wiped out and overheated from cycling in the intense equatorial sun all day. I pedaled into town thinking, "I want ice cream."

We checked into a hotel, and I headed out for three liters of ice cold soda and ice cream. We got the soda, but she refused to sell the ice cream.

"If I open the ice cream freezer all the cold will escape. I'll start selling it later — once it cools off."

Later, once it cooled off, I wouldn't want ice cream. I wanted it immediately after our long ride under the blazing sun, not after I had showered and cooled off.

I was not impressed with Peru.

I told myself I was making it all up; there was no way one hundred miles could make such a difference. I figured my perception had been colored by the dozens of emails we had received before we reached this country.

In the weeks before we arrived at the border, my inbox had been filled with emails from friends and acquaintances writing to warn us about thieves. "Be careful in X region" or "Get a police escort through Y town" or "Never, ever let your guard down — ever." We probably got twenty or thirty emails from various people warning us about thieves in Peru. I hadn't gotten a single warning about any other country. None. Not a one.

We had been in Peru for a total of four days and I knew it wasn't fair to judge a country based on such limited experience, but I couldn't help it. In four days, we had been robbed for the very first time, been nearly run off the road multiple times, served inedible food, slept on ladders, and now we couldn't even buy ice cream.

I could only hope things would get better.

Cycling under the intense rays of the sun, I thought about some comments that had been left on my blog. When I wrote about Davy's toys being stolen at the border, a few people responded saying the local population was so poor that thievery was the only option they had available. I didn't buy it.

I thought back to my time in Ethiopia where we lived for seven years. It was one of the poorest countries in the world yet people didn't steal like we had heard about in Peru. We had seen more poverty than most people could ever imagine and had found that, almost always, the poorer the people, the more honest they were. Poverty may have been rampant in Peru, but that didn't mean they needed to steal. I had no explanation for the warnings we had received.

By the time we arrived at the junction for Talara, we were beat; we had cycled a tough forty-four miles with a 1500-foot climb onto a plateau. We stopped at the junction, trying to decide what to do. We weren't sure how far it was into town, but could see a good three miles and it wasn't there. Besides that, our map indicated that Talara was down by the ocean, which meant that we would have to climb back up in the morning.

"Let's go camp in the desert tonight," John suggested.

"We have to go into town," I countered. "We are out of food entirely and nearly out of water. We can't go on without resupplying."

We hatched a plan to find a campsite a mile or so from the junction, then I would jump on a bus and head into town for water and food.

Unfortunately, our plans didn't seem to be working well those days.

We pedaled one mile. Then two. There was no place to camp. Three, four, five. Still nothing. Seven miles from the junction, John finally pulled off the road into an old dry riverbed. We were home for the night.

We were, as far as I could tell, about eleven miles from town, had almost no water, and no food. And it would be getting dark soon. Daryl and I headed out to the road.

One car zipped past totally ignoring our pleading hand signals. Another one did the same. A pickup with an empty bed zoomed by. Daryl and I attempted to flag down each and every vehicle that passed — trucks, buses, vans, pickups, and cars. We desperately tried to beg a ride from each one. *Nada*.

We walked two miles back toward town begging a ride from every vehicle that passed before a truck finally stopped. "Peruvians don't stop," the driver said. "I'm Ecuadorian. Ecuadorians help each other."

Our trucker friend only had permission to be on the road from six in the morning until six at night. It was already 6:30. Our Road Angel was headed to a small restaurant up the road where he would spend the night; he would take us there.

As luck would have it, the *señora* at the restaurant agreed to pack up four fish dinners for us and a small shop next door had water and cookies for breakfast. It wasn't ideal, but we could make it without going into town, which was a good thing as I now knew there was no way we would find a way in anyway.

But then came the problem — how in the heck would we get back out to John and Davy? It was pitch black and there was no way we could walk carrying fifteen liters of liquid plus four fish dinners.

Just then a truck driver pulled up to the store to buy water, and I asked him if he would do us a favor. He was more than happy to take us 'home.' In fact, he had seen us struggling up the big climb earlier in the day and had been wondering about our journey.

It was delightful to finally reach camp and eat our fish dinner under the twinkling stars of the desert before climbing into our tent for some much needed rest.

"Nancy!" John woke me from a deep sleep early in the morning. "It's raining!" Seeing as how we were now deep in the desert, we hadn't put the fly on the tent, so we scrambled around furiously packing our sleeping bags before they got too wet.

When I climbed out of the tent into the pre-dawn darkness, I discovered not one, not two, not even three, but FOUR flat tires from when we pushed the bikes through the desert to our campsite the night before. Mosquitoes swarmed over my sweaty body and I swatted and smacked at the critters invisible in the darkness.

It was 9:00 in the morning by the time we had repaired our tires and started on the road, with wind whipping at gale force levels—in the wrong direction. We battled the headwinds and kept pedaling even though we could only go five miles per hour on flat roads.

Finally, we arrived into Sullana, a town I had been warned about by dozens of Peruvians. "Don't stop in Sullana," they all said. "The town is full of thieves. Go straight to Piura." We had no choice but to stop in Sullana because we were too bloody tired to continue on another twenty-five miles.

Amazingly, we found the best little hotel we had seen so far in Peru with wonderful friendly owners. The father happened to be the colonel in the local police force, so nobody would mess with his house. But even so, he warned me, "Never walk outside with your fanny pack on. They will hit you and throw you to the ground and yank your fanny pack off your waist. There are lots of thieves here in Sullana."

We had only been one week in Peru and I had a feeling it would be a long haul to the southern end of the country.

DAY 634 We arrived in Piura early in the morning after a short ride from Sullana. I stashed my bike in the hotel and headed to the market where massive riots had erupted two days earlier, killing six vendors. The government was forcing the vendors to relocate into the desert but the vendors claimed the location was inadequate. I could feel the tension in the air; I had never felt so much nervous tension anywhere.

The market was closed when I got there — all the metal doors rolled down and locked shut. People milled about, standing in small groups chatting. One stall was open and there was a single old man working in there, although it was pretty much emptied out.

"Are you moving to the new market?" I asked him. "Is that why your stall is empty?"

"I'll never move to that market," he responded. "There is no way I can move there. I've emptied my shop in fear of looters, so now I'm taking advantage of that to clean."

Within minutes, I was surrounded by vendors who sold clothes or shoes or fans or radios. Vendors who simply wanted to sell their goods so they could put food on the table for their families.

"We can't move to the new market," they repeated. "We'll never sell anything!"

"You want to see the new market?" one of the women asked. "I'll take you out there so you can see where they expect us to go. You want to go?"

My life was getting carried away in directions I never dreamed of. I had no idea what the next six hours would bring.

I hopped into a taxi with three women and twenty minutes later we pulled up to a field in the desert marked off with lines of chalk. "This is it," the women said. "This is where we are supposed to come to sell."

"This? Here?" I asked. "But how? This is just a plot of land out in the middle of the desert!"

"Exactly," they replied. "Look at this! It's just dirt! There is no electricity or water or bathrooms! There is no floor. Where are we supposed to put our clothes? See how small these plots are? How can we fit a whole shop of clothes in this tiny space? And who will come here? Who is going to travel twenty minutes into the desert to come to a market where everything is laying in the dirt? How are we going to sell our goods?"

"All I want to do is sell clothes so I can put food on the table for my children," one of the women, Maria, told me. "I'm just a simple woman and only want to feed my children. That's all I ask for. But we can't move out here — it's just desert. How can I sell clothes in the middle of the desert?"

"Please tell our story," the women pleaded. "Somebody has to tell our story. The local press makes us out to be lunatics. They tell everybody that

Juan, a vendor in the market in Piura, spent a lot of time talking to me about what happened. His son was shot by government forces and was in the hospital in a coma. I later heard that he pulled through.

we have a great big beautiful market and that we are crazy. But *you* see. You are *here* — you can see this is inadequate. Please tell our story!"

After returning to town, the vendors took me on a tour of the market where the riots happened and pointed out bullet holes in the walls of shops. They showed me makeshift memorials for the fallen vendors. Grief and sadness and confusion reigned unchecked through the crowds. They dragged me to the hospital where I talked with a vendor with a bullet lodged in his belly. I talked with the father of another victim, a young man who was shot while working in his store and was in a coma.

I tried to talk with the police, but they refused. The mayor was busy in negotiations with the market leaders so I couldn't talk with her, but my life was changed by a peaceful group of vendors who simply wanted to put food on the table for their children. They were a hardworking group of people who had been devastated by the events of the past few days.

I was heartbroken. I wanted to help in some way — to somehow intervene and make it all better for the vendors — but I knew there wasn't much I could do. I could write a story in my blog, but I was only one woman with little influence. In the end, it was their battle to fight and I wished them well as I pedaled out of town into the Sechura Desert.

One hundred forty miles away lay Chiclayo. In between was the longest stretch of desert we had attempted. We hoped to make it across in two days, but planned for three. We had been told there were small restaurants every thirty or forty miles so we would be able to get food each day, but it was bleak. Very bleak.

As we cycled out of town we noticed an immediate change in vegetation. Within a few miles, it was true desert — not like the desert we had up in Idaho. We pedaled past mile upon mile of blowing sand with not so much as a small bush or blade of grass. Nothing lived out in that desert.

The first thirty miles were flat with very little wind and were pretty easy. But then, everything changed. By the time we set up camp in the desert the wind was howling directly in our faces. In fact, when I brushed my teeth that evening, the toothpaste landed a full six feet from my side.

We awoke to wind the following morning. Yesterday's slight breeze was nothing but a puff of air compared to what we woke up to. We had wind. Wind with a capital W. Gale force gusts that threatened to blow us off the road.

On top of that, three of us woke up with diarrhea. Unfortunately, we were in the middle of the desert and simply could not take the day off. We packed up and headed out into the wind.

We struggled along for a while, weakened by sickness, battling the horrific headwind. "I can't do this anymore," Davy said as he climbed off his bike and collapsed on the side of the road.

Daryl took the single and Davy took the back seat of the tandem. Daryl hated riding the single bike in the best of times, and with that wind, it wasn't exactly the best of anything. I rode ahead of him to break the wind, and he plodded along.

Every mile Daryl dropped the bike and lay down on the side of the road for a break. In the stark desert, shade was nearly non-existent, but he climbed under small bushes if they were available. When they weren't, he crawled under my trailer to rest and recuperate a bit before pushing on.

Slowly, but surely, we made progress and ended the day with thirty-three miles behind us. It wasn't as far as we had hoped for, but it positioned us to be able to reach civilization the following day. Fortunately, we were all feeling better by afternoon.

Even after such a grueling day, Davy and Daryl had no shortage of energy. "Can we, Mom? Please?" As soon as the tent was set up, they were off to the sand dune in the distance.

An hour later, just after the sun had disappeared for the night, they reappeared looking like sandmen covered head to toe. Sand covered their faces, necks, arms, and legs. Sand in their hair, ears, noses, and belly buttons.

Northern Peru was a very poor area. Very few people had cars, but relied on donkeys to get around.

Sand, sand, sand.

And that presented a problem. How in the heck could we clean two boys with sand adhered to all their sweat and sunscreen without water? We had enough water to get us to the next restaurant, but certainly not enough to clean a couple of kids.

In the end, John brushed as much sand off as possible. "Ow! That hurts! It's like you're rubbing me with sandpaper!" Then I wet my wash cloth with a bit of water to wash the rest off. I ended up using nearly two bottles of water, but figured it was worth it to keep the sand out of their sleeping bags. I hoped I'd be saying the same thing the following day when our water supplies ran low.

After a tough three-day desert crossing through the most remote part of the Sechura desert, we landed at a hotel where we locked ourselves inside for three days — vegetating and working up the courage to get back on our bikes.

And when we did, we discovered just how fickle Peru was. It was, beyond a doubt, the most inconsistent place I had ever seen. The winds were erratic, the drivers were fickle, the food was unpredictable, and the hotels varied widely.

Our experiences with food left us confused. Some places it was good — surprisingly good in fact. In other places, the food was awful — leave-it-

It was very hot cycling through the Sechura Desert in northern Peru, and there was absolutely no shade whatsoever. Daryl, in desperation to get out of the sun, crawled under the only bush for miles around.

on-the-plate-and-forget-about-it bad. There didn't seem to be any way to predict; some of the most run-down restaurants in the middle of nowhere had the best food and fancy places in the cities were terrible. There didn't seem to be any kind of pattern.

And then there were the hotels. Some nights we stayed in old, run-down grungy hotels that we paid an arm and a leg for. Another night we stayed in a veritable palace with a garage for the bikes, hot water in the showers, comfortable beds, and strong fans. And we only paid $12 for the two double rooms. We wished we could find places like that more often.

The winds seemed to blow whenever and wherever they wanted. We had been warned over and over again about the coastal headwinds, but then one day we had a tailwind and the next hardly any wind at all.

DAY 642 We were totally confused about Peru, but there was one thing we weren't confused about at all: we were arriving into the black hole for bike tourists. We had been warned about Paijan more times than we cared to think about and were extremely nervous as we approached

The sand formations were really quite beautiful in places.

the city. According to reports flying through the cyclists' grapevine, there was a family with a mototaxi who robbed bike tourists regularly. They watched cyclists go through town, waited just long enough for them to get out into the middle of corn fields five miles away, then drove out and stole everything. We had heard dozens of reports of bike tourists who had lost everything. General consensus was that nobody should ride a bike through Paijan. Nobody.

And that posed a problem for us. Davy and Daryl were determined to break the world record, which meant they needed to pedal the whole way. We could turn left, head up about 12,000 feet in the mountains, then drop back down south of Paijan, or we could go right through. We chose the latter.

"Okay guys, listen up," John told the boys as we took a break on the side of the road before entering the city. "We need to stay right together here. Davy, stay right on my tail as we enter the city; Mommy will stay behind you. We think there is safety in numbers and they will be less likely to attack a group than a single person. Got that? There should never be more than ten feet between our bikes. We'll form a nice tight paceline and go into town together. If we see a police car, we'll flag them down and ask them to escort us."

We were nervous and stayed very alert to what was happening around us. We were particularly nervous in that not only would we ride through

194

town, but we also needed to spend the night there. Most cyclists could make more miles than we did, so they could have made it all the way to the next town. We couldn't.

Constantly checking our rear-view mirrors to see if a mototaxi was approaching, we made our way to the center of town with no incident at all. There was only one hotel and we knew our most vulnerable moment was as we unpacked and stored the bikes.

"I'm staying right here with the bikes to protect them," John said when we were ready to move in. "Davy, I need you to stay here with me. Get right there on the other side of the bikes. We need to do this carefully — there is most likely a thief standing somewhere watching, just waiting for the moment we're distracted." Davy positioned himself on the other side of the bikes and guarded them like a mother hen.

"Daryl," John ordered. "Take these panniers up to the room. Nancy — grab the dry bags."

Daryl and I worked together to take off one set of panniers at a time and haul them upstairs. Rather than our normal routine of quickly dismantling the bikes, we did it deliberately and carefully, being certain not to set even one single item on the ground where a thief could dart in and grab it. It took twice as long as normal to get settled in our hotel room but, fortunately, all was well.

Early the next morning we readied ourselves to leave town. Heading into town wasn't all that bad since all the robberies happened on the way out. Now we were on our way out to the cornfields. We decided to ask for a police escort.

"Good morning, sir," I said to the police chief. "We're cycling through the area and I wondered…."

"Not a problem," he interrupted. "Are you ready now? Which direction are you going?"

Obviously, the police were used to escorting cyclists through Paiján.

"Better safe than sorry," the police chief said. We agreed.

An officer in a police car stayed just behind us as we moved south. Once we were out of the danger zone, the officer turned around and we were on our own.

Later that day, we made it safely to the famous *Casa de Ciclistas* in Trujillo. For something like twenty-five years, Lucho had been opening his home to cyclists and there was a long legacy of hospitality there.

Throughout South America individual people who supported cycling opened their homes to bike tourists. Lucho's house was perhaps the most famous of the *casas*. Bike tourists arrived at Lucho's house planning to stay one day and finally left three weeks or three months later.

It was a place we had been looking forward to for many months. We had made it.

Unfortunately, the house was full and the four of us didn't fit, so we moved over to a hotel.

My mental state was starting a downward spiral and I was having a hard time keeping it under control. After being so excited about staying at the *Casa de Ciclistas* for so long, we were sorely disappointed that we couldn't. Our bikes needed work and we had agreed to hire Lucho to do it. Unfortunately, he was busy with other projects, so we sat around the *casa* all day every day waiting for him to find time to fix our bikes. It had been one heck of a three weeks since we entered Peru and I was starting to question why we were putting up with it all.

And then the ATM ate my debit card. That was the proverbial straw that broke the camel's back, and I lost it. I looked back at the struggles of the previous twenty-two days — the headwinds, the sickness, the sand, and the horrible drivers. And then I looked ahead and saw another thousand miles of coastal desert with endless headwinds and sand blasting into our legs like BB's, on a seemingly-endless battle against Mother Nature.

It was us versus Peru, and I figured the odds were about even. If we managed to cycle out of the southern end of Peru, it would be the biggest victory of my life. I knew that, if that day ever came, I would have worked harder for it than I had ever worked in my life.

For years I had heard people talk about how bike touring was nine parts mental and one part physical, but I didn't understand that earlier. Bicycle touring had never been a mental challenge for me until now.

Our journey was no longer fun. It had become a test of wills. It was a matter of who could hold out longer: the Vogel family or Peru?

I told myself I was living my dream. I was extraordinarily lucky to have the opportunity to explore the world with my precious children. I knew I had absolutely no right to complain.

But I still felt like crap at that moment. I felt like I had been dragged through the mud, spat upon, kicked viciously, and discarded for dead. I felt like nothing — absolutely nothing — was going our way.

I knew, intellectually, that it wasn't Peru's fault. I knew, intellectually, that there were wonderful people in Peru and great scenery and good food, but I wasn't seeing it. All I wanted to do was run back to Ecuador with my tail between my legs.

I was torn. With every cell in my body I wanted to continue on to support my sons. Davy and Daryl were determined to cycle all the way to

Patagonia, and I didn't want to be the cause of them having to stop. What kind of mom was I to consider taking my babies' dream away?

But still, I had to admit that I hated it. Life sucked. Bike touring sucked. Peru sucked.

As we walked along the streets of Trujillo, trudging once again to the *Casa de Ciclistas* in the hopes that maybe, just maybe, Lucho would have time to work on our bikes, I was bitching, moaning, and complaining once again.

"Mom," Daryl said with all his twelve-year-old wisdom, "It's not going to do any good to complain about it. All you can do is keep going and things will get better."

The truth of Daryl's words rang hit home with me. I had been complaining too much and I vowed to stop. I vowed to make the most of every single day and do my absolute best to love what I was doing. It would be a struggle, but I was going to try. Our dream was worth it.

We were working together, as a family, toward a common goal. In today's society that simply didn't happen anymore. I was fortunate that I could be out there in the Peruvian desert with my husband and sons. It wasn't always easy, but is any dream easy?

I told myself I could be back home sleeping in my own bed every night. I could be spending every day in a local school dealing with unruly teenagers. I could be sending my boys off to school every morning and not seeing them again until we were all ready to collapse into bed. But I wasn't. I was living my dream. Our shared dream. And I didn't want to forget that.

I set my sights on Lima and decided I wouldn't give up until then. If I still hated it, then I'd stop. That gave me five hundred miles to think about it. It might be a miserable five hundred miles, but I knew I could do it. I wouldn't give up just yet.

Chapter 16

We Interrupt This Nightmare to Remind You Why You Did This

Peruvian Coast

Eight days after arriving into Trujillo, we climbed back on our bikes to leave. I had gone through an attitude adjustment and vowed not to complain. Peru hadn't defeated me yet.

That didn't last long.

It was actually a fairly easy day. The wind gods were with us — or at least they weren't against us. We wanted to get as many miles behind us before they kicked up, so passed right through the only small town we would pass that day even though I knew I needed to eat and drink. Two miles from our goal, I ground to a halt and collapsed over my bike.

"I can't make it," I mumbled "I'm about ready to pass out."

I stood in the intense sun with my head resting on my handlebars. My head was spinning and the only thing holding me up was my bike — which wasn't a good thing as it only had two wheels.

John and the boys scrambled into action. Daryl hopped off the tandem and grabbed Davy's bike. Davy, the bigger and stronger of the two, grabbed my bike from me. I stumbled through the sand to a spot of shade

under a tree while the boys took the bikes up to a mile post to park for a while.

I ate a few bananas and drank a liter of water mixed with rehydration salts. It took a while before I recuperated enough to continue on for the last few miles of the day.

One thing I had learned since entering the

Peruvian desert was that sometimes plain water just wasn't enough. From the very beginning, the only liquid we drank was water while on the road. When it was hot, I drank up to three gallons of water every day. We carried packets of rehydration salts which we added to the water if we were feeling dehydrated. That was all we needed all the way, including in the Central American jungles. But in Peru, it didn't even come close.

I couldn't explain how it helped, but I had learned to strap a bottle of soda to my trailer every morning and we took sips of it throughout the day in addition to the water. That strategy had gotten this far, but now, even the Inca Kola hadn't done the trick.

Maybe Peru would defeat us after all.

We fell into a routine. Every morning we woke up early in order to hit the road at the first sign of daylight. Getting on the road early was imperative for two reasons: the heat and the wind. We had quickly learned that heat was a constant and the wind was as well. The only question was what time the wind would start.

We had a bit of a reprieve from the wind early in the morning, so we pushed hard to take advantage of every moment without the headwind, but once it started we dealt with the demoralizing factor of battling an unbeatable foe. Villages were generally spaced a distance that was doable in one day, although there were days when it was a long, long day.

We put blinders on and focused with single-minded dedication on what we were doing. Our routine varied little: get on the road early, ride into the headwind all day, stumble into the next village in late afternoon, get dinner, buy food and water for the next day, shower with cold water, and collapse into bed. Every three or four days we took a day or two off. On those days we stayed in bed and watched TV.

Food for our time on the road had become a major challenge. Although we could readily find restaurants in the towns and villages, finding food that we could pack in our panniers to eat on the road was difficult. I finally settled on picking up four pounds of tangerines and two pounds of fresh peas from the market along with two dozen bread rolls from a local bakery each evening. That provided nourishment to get us to town the following day.

As difficult as that part of our journey was, it was also magical in many ways. Every morning, just as the sun was barely peeking over the horizon shadows highlighted the sand formations surrounding us turning them into some kind of fantasyland. The scene changed every half mile and I wished I had to way to lock it in my brain forever. The shadows over the sand

Davy and I entering the town of Chimbote where we would spend the night. It was always strange to enter a city after days out in the middle of nowhere.

dunes stretched forever and, when we crested the top of a major climb, we could see mile upon mile of desert extending out in front of us.

Now, with the benefit of hindsight, I consider the Peruvian coast to be one of the most beautiful areas we passed through. The desert was stunning — stark as all get-out, but gorgeous nonetheless. Each day we left town and knew we wouldn't see a single blade of grass or bush or anything green at all until we arrived at the next village. Just sand, sand, and more sand. And wind. Each day was like the one before — the same endless sand and the shadows stretching on forever.

Tons of sand blew from the coastal side of the road to the other, creating massive sand dunes. We quickly learned just how much it hurt when itty bitty bits of sand blasted into your unsuspecting skin. Frequently, we came across road crews moving sand from one side of the road to the other with a big tractor. "If we don't get out here for three days," they told me one day, "the road will be closed. Too much sand builds up and cars can't get through any more."

Depending on the direction and strength of the wind, we were buffeted around like balls bouncing in a pinball machine each time a truck whizzed past. John and I, with plenty of weight on our bikes, were merely blown around a bit. Davy was a different story.

When those conditions existed, poor little Davy flew around like a drunken seagull. Each time a truck blasted by, he was sucked into the draft, and spit out again with tremendous force. Even when a truck wasn't barreling past, he was zigging and zagging as he battled the wind. It was a fairly dangerous situation and we weren't quite sure what do to about it.

One solution to the problem would be to weigh the kid down. We could put some rocks in his panniers, or better yet transfer some of the weight from John's and my bikes to his. With more weight, he would be better able to hold his ground against the brutal gusts. But that would also make it harder for him to pedal up the hills.

In the end, we weighed him down a little and trusted in providence to take care of him. He had managed okay so far; we trusted he could manage a bit farther.

And then there was the clunk in my rear hub. We had discovered small cracks in my rear rim and were keeping our fingers crossed it would make it to Lima. Now, my hub was clunking and clanking as I battled the winds. Would my wheel hold together long enough to reach the capital city?

Each afternoon, we pulled into a new small town and started the aggravating search for a hotel. Every single day for ages we had spent at least an hour looking for a hotel when we arrived into town.

Throughout Central America, Colombia, and Ecuador, hotels had been fairly consistent in both quality and price; we never looked at more than three hotels before deciding on one. In Peru, we accepted the fact that every day would end with an agonizing hour or more hunting for a place to stay. We would look at fifteen comparable hotels and fourteen of them cost around US$50/night. The other one cost US$20. The trick was to find that one.

When I managed to find a wonderful hotel, I loathed the idea of giving it up knowing just how hard it would be to find another decent one.

DAY 671 As had become our practice with big cities, we wanted to pass through Lima on a Sunday as that was when traffic was lightest. We actually made pretty good time cycling through the massive city and the traffic wasn't bad. By eleven in the morning, we were south of center and heading out.

And then we saw a Pizza Hut. It was almost like some kind of magnet drawing us in, but it was closed.

We continued on, but by then we had one thing on our minds — pizza. We were a family on a mission — a mission to find pepperoni pizza.

With each mile we cycled, my hopes dwindled of ever finding Pizza Hut; we knew that Lima would be our only hope as small villages didn't have American franchises. We could have opted to stay the night in Lima, but wanted to get out the tail end before traffic picked back up.

All four of us pedaled with one eye on the highway and the other scanning the roadside for that Pizza Hut sign. After what seemed like forever, we found one! It was a little bit of heaven on earth. In Lima, anyway.

With bellies stuffed full of pepperoni, we climbed back on our bikes for the trek to the edge of town. By the time we stopped for the night, we were poised for an easy escape the following morning. Lima, the largest city we would cycle through on our entire journey, was behind us.

We flew as though we had sprouted wings. The road south of Lima was flat and in great condition. Winds were minimal for once and we barreled along the road...

...until we were flagged down by a group of men. As we whizzed along the road, one of them stood up and shouted, "Want something to drink?" as he waved an Inca Kola bottle in the air. What cyclist could pass that up on a hot, sunny day?

His name was Roberto and we shared a soda, studied our map, and chatted for an hour or so before parting ways.

Thirty minutes later we pulled into Chincha and pedaled past dozens of roadside stalls selling the wine the area was famous for. And then there he was flagging us down again.

"Welcome to our office!" Roberto greeted us. "We're just putting the finishing touches on the office now; it'll be open within two weeks. We were just thinking that our office isn't much, but we do have some beds upstairs and a shower. There's TV with cable. If you want, you are more than welcome to stay here tonight."

It was a delightful surprise to nestle ourselves into the unfinished office and spend the afternoon drinking *chicha* with a great group of people. It was those unexpected little turns of events that kept me going.

Just like back in Honduras, we made the decision that it was better to actually fly back to the USA to pick up what we needed rather than risk mailing it. Eddie Bauer had recently come on board as a sponsor and they were sending out winter clothing and two tents to replace our small, worn-out tent. We needed new tires for all three bikes, and I needed a whole new rear wheel. The gasket for our stove had worn out and, of course, we needed a new Nintendo DS to replace the one stolen at the border.

Pisco, Peru, would be home for John and the boys while I flew to the USA. I purchased tickets, confirmed and double-checked the reservations, and couldn't wait to get a taste of my home country.

We managed to find a wonderful small hotel with a pool and ping pong table; I was confident that John and the boys would be very comfortable. The owners of the hotel, who lived there as well, were friendly and helpful. It was as good a situation as we could find. I knew they would all be bored waiting for me, but it couldn't be helped.

Then I got a niggling little idea in the back of my mind. What if a local school allowed Davy and Daryl to attend classes? They could meet other kids, get out of the hotel during the day, and learn more Spanish. It was a long shot, but I figured it wouldn't hurt to ask.

The owner of our hotel took me to her kids' school to talk with the director. I explained our situation and she was thrilled! The boys had permission to go to a Peruvian school for a few weeks. It would be good for her students to get to know kids from another country, and it would be great for Davy and Daryl to establish friendships with Peruvian kids. Their time in Pisco wouldn't be so boring after all.

Our break was perfect. I delighted in Starbucks and New York pizza and bead shopping and visiting friends and family while John enjoyed plenty of hours of uninterrupted time to get his videos and photos in order. It was exactly what we needed after our battle with the Peruvian coast.

"We thought going to school was a bad idea but it turned out not to be that bad after all," Davy journaled. "I still would have preferred not to go to school but I made some friends and they seem nice enough. They have a nice stand where you can buy drinks and little Styrofoam plates of food, and chips. I usually get a Coke and a plate of *salchipapas*. *Salchipapas* are a plate of French fries and some little pieces of sausage."

After three weeks, we were ready to move on. All we had to do was get organized. That's all.

Unfortunately, getting organized was an enormous task. Everything was taken apart, and I do mean everything. Although we had completely disassembled the bikes a few times on our journey, this was the very first time we had completely emptied the panniers.

It was mindboggling to look at the enormous pile of little odds and ends we kept stashed in the pockets of our panniers. They didn't seem like much — extra shoelaces, Q-tips, eyeglass holders, chapstick — but when we took them all out of their hiding places, they seemed to explode and fill the room.

On top of the itty-bitty items that were generally stashed in pockets of panniers, I also took out all our winter stuff to sort. All those hats and gloves and neck gaiters, tights and long underwear, wool socks and sweaters; they all came out. That stuff hadn't seen the light of day since Texas. In addition to the old winter gear, we also had our new Eddie Bauer winter gear to pack. It wouldn't be long before we were up in the midst of the Andean winter and would need it all.

Getting it all off the bikes and out of the panniers had been a chore. Getting it all back on was next to impossible. Since Davy and Daryl had grown too much to make one tent comfortable, we now had two. We loaded Davy down more than he had ever carried before. We figured he was strong enough to handle it.

DAY 701 Fifty miles away, we reached Ica, famous for three main sites. We charged off to the sand dunes, where we went sandboarding. Strapping ourselves into dune buggies, we raced out into the desert before waxing our boards and surfing down the massive dunes. Davy and Daryl couldn't get enough and were the first to jump out of the dune buggy when we reached the top of another massive run.

Next stop was the regional museum where we were fascinated by the well-preserved mummies and conehead skulls. From there, we went to Dr. Cabrera's Stone Museum to see thousands of mysterious carved stones that have appeared in the desert over the years. The stones depicted very advanced medical knowledge like heart transplants and detailed anatomy. Nobody knows how or when the stones were carved, and the coneheads were a mystery as well. Our curiosity had been piqued.

"I could buy the alien theory," John said as he took a bite of rice and eggs the following afternoon, "but it's not all there. I mean, if there had been this super-intelligent society around here — smart enough to know how to do heart transplants and build spaceships — surely there would be some trace of their society besides just carved rocks. Like cities or medical tools or parts of their spaceships or something."

"But there are 50,000 stones, Dad!" Daryl added as he crammed beef stew in his mouth. "50,000 carved rocks have been found — and who knows how many more there are? That's a LOT of rocks!"

"Maybe all this is a big joke and it was just shepherds carving the rocks," Davy added.

"But how would shepherds know how to do a heart transplant?" I asked.

The mysteries of the area had captivated our imaginations, and there was still more to come.

I could hear the drone of small planes off in the distance and figured we were approaching the famous Nazca Lines. Although I had heard stories of needing to be up in the air in order to see the lines scratched into the surface of the earth two thousand years ago, I figured we would see them if they were close to the road. The way I figured it, going at our slow pace there was no way we could miss the designs.

As we climbed a small hill, we started seeing the planes buzzing over the road ahead of us. "There they are!" I said. "Those must be planes flying over the Nazca Lines. We'll be able to see them soon." We couldn't wait.

Once we broke out onto the plain, we could see scores of planes flying over the large flat valley, one after another. Every five minutes like clockwork another plane arrived, and we could see them circle in one spot before moving on to another. The lines had to be right there, and yet we couldn't see anything.

"Where are the lines?" Daryl asked as we pedaled along the sparsely trafficked road.

"They're right here, but I don't see anything."

Up ahead, we saw a large observation tower, so we parked our bikes and climbed up. All it took was to get ten feet off the ground and the lines magically appeared. As we climbed higher, the entire pattern came into view. Amazingly, we had been cycling a mere ten feet from one design, yet hadn't seen it at all.

"I can't wait to fly over the lines!" Daryl said as we taxied to the airport the following day. "This is one of the few tourist things I want to do."

We flew over the lines in a small plane and saw them in all their glory. I was amazed to think each line was only five inches wide and less than an inch deep, yet they were crystal clear from up above. Nobody knew who made them or why, we only knew they were there and had been, most likely, for thousands of years.

The Nazca Lines were a mystery of astronomical proportions. How did the ancients make those lines in the sand that withstood thousands of years of wind and rain? *Why* did they make them?

Our basic presupposition was that people on earth two thousand years ago didn't have airplanes. They didn't have helicopters or hot air balloons either. So how, I asked, could they have seen the designs? And if they couldn't, who could?

Many people felt the Nazca Lines were religious symbols meant for the eyes of the gods; others felt the area was a gigantic calendar of some sort, but many felt the Nazca Lines were landing strips for alien spaceships.

As we pedaled away, my mind was reeling. Intellectually I wanted to maintain the alien theory was hogwash. Aliens? Really? On earth? Who are we kidding? And yet, maybe there was something to that theory. Maybe there was some sort of extraordinarily intelligent species on earth thousands of years ago. They had conical heads and carved rocks to teach us what they knew, and they flew away in their spaceships. Who was to say there wasn't?

I couldn't believe how far I had sunk. For an ex-healthfood junkie to stand in the desert watching her sons eat Oreos for breakfast… well, words failed me.

Once upon a time I was one of those whole grain eatin', moccasin wearin', organic spoutin' granola types. And in southern Peru I handed my beloved boys Oreos and chocolate bars first thing in the morning.

To be fair, I had little choice. We were finding it very difficult in Peru to find semi-healthy food to carry with us on the bikes. We passed restaurants on a fairly regular basis and could eat rice and chicken at those, but finding healthy food to eat on the road was a struggle.

The day before we had eaten everything I had with me when the town we were aiming for was one of those clearly marked, but non-existent, towns our map was famous for. When we finally arrived at a restaurant after fifty-eight miles of riding, I knew I needed to resupply my panniers.

But just what was I to put in them when all they sold was rice, chicken, fried eggs, and Oreo cookies?

So I stood there in the barren desert that morning and guiltily handed my boys a bagful of Oreos for their morning meal. We had come a long way from the days of tofu french fries and quinoa stew.

We were on a mission. In a few hundred miles we would reach the point where we would turn left to leave the coastal desert behind us and climb back up into the Andes. We were psyched. When we left the mountains more than a thousand miles earlier in Ecuador, we couldn't wait to get down to the flat desert. Now, we were tired of the desert and couldn't wait to get back into high country.

As we cycled away from Nazca, we had decided to make one big push to where we would leave the coastal road. We would take a few rest days here and there, but mostly we planned to just go.

We arrived into one small town and John somehow pulled a muscle in his back and we were stuck for four days. He got better and we packed up and took off and made it fifty-five miles before I got sick and we were stuck again.

A few days later, we got back on the road and spent the day inching our way up a narrow track carved into cliff sides overlooking waves crashing into the rocky shore, and then racing back down to the coast.

It was a tough day and I didn't even want to think about how many thousands of vertical feet we had climbed, but it was stunningly beautiful. Bright teal-blue water, white frothy waves, dark black rocks, and tan sand. A veritable feast of eye-candy.

And then came the *POP* of a broken spoke. There were few noises in the world uglier than the sound of breaking spokes.

Spokes pull on the rim from both sides, keeping the wheel straight and true. The problem with my broken spoke was that, at that particular spot, there was no spoke pulling the rim into position, which caused a bulge. If I rode on it, the rim would actually bend and would never be straight again.

We pushed on, trying to make it to town.

POP

That most definitely wasn't good. Two broken spokes spelled trouble. My front wheel was now so far out of true that the brake was catching with each revolution of my wheel, making the bike jerk.

"You're screwed, Nancy," John said as he rode alongside me, watching my bike lurch with each revolution of the wheel. "The trouble is that once one goes, it puts stress on the others, and they'll pop as well."

We made the decision to bag our plans to make it into town and pulled into a canyon to camp and fix my wheel.

As it turned out, it wasn't the spokes that had broken, but the small nipples that held the spokes in place. We were able to pull out some new nipples and replace them but, as John was truing the wheel, another nipple disintegrated in his hand.

We only had five days to the next big city where we figured we could find a bike shop to replace all the nipples, but could we make it? And once we got the spokes fixed, would my bike make it another five thousand miles to the end of the world? What about the other bikes? They were all showing signs of wear and tear.

"Nancy!" John shouted in the morning as I rubbed the sleep out of my eyes, "You've got three broken spokes!"

Three busted spokes while the bike sat overnight and wasn't even moving. Three more spoke nipples had popped under no stress at all. The aluminum had failed catastrophically at 12,500 miles. My bike was unrideable.

"You guys can stay here while I hitch into town and see if I can get it fixed," I suggested. "There's a small town in ten miles, so I'll see if I can get it fixed there. If not, I'll continue on to Arequipa. It could take until tomorrow before I get back."

"We can't stay out here until tomorrow," John replied. "We don't have enough food and water for a whole day. We need to get into Ocoña, at least."

"I suppose I could hitch in with my whole bike while you guys ride in. It doesn't really matter if I ride the whole way — the world record isn't for me anyway."

As we worked together to push my bike to the road, another spoke nipple popped. With so many spokes flopping around, the wheel wouldn't even spin. We could only hope that we could get the wheel rebuilt in Ocoña. John and I piled the bike and trailer on top of bags of onions in a large truck we flagged down, I climbed up on the onions as well, and we said goodbye.

A while later, I unloaded my bike in the center of Ocoña and discovered yet another busted spoke nipple. Where would it end?

I managed to find a small bike workshop in town and the mechanic was able to rebuild my wheel with steel nipples. I was thankful it was the nipples that broke rather than the spokes; there was no way I would have found spokes to fit my bike in Peru. Nipples were universal.

Hours later, John and the boys appeared after battling headwinds so stiff they were in nearly bottom gear going down the cliff side. Fortunately, they only had to ride nine miles.

We were looking forward to our final thirty miles of the Peruvian coast. It had been a difficult 1500 miles and had pushed me far beyond what I thought I was capable of doing. When I had hit bottom farther north, I wondered if I had it in me to continue on. Peru had challenged me with her headwinds, blowing sand, and long distances, but I had successfully beaten her so far. I could only hope I could triumph over the high Andes as well.

Our primary concern, however, had become my bike. My trusty steed had gotten me 12,500 miles from Alaska, but was showing the stresses of what she had endured. My rear wheel was brand new, so should make it to Ushuaia, but I was concerned about my front one. Only time would tell.

For now, we relaxed and enjoyed our final miles of the coastal desert. We would miss the dancing shadows on the sand dunes, the early morning magic in the desert, and the lovely views of crashing waves. We would not miss the headwinds and blowing sand. The Andes were upon us once again.

Chapter 17

Into the Andean Winter

SOUTHERN PERU

I was nervous about the Peruvian Andes. We had managed in Colombia and Ecuador, but now we were headed into the high Andes in the dead of winter. Once we reached the *altiplano*, a high flat plain nestled between two arms of the Andes, we wouldn't drop below 11,000 feet for months until reaching Argentina thousands of miles away.

Less than three hundred miles from the coast lay the highest mountain pass of our entire journey at nearly 15,000 feet. It would be one solid climb up before dropping down onto the *altiplano*. We set off early in the morning to start the ascent.

By the time my odometer clicked to thirty-five miles, the sun was making a rapid nosedive toward the horizon. Although we figured we were close to town, we pulled off the road to camp. Day one of our ginormous climb was over. As near as we could tell, we had climbed around three thousand feet.

Day two of the climb lasted a full thirteen miles before we found a hotel and decided to call it a day. Our legs, unaccustomed to the mountains, were jelly from the previous day and were ever so happy to get off the bikes.

When the alarm went off, we packed up and headed down to our bikes where John discovered a flat tire on Davy's bike. That should have been a sign to climb back into bed, an omen of things to come. Unfortunately, we didn't listen.

After nine miles, Davy and I stopped to

210

wait for John and Daryl. As they rolled up, John said, "We need to have a serious talk with Daryl. He is sick and by pushing on he is only going to get worse." He had had a rough night, but insisted he was fine in the morning. Obviously, he wasn't. Seeing as how we were then in the middle of the desert with absolutely no shade in which to set up the tent, we pushed on to try and reach a hotel.

A few minutes later, Davy's tire was flat again. I pumped it up and crossed my fingers that it would hold.

We had plummeted down into a canyon first thing in the morning and now had to climb back out. We climbed up through a very narrow, but incredibly beautiful, canyon. Davy's tire went flat again. I pumped it up once more. Daryl complained of a tummy ache.

As we rounded a curve in the canyon, a big gust of wind blasted us and I felt my hair blowing in the wind, but under my helmet my hair shouldn't blow in the wind. I reached up and discovered I didn't have my helmet on; it was back down where I had taken a video of John. I turned around and raced three miles down the canyon but couldn't find my brand new white helmet that I brought back from the USA. Then I had to climb three miles back up to where the others were waiting for me.

When we finally broke out of the canyon, I heard Davy's tire go, "Psssssst." His tube was shot. I took off his tire and replaced the tube with one of our precious spares. That meant we were down to only one spare, and we couldn't find replacements in Peru.

By the time we reached town, we were done. Physically and emotionally fried. And we still had over 10,000 feet to climb.

DAY 725 "I think we made a mistake coming this way," John said as we struggled up the hill.

Duh!

I had asked about the route to Arequipa earlier. "There are two roads," the truckers said. "Go left to go up a canyon and straight to the city. If you turn right, the road is much prettier, but longer, very steep, and with a lot more climbing."

I figured it was a shoe-in; with all the climbing we had coming up, we would take the easier route. But John? As soon as he heard the words 'prettier' and 'no trucks,' he insisted on turning right. This route would take us up a minor pass before dropping down into the city. "We're climbing a 15,000-foot pass," John reasoned. "What's an extra thousand feet?"

For eight miles we climbed through a wide valley. Up. Steep up. And

The road leading from the Pacific Ocean into the Andes was full of switchbacks, twists, and turns.

that was after seven miles of climbing to reach the junction.

As we came around a bend in the road, we suddenly had a view of the road ahead in all its glory, and it scared the pants off us. Steep switchbacks heading to who-knows-where. We called it a day.

"Today we had a long, fairly uneventful climb," Daryl wrote that night. "After a long day, we started looking for a place to camp. Daddy saw a ravine that would make a good place to camp so we parked the bikes too look for a way in. When Daddy sat down, he sat right in a cactus. Mommy and Davy were laughing really hard. I couldn't help a few chuckles, but I thought it was rude to laugh and it wasn't that funny anyway. Then we found a path down into the ravine. Later, we made a campfire. We had a lot of wood. It was a good fire."

We spent the night tucked away in our outrageously spacious tents enjoying the peace and quiet of the desert. We were high enough in the mountains to enjoy chilly temperatures, which made for great sleeping weather. I was glad to have left the heat behind.

"We need to stage an intervention for John," I thought as I pushed my bike through deep sand back to the road in the morning. "Maybe that would knock some sense into the man." The man was nuts.

The road had been steep the day before, but what we did was peanuts compared to what lay ahead. All four of us were leaning into our handlebars, pushing with our entire bodies when a pickup came racing down the hill. The driver slammed on his brakes and backed up until he was beside us. "It's too steep here," he said. "You need to go back down and go to Arequipa the other way."

I figured he was probably right, but John was adamant we continue on.

But finally, somehow, after nearly three hours of pushing, we managed to reach the tunnel indicating the top of the pass, two miles from our campsite. We had made it over the pass. YEEHAW! But really, it was more of a pathetic little yippee! as we didn't have the energy for a real cheer.

We passed through the tunnel and were rewarded with spectacular views of the mountains surrounding Arequipa. We raced down the twisty, winding road into town.

We had been on the road two years. Twenty-four months of steadily making our way southward. Even though it had been hard in many ways, as I looked back upon those two years I saw 104 weeks and 13,000 miles of magic.

As I ground my way up the mountain, I thought about how Davy and Daryl had changed during that time. My mind went back to the day we had climbed aboard our bikes for the very first time. The boys looked so small and vulnerable and I wondered what in the hell I was doing taking them on a bicycle ride to the ends of the world.

Then I fast forwarded to the time in Panama when Davy had escorted me when I was sick and I realized that young man was the very same person who just yesterday had been so tiny and vulnerable. Now he was a strong, confident young man who was able to take care of me should I collapse by the side of the road.

In Ecuador my sons had taken off on their own and shown me how capable they were of navigating the world. They weren't afraid to tackle new challenges that might intimidate others. I took great comfort in the fact that my sons, once so small and fragile, had grown and matured into young men.

Now, I looked at my boys again — so determined to reach the end of the world, so confident in their abilities, so uncomplaining about the demands of our journey — and I was humbled. I tended to grumble and complain when times got tough, but Davy and Daryl showed me a wisdom I couldn't come close to achieving. They somehow knew when it was time to bicker (chore time) and when it was time to jump in and give it everything they had.

Davy and Daryl could climb the highest mountain and wrestle their bikes through the deepest sand because they were determined to get to Ushuaia and that was what they had to do to get there. They had dreamed the impossible dream and I knew they would reach the unreachable star. Nothing could stop them now.

I thought too about all the lessons John and I had learned. Mainly, we had learned that we would never know everything. No matter how many months we had been on the road or miles we had pedaled, there were times when we would face a new situation we didn't know how to deal with.

All our thousands of miles of bike touring had prepared us for a lot. We knew how to anticipate most possible situations, but there were times when we came head-on into a situation that we had never faced before and had no idea how to deal with. All we could do was lean on our past experience, create a solution to the problem, and hope it worked.

We couldn't plan for every eventuality. We could plan and plan, but sometimes we simply hadn't hit upon the perfect solution — yet. We needed to use each failure as a learning opportunity to add knowledge to our bank.

Most importantly, I had learned I could push myself beyond what I thought were my limits. I was stronger and more resilient than I thought I was. As long as my *why* was strong enough, I could go places I never dreamed I could.

After a four-day break in Arequipa, we were ready to tackle our sixth day of climbing. We had climbed to about the halfway mark of our highest pass, but knew the second half of the climb would be the hardest. I stuffed our panniers with countless packets of nuts and raisins, cookies and crackers, pita bread and canned salmon. Water bottles were filled and extra water strapped to the bikes. I had pulled our winter gear from our panniers and stashed it where it was readily available.

We still had 7,000 feet to climb, and at high altitude it would be a challenge. We planned to take it slow and easy and gradually make our way up the mountainside. We had no illusions it would be easy, but figured we were up to the task. If we survived the Peruvian coast, surely we could survive the Peruvian Andes.

Altitude sickness is not something to take lightly, and we were all concerned about how well we would handle it. After John suffered from a terrible headache our first day out of Arequipa, we bought some coca leaves to chew. Local people regularly chewed the leaves cocaine is made from and claimed it helped tremendously with the altitude. We rounded up a big bag of leaves for John to chew as we ascended farther.

214

After a long day in the saddle, we pushed our bikes through the deep sand of a river bed to a camping spot.

We were moving up and our lives were changing. Rather than the stark desert from the coast, now we had plenty of cacti and bushes around, which was a good thing as it was also cold in the evenings. We utilized dead branches from the bushes as firewood to keep us warm.

It was delightful to sit beneath millions of twinkling stars, toasty warm next to a roaring fire. The boys made torches and played with the fire. John and I sat side-by-side and enjoyed the peacefulness of our surroundings.

The morning temperatures told us we were getting higher. We waited for the sun to thaw us out before hitting the road each morning.

It was slow going made even slower by the many breaks we took. A few days out of Arequipa, we had made it a grand total of seven miles by noon. As we came around a bend in the road, we could see a climb spread out before us — eight miles of switchbacks snaking up the hillside starting from an elevation of 11,350 feet.

The excitement and euphoria of our journey had long since worn off and we were functioning on basic deep-down grit and resolve. How badly did we want our dream? Was reaching the end of the world really that important? The world record, as I saw it and I assumed the others did as well, was secondary to our simple determination of doing what we said we would do. We had set out to ride our bikes from one end of the world to the other and, by golly, we were going to do it.

Seeing as how we were nearly out of water and there was no way we could do that climb without water, we parked the bikes and the boys and I prepared to hitch a ride up to the town.

"Why don't you just stay up there?" John said to Daryl. "There's no way we'll make it up on the tandem so you'll be walking anyway. Just find a restaurant and wait for us up there."

Daryl didn't pause for a second. "No," he told his father. "If I do that, then I won't get the world record. I'll come back down."

I was stunned. I hadn't heard a peep from either kid about the record since Central America, but it was obviously on their minds. They were still, after two years, determined to pedal every inch of the way.

The kids and I picked up a bunch of water and four meals to go before jumping on the bus to go back down to John and the bikes.

And then we faced a dilemma: head up and hope there was some kind of camping spot somewhere? Or call it a day and head back into the canyon beneath us? We called it a day.

It was a lovely lazy afternoon. Davy curled up in the tent to read, John played solitaire, Daryl collected firewood for a big bonfire in the evening, and I found a lovely little rock in the sun to sit on and write and play with my beads. It was just what we needed.

The climb was much more than we anticipated — 2500 vertical feet in eight miles. To make matters worse, we faced a horrific headwind nearly all the way up.

When we were nearly at the top the wind stopped and as soon as we reached the flat plateau on top, an awesome tailwind picked up. We flew along the plateau, slamming on the brakes every mile or so to take photos or videos of the many vicuñas, a high-altitude cousin of the common alpaca, dotting the landscape. What a change from the painfully slow ascent!

We ate a quick lunch in the tiny settlement of Cañahuas, stocked up with food from kiosks lining the road, and pushed on.

Six miles later we pulled off the road and pushed our bikes through sand and bushes down to a riverbed to camp. Seeing as how we hadn't showered for four days, and it looked like we would be camping out at least another two nights before we would find a hotel, John and I marched the boys down to the glacial river to wash up.

"No way, Mom!" they protested. "I'm not getting in!"

"Hurry up!" I urged. "The sun is setting quickly. It'll be really cold soon. Take advantage of the sun while you can." I coaxed the boys to strip down to their bike shorts and lean over the stream while I washed their hair and faces. I gave their bodies a quick sponge bath and sent them on their way.

"Aarrrrggghhh!" John shouted as he splashed the frigid water over his body. "This is crazy!"

As cold as the water was, it felt wonderful to be clean.

"Today we left our camp early," Davy wrote in his journal once we were all tucked in for the night. "We climbed for about eleven kilometers. We went up about 2500 vertical feet in that climb. Finally we made it to the top and almost

Vicuñas live very high in the mountains. Their wool is super soft, but each animal provides a little wool. The vicuñas are not domesticated at all - they live wild.

flew over to the tiny town of Cañahuas. We ate lunch and bought bread and other stuff, then we left. We went down to the river and went up a bit, then stopped and found a good place to camp. I had to take a sponge bath in the river that can give you hypothermia. My head went numb after about five bowlfuls of water. Then we came into our tents for the night."

Finding accurate information about the road ahead was a continual battle. We talked with hotel owners and shop keepers about where we would find food and water, and we talked with drivers to find out about road conditions.

We had found, in general, that truck drivers were the most accurate sources of information. We sought out drivers hauling heavy bags of cement or other very heavy loads and asked them for the low-down. They knew exactly where the climbs were — usually.

As we climbed into the Andes, I asked a group of truckers about the road. "The top of the climb is at kilometer 102," they all agreed. "From there, you'll be on the *altiplano* and it'll be mostly flat all the way to Juliaca and Puno."

We set our sights on kilometer 102.

When we reached that marker, it was, indeed, the top of a climb — *A* climb. We descended a thousand feet down to the river and camped out knowing we faced another climb in the morning.

"Nancy! It's snowing!" John shouted early the next morning. "It's snowing in the tent!"

Sure enough, the insides of the tents were lined with a thick layer of frost. Every time we moved, snow fell, getting everything wet.

"It's twenty-six degrees!" John said when he looked at the thermometer. "And that's *inside* the tent!"

It was seventeen degrees Fahrenheit outside — our coldest morning yet. Prior to this, the coldest was twenty-two degrees in Wyoming, but that night we had camped next to a post office so the kids could take shelter as soon as they got up. This time, there was no escaping the cold.

We piled every layer we owned on and packed up, thankful for our warm winter gear.

DAY 733 As promised, we had a climb out of the river valley, but it was nowhere near the six miles we had been told. After seven miles of climbing we found a small restaurant and I asked again about the road.

"The top is just around that bend over there," the woman said, pointing about a mile away. "After that, it's flat or down all the way to Juliaca."

A mile later we came to a viewpoint and the sign said we were at 4320 meters (14,173 feet). We figured we were close. Wearily, we pedaled on until we came around a bend in the road and...

...the road climbed. A lot.

At 4422 meters (14,508 feet) we crested the top, or so we thought. Then we looked ahead and saw the road plummet down before climbing again.

We descended to about 4100 meters, and climbed back up before looking ahead at the next descent and climb. We called it a day and set up camp on a plain at 4425 meters (14,518 feet) under the watchful eye of Pedro the alpaca herder. We knew it would be a cold night as we were 2000 feet higher than the previous night.

I piled on two pairs wool socks, two pairs of wool tights, two wool tank tops, three long-sleeved wool shirts, my down vest and two wool hats, and climbed into my sleeping bag. I was still a bit uncomfortable in the wee hours of the night, but not too bad. I could only hope we would start our descent soon.

It was COLD! We headed up into the worst winter on record and were thankful for our down jackets.

It was winter. Big time winter. Our cycling days were so short I felt like we would never make progress.

It was too cold to pack up before the sun hit our tents and started to thaw the thick layer of frost that built up overnight, so that cut a few hours off our riding time in the morning. In the evening, it was completely dark by 5:15.

We walked the tightrope of time, trying to figure out the latest we could pull off the road to camp, knowing we still had to get camp set up, dinner cooked and eaten, teeth brushed, and the dozens of layers of clothing we needed for the night put on.

Perhaps the worst part of dealing with cold temperatures, though, was not being able to drink enough water. Every morning our water bottles were frozen into solid blocks of ice. As we cycled we took small sips of ice water as the sun slowly melted them, but what I really wanted was a great big gulp after pushing up the hills. Over time, I felt my body becoming more dehydrated each day.

It was also difficult to spend so many hours curled up in our sleeping bags. We were in the tents by five and tried to read or play cards, but that only lasted a short while before our hands were too cold to continue. Even with winter gloves on, my hands couldn't handle holding a flashlight and book for more than thirty minutes. The only thing we could do was curl up and sleep (or attempt to) from six in the evening until seven the following morning.

The good news was that I could finally carry chocolate without risk that it would melt all over my panniers. The bad news was that frozen chocolate wasn't nearly as tasty as warm chocolate.

One afternoon, as dusk was upon us and cold nipped at our hands and feet, we pushed our bikes into a meadow to look for a place to camp. As we pulled tents and other gear off our bikes, Gregory, a land owner who boasted he had four hundred head of alpaca, approached. Gregory was a nice guy and was happy to have us stay on his property; he even invited us to stay in his home, but we declined since his house was little more than a pile of rocks with a roof on it. No electricity, no running water — just the basics.

It had been far too long since we had seen any vestiges of civilization, and we couldn't wait to reach town where we could take hot showers and sleep in soft beds, and yet all Gregory had was a frigid stream running through his property and some old blankets piled atop rocks to sleep on. We were probably much more comfortable sleeping in our Eddie Bauer tents, on our blow-up mattresses, and under our down sleeping bags than Gregory would ever be. I couldn't imagine sleeping in a stone house with a ten-degree wind howling through it. I was even more grateful for the equipment we carried.

It had been an agonizing four days above 14,000 feet climbing hill after hill after hill. Each time we crested what we thought was the top, we descended 200 or 1000 feet before climbing back up, a few meters higher each time.

After days of being assured we had crested the top of our climb and were on the downhill side, we finally did cross the pass — at 4528 meters (14,856 feet). There was a big ol' sign telling us so.

And then came our final descent into town — *wheeeeee!* Pure, unadulterated descent. Not a single pedal stroke for twelve blessed miles.

"I'll gladly pay more for a really nice place with a hot shower," John said as we pulled into town.

"I don't care what it costs," I said. "We're staying in a nice place tonight!"

The shared "first class" bathrooms at a hostel we stayed at!

"I can't wait to lie in bed watching TV," Davy put in his thoughts.

"And have a real bathroom!" Daryl added.

It had been eight days since we left Arequipa, and all four of us were filthy, exhausted, and ready for a bit of luxury.

Luxury, however, wasn't going to be found in Santa Lucia. We did end up in a hostel, but only because we were desperate. Under normal conditions, we would have taken one look at that dump and headed for the hills to camp.

Now, as exhausted as we were, we checked in, piled all the bikes into our tiny, grimy rooms, took showers in barely tolerable water in bathrooms that hadn't been cleaned since dinosaurs roamed the earth, and looked forward to sleeping in real beds. Granted, they were old and sagging and had grubby blankets, but sometimes beggars can't be choosers.

It wasn't anywhere near what we had hoped for, but at least we were in some sort of a building rather than our tents, although it was barely a step up from camping out.

"This feels so weird," Davy said as we flew along the flat plain of the *altiplano* toward Lake Titicaca the next day. "It's been flat for twenty miles so far and they tell us it'll be flat for another twenty! I can't believe it!"

After three hundred miles of climbing steadily and never having more than a mile or two of flat ground since we left the coast, it felt bizarre to not have to change gears on the bikes at all. Somehow, I just couldn't seem to wrap my mind around that one.

We were looking forward to taking a week or more off the bikes. "We deserve this week off," Davy told me as we pedaled side-by-side through the *altiplano*. "We really deserve it!"

We planned to store our bikes and take a bus to Cuzco to visit Machu Picchu and climb on the wonderful Incan ruins during our break. What we didn't plan was to be there with massive crowds. It hadn't even occurred to us that we would be visiting the famous ruins on the winter solstice, the same day thousands of others visited as well. We hadn't even considered the idea that we would be in Cuzco for the Inti Raymi celebration that brings in hundreds of thousands of tourists each year. For a family used to being on our bikes in the middle of nowhere, it was quite a shock to our systems.

Our side trip to Cuzco wasn't all bad though. We met up with Anna and Alister, other PanAm cyclists whom we had first met in Moab, then celebrated the boys' twelfth birthday with in Quito. Now, they were in Cuzco. We also met up with a reader of our blog who graciously offered to bring down some replacement tubes and water bottles. After having been just our tiny family unit for so long, it was wonderful to swap stories with other travelers.

Even so, it wasn't long before we were feeling suffocated by the massive crowds in Cuzco and longed for the peace and solitude of our bikes. Our week off was just what we needed to convince us our bikes weren't as bad as we had come to believe.

"I'm exhausted," John mumbled as he collapsed off his bike the day we started cycling again. "I just can't seem to catch my breath."

That was bizarre. I was pedaling just fine up the minor climb, and John was struggling. That simply didn't happen.

"I wonder if you are fighting something off," I suggested. "On a climb like this, you should be way ahead of me."

Sure enough, once we got to Puno, the poor guy couldn't warm up; he shivered as the boys and I hauled everything up to the hotel room. He shivered as we sat in a Chinese restaurant for lunch. As soon as he got back to the hotel, he curled up in bed.

"Nancy," he mumbled a few minutes later. "Would you get my sleeping bag off my bike? I can't breathe with all this weight on me." He had

Machu Picchu seen soon after we started climbing Machu Picchu Mountain.

climbed into bed under four Peruvian blankets, which felt like sleeping under a pile of bricks. We all pulled out our lightweight sleeping bags that night. In fact, we pulled out our sleeping bags every night for a very long time.

John's illness continued into the next day, but after that he was well enough to manage a tour to the floating islands in Lake Titicaca. We enjoyed the boat ride out and the boys had a blast trying to run on the soft surface of the reed islands. People have lived on the man-made islands for thousands of years and, when they needed a new island, they simply cut a big chunk of reeds from the shoreline and towed it into position. It was always fun to see the boys learn about different ways of living.

DAY 750 John was better and we were antsy; the Bolivian border was nearby and we were excited to cross it. Of all the countries we had been through, Peru had come the closest to defeating us. The coastal desert was a challenge of epic proportions, yet we had somehow managed to get through it. Right on the heels of the desert, came our highest pass ever. We were exhausted mentally and physically and somehow hoped that crossing that border would revive us.

We were only about fifty miles from the Bolivian border when my bike fell apart. Or maybe I should say continued to fall apart. It seemed like every time I turned around something else broke. I had no idea how I could make it another 4500 miles to Ushuaia.

This time, it was my seat post clamp. As I pedaled along the flat highway, I noticed my seat slipping lower. "I must not have tightened the seat clamp enough," I thought as I pulled out my allen wrenches to tighten the tiny ring that held my seat at the desired height.

The clamp fell off into my hand.

I rode the last nine miles into town with my seat all the way down like riding a tiny kids' bike. With each pedal stroke my knees nearly hit my chin and I had to walk up even tiny little hills.

As soon as we pulled into town I deposited John and the boys at a hostel and took off to find a bike mechanic. I figured I would end up with massive amounts of duct tape and wire holding it together. "I think I might be able to find something," the mechanic said after inspecting the broken piece. "I'll be back."

Twenty minutes later he showed up with a seat post clamp! Somewhere he found an old bike and took it off. It worked! It was a bit too small, but creative use of a pliers and an extra-long bolt solved the problem.

It looked like my bike was good to go. We just hoped the new clamp would hold, which I was fairly certain it would. "The old one was made of aluminum — no wonder it broke," the mechanic said. "This one is metal."

With my new seat post clamp installed, we took off for the Bolivian border. In just a few short miles, we would reach the end of Peru. As I pedaled, I thought about how it wasn't all that long ago that I was fairly certain Peru would beat us. I felt like the country was beating us down, kicking us like dogs, and doing everything possible to make us miserable. I didn't think there was any way I would cycle out the tail end of that country.

And now, we had done it. We had conquered Peru against all odds. It had taken us just over four months, but we survived the blowing sand and headwinds. We made it over an impossibly high mountain pass. Most importantly, we hadn't given up, even though I had been tempted more times than I cared to count.

We had put on blinders, focused on our goal, took itty-bitty tiny steps, and managed to make it to the bottom of the country. Now, I looked ahead at the flags flying at the border through tears welling up in my eyes. Peru was behind us. Finally.

Chapter 18

A Detour Leads to a Crossroads

BOLIVIA

On our 754th day on the road, we pedaled into our 13th country full of wonder. Wonder at the simple fact that we had made it, and wonder at the magnificent sights of Lake Titicaca.

It had been a full day of climbing hills when we pulled into the tiny town of Tiquina, on the straits between the two segments of Lake Titicaca. By that point, it was around two in the afternoon and we had been warned about a six-mile climb on the other side. It was clear we wouldn't be able to push on.

We managed to find an *alojamiento*, a local hotel of sorts, and the kids and I trotted off behind the owner to check it out. We tiptoed along a muddy footpath strewn with debris to the back of a decrepit building and climbed stairs that looked as though they hadn't been cleaned since the Great Depression. The owner pushed open a door covered with green slimy mold to reveal the grungy room. The floor was caked with layers of dirt. I had no idea that much grime could cling to walls. The single bed in the middle of the room was so filthy I couldn't imagine touching it, let alone sleeping in it.

"And the bathroom?" Daryl asked. "Where is the bathroom?"

"Bathroom?" the man asked, surprised that we might need one. "It's downstairs, but you'll have to pay."

We headed out, hoping to find someplace else.

Our first stop was the Navy base. "Hello Captain," I said. "I wonder if it might be pos-

225

sible to camp here for the night. We're stuck here in Tiquina and need a safe place for the night."

"I'm sorry," came the response. "The commander is gone right now, and I don't have the authority to give you permission."

Our next stop was Town Hall. "I wonder if it might be possible to camp in that vacant building over there; the captain of the Armada mentioned it might be a possibility."

"The guy in charge isn't around right now," the woman responded. "I'll look for him."

Thirty minutes later he was still missing and we were still homeless. I gave up on them and headed off to the local Nazarene church. Behind the church and way up on the third floor of a construction zone, I found the pastor.

"We're a family traveling on bikes and are stuck here for the night. I wonder if…."

"Not a problem!" the pastor assured me. "Come on over!"

We spent the night comfortably nestled in a room in the parsonage. Daryl and I shared the one small bed while John and Davy slept on the floor in their sleeping bags.

It amazed me how we always managed to find a safe place to sleep — always. We were generally in hotels, but had many days where people were gracious and helpful and allowed us to throw our sleeping bags on their floors. It was reassuring to know people the world over were willing to help a stranger in need.

The following night we, once again, needed to rely on the kindness of strangers.

We got a late start after chatting with the pastor of the church, playing soccer, and eating a good breakfast at the town square. Then we had to get a ferry across the straits of Lake Titicaca.

We dealt with rolling hills the whole day and the altitude affected our ability to get enough oxygen to our muscles. In addition, it was our fifth day in a row on the road, something we very rarely did. Getting up even tiny climbs about killed us.

It was late in the afternoon when we arrived into Batallas and looked for a hotel. People directed us to the only *alojamiento* in town, but the owners weren't there. We were starving by that point, so we headed to the plaza for chicken, then went back to the *alojamiento* — still locked up tight. What now?

By that point it was very late in the afternoon and would be too dark to

Davy, Daryl and John ride along Lake Titicaca in Bolivia.

ride within 45 minutes. Should we wait and hope they showed up? Or continue on in hopes of finding another place to stay? In the end, we climbed back on our bikes and headed to the main road to pedal south, frantically looking for a local house where we could ask permission to camp.

Every person I asked directed us farther on. "There's a hotel just right up the road," they said. We continued pedaling, but I started to wonder if said hotel actually existed.

Finally, just as the sun bid us goodbye, we pulled up to the tiny place with an old, faded sign that said *HOTEL*, staggered off our bikes and into the restaurant. As it happened, it wasn't a hotel at all but a small restaurant. The owner happened to have a lovely little courtyard just perfect for two tents.

Providence had done it again. No matter where we were, no matter what our circumstances, we managed to find a safe place to sleep. Why did I worry?

The following morning, we awoke with luxury on our minds. Ever since we left Puno a couple weeks earlier, we had been in small villages, which we loved. We loved the friendly people, the rich

227

Davy with La Paz in the background. We descended 1,400 feet from the edge of the altiplano down into the huge metropolis of La Paz.

culture, and the small town feel. I wouldn't give those experiences up for the world, but I also knew it was draining. In small villages, we didn't get time alone and were constantly entertaining the local people. Food was, while certainly adequate, not what we could get in the cities. Lodging meant camping out or sleeping on floors in our sleeping bags. Showers were non-existent.

We had been invited to stay at the home of some readers of our blog from La Paz. They were out of the country for the summer, but had offered us the use of their home. We pushed hard to get there.

"I wonder if they'll have a DVD player?" Daryl asked as we cycled toward the capital city.

"Or maybe they'll have a Wii," Davy added.

"I call first shower!" John said.

"I get the softest bed!" I added.

La Paz is situated in a hole in the *altiplano*. All around the high flat plains of the *altiplano* extend for miles, but the city itself lay two thousand feet below. As we approached the drop off and readied ourselves to plunge into the canyon, we could see the massive city sprawling across the hillsides.

It was an eighteen-mile descent through the hectic craziness of the city to Barbara and Rainier's house, but it was worth every cramped hand muscle. The house was pure, unadulterated, blissful decadence.

In the morning we rolled out of bed and headed to the dining room where the maid had tea waiting for us. John and I looked around bewildered, not quite sure how to handle it all.

"Do you have dirty clothes?" Sixta, the maid, asked me.

"Thank you, but I can wash them," I responded.

"No," came the reply. "You guys rest. I'll wash them — I'm happy for something to do. For months now it's just been me and the dog in this great big house. I'm happy that you are here!"

I couldn't quite figure out what to do with the luxury.

I was astounded by the little things. The pot of water that was perpetually hot in the kitchen. The stove that got hot with just a simple turn of a knob. A refrigerator to store cheese and butter. Butter! Real creamy butter! Down comforters on the beds. They even had some funky heaters that went under the sheet to heat us from the bottom! Toilet seats that were clean and not freezing. Hot water that came from the faucet. A DVD player and hundreds of DVDs.

If I thought I was awed by the house and maid, I was blown away by the supermarket. I wandered the aisles throwing pancake mix, cheddar cheese, whole grain bread, and Newman's Own spaghetti sauce in my cart. I couldn't imagine we would ever want to leave.

The kids had their own priorities. "Today is our first day in La Paz!" Davy wrote. "It feels so good to be off the bikes for a day! I never thought it would feel so good to be off the bikes — biking at this altitude is hard!

"I got up at 6:20 in the morning and the first thing I said was, 'Dad? Where's my math?' I said that because Mom was going to go to an internet cafe for a LONG time, and we can't go to the internet cafe unless we have done our math. I did my math and then Mom and I went to the store to buy some food. When we got back Daryl STILL hadn't done his math so Mom and I went to an internet cafe without Daryl."

La Paz was decadent. Pure decadence.

What wasn't so nice was the firestorm that was brewing around the world. I had learned ages earlier that people who disagreed with what we were doing could and would take my words out of context and create stories out of thin air. They would also pick out one short phrase from my blog and build a bizarre scenario from it.

In order not to give them fuel for the fire, we were very careful how we phrased things in the blog and had kept certain incidents a secret. It was like walking a tightrope, never knowing which particular blog entry our critics might grab hold of.

Those people, whom we had never met and had no idea who they were, became stalkers and made it their life mission to discredit us and expose our abusive ways to the world. They were convinced John and I were using and abusing our children, and would go to great lengths to rescue them from our grip.

When I flew to New York from Peru, I was interviewed on the NBC NY Nightly News and the clip was put on the NBC website. Our stalkers immediately left comments. "Shame on you, NBC! Don't you vet your stories at all? These parents are abusing their children and you've just given them air time?"

Every article written about our journey on any website was sure to have critical comments from the group. They followed us everywhere, stalking us.

When Parade Magazine wrote and asked to do a feature article about our journey, we were a bit concerned, but agreed anyway. It was an enormous honor to be featured in Parade and we wouldn't let the stalkers scare us away.

The Parade article came out while we were in La Paz, and was a very nice, uplifting story. They did a great job on it, and we were pleased.

Unfortunately, what followed was not nice, and we found ourselves at the center of a scathing media storm. One blogger asked, "Whose dreams are they really following and at what cost?" Another said, "Forcing children to live their lives on bicycles to make their parents' lifestyle choice possible is quite simply long-term child abuse and exploitation."

The Guardian newspaper from London interviewed us, and then approached a child psychologist to see if a journey of this magnitude could be beneficial to children. "The 10 to 13 age bracket is a critical one in terms of the child developing social skills, interacting with peer groups and making the transition to senior school. It's also usually a time when the child develops a sense of self and you start to see them separating from the parents as they begin to work out how they fit in with the rest of the world."

My head was spinning. Was I doing the best thing for my children? Was I being unfair to them to take them out of school for so long? Although the boys talked with many people every day, it was true that they didn't have any long-term friendships; was that fact doing them irreparable damage? Did the benefits of our journey, of which there were many, outweigh the negatives? I lay awake in bed pondering the advantages and disadvantages of our lifestyle.

In the end, I came to the conclusion that the childhood we were giving our children was the best *for them*. It wouldn't be the best for every child, but for Davy and Daryl, it was an incredible experience. There were advantages and disadvantages, good points and bad, but when we looked at it in its entirety, we came to the conclusion that our life on the road was the best thing going for our boys.

I understood there was a price to be paid in order to do what we were doing. Our sons missed playing on soccer teams and being a part of the swim team. They missed sleepovers with friends and Boy Scout campouts. But they gained other things. They got to climb Mayan pyramids and explore Incan ruins. They swam with sea lions and scuba dived with turtles. They danced at Carnival and burned *viejos* at New Year.

I realized that every time we made the choice *to do* something, we made a parallel choice *not to do* something else. It was all about weighing the options and figuring out which option had the most benefits. There was no right or wrong; there was no one choice. Each person needed to make that choice for herself. And my choice, for my family, was to continue biking the Americas.

We had enjoyed our five weeks in La Paz. We hung out with other cyclists, and John got his entire mouth refurbished by a German-trained dentist that came highly recommended. I had my old crown replaced. We pored over maps and planned our route to Argentina. After five weeks, we were missing our bikes and ready to move on.

After climbing up out of the canyon to the *altiplano*, we arrived into the town of El Alto and looked around at various hotels. We chose the one that was, by far, the best of the bunch before unloading our piles of gear and hauling them up to our fourth floor room.

About ¾ of our gear was upstairs — along with Daryl — when the owner blocked our way.

"We don't have any rooms available," he said.

John and I stood with our arms full of panniers and thought, "What the heck?"

"There aren't any rooms," the owner repeated.

"But... but... but..." I stammered. "We've already got most of our gear up there — plus a kid!"

Apparently, the daughter wasn't supposed to rent any rooms as the family was about to take off for the day. Once the Dad arrived on the scene, he took over and told us we couldn't stay. We begged and pleaded and promised we wouldn't trash his hotel in his absence, and managed to convince him to let us stay.

DAY 793 "This looks like home," I thought as I pedaled south through the *altiplano* the following day. The desert of southern Idaho looked very similar with its wide open spaces lined with grasses gently swaying in the breeze. The only thing missing was sagebrush.

I found a beauty and tranquility in the desert; there was something about it that drew me in. I knew some felt it was ugly with the scrub brush being the tallest thing around, but I loved it. It was home.

"This reminds me of the tundra," Davy interrupted my reverie. "Remember when we first started our trip and it was just flat tundra forever? This is almost the same, but we're a lot higher now."

I didn't relish the idea of the frigid temperatures, high altitudes, or unrelenting sun of the *altiplano*, but the wide open plateaus with sweeping vistas of snow-capped Andes delighted me. Having the freedom to explore the land and discover hidden treasures that could only be found while riding a bicycle made it all worth it. Whether it was an alpaca herder who was honored that we spent a night with him or bright green cactus growing in intricately fine sand with 21,000-foot peaks in the background, each day brought new and unexpected adventures. It was even more special when colorful and rugged people who eked out a living in the sparsely populated wonderland welcomed us to their homes.

"Today was VERY dusty," Davy wrote in his journal. "At the beginning it was very nice riding. We had a tailwind and went very fast. Then after a while the line of hills that blocked the side wind ended and we had a SUPER bad side wind. It blew dust over the road so thick that you couldn't see fifty feet, but that was only at times. Half the time all you had was a side wind and another quarter of the time some dust was being blown across the road. Then we finally made it to Oruro. It was a very dirty town. That was most likely because there was wind going down some of the streets like crazy."

"Where are you headed from here?" asked Ami, the hotel receptionist in a small hotel in Oruro as we checked in.

"Tomorrow morning we'll head out for Potosi!" I told her. We were excited to be continuing south through the *altiplano*.

"You can't go to Potosi," she replied.

That made no sense. Potosi was the fourth largest city in Bolivia; of course we could go there, or so said my American mind.

"Potosi is completely blocked off. You can't get in. There is a strike going on and the entire city has been sealed off — nobody in, nobody out," she continued. "The big news around here is that a group of tourists finally managed to escape the city yesterday after being trapped for thirteen days." Ami handed me a newspaper with the story on the front page. A group of thirty-seven tourists had finally been allowed to leave after being held in the city for two weeks.

"We can get through," John said. "They'll block the road for cars, but we'll get through on the bikes. In fact, it's perfect! The road block will mean no traffic so it'll be perfect for us."

The more we learned, however, the less we thought it was wise to continue on. We could most likely get through, but everything was closed — all stores, all restaurants, and all hotels. Once we got into the city three days away, then what?

We decided to hang out in Oruro until the strike was resolved.

"It's getting worse," Ami told me when I walked downstairs for breakfast. "The news says they've taken control of the hydroelectric plant and are threatening to shut off power to the city which would also affect the water supply. The news reports are saying there are already serious food shortages in the city. It's a good thing you didn't go."

It was Day Fifteen of the strike designed to pressure the president of the country into providing development projects in the city. The local officials had shut down the city and vowed they wouldn't relent until they got the promises they wanted. We sat tight, watching the news, hoping they could resolve their differences.

"You guys need to leave," Ami said as we descended from our room on Day Seventeen. "Word on the street is that they will close Oruro if the president doesn't meet their demands."

We scrambled into action, getting the bikes out of the storeroom, packing everything, hauling it all down, and loading the bikes. I ran to the ATM to get more money out, just in case. Within two hours of hearing the rumor, we were off. Off for a scenic tour of Bolivia.

Our plan had been to stay on the *altiplano* between the two arms of the Andes, and we had planned our route impeccably. We knew where the water and food sources were and knew exactly what to expect. Now, that plan had been aborted and we had changed gears. The only other route we could take involved going up and over the eastern arm of the mountains, and then dropping down into the Amazon basin before turning right and heading south to Argentina. It would be a 400-mile detour, but we had little choice.

We knew nothing about our new route. Our map showed a line on the map, but we had no idea where we would find anything. I was nervous as we pulled out of town, knowing we were sorely unprepared for what lay ahead.

Thirty miles later we pulled up to a small restaurant and started talking with a bunch of truck drivers. "Where are you going?" they asked.

"Cochabamba," I replied. "How's the road?"

"You'll climb for another forty-five miles," came the reply. "The top is at around 5000 meters."

I was aghast; 5000 meters was 16,400 feet! We pedaled away hoping they were wrong.

High-altitude climbing was hard. Climbing was tough enough at sea level, but at fourteen thousand feet, it was insanity. We gasped for air as we pounded the pedals and slowly made our way up.

Fortunately, the truckers were wrong and we topped out at 4494 meters (14,744 feet). Even so, that was higher than the highest peaks in Colorado.

Bolivia was proving to be a tough country as services were basically non-existent. Hotels of any kind were only available in the largest cities, and we had heard from other cyclists that they stayed at schools and health centers, but we bombed out in that arena.

One night we pulled into a small town and found the woman in charge of the local school. "I wonder if it might be possible to put our tent up at the school," I asked. "It's getting late and we need a place to sleep."

"There is no space at the school," she told me even though I could clearly see a very large field behind the school across the street. "Just up the road there is another village; you should be able to stay there. It's just right up there where you see that big patch of shade less than a mile away."

"But is there a school there?" I asked. "So close to this one?" We were in a rural area and the idea of two schools within a mile of each other was outrageous.

"There's a school there. Go there."

We rode away knowing full well there was no village one mile away and, if there happened to be, it surely wouldn't have a school. We found a place to pitch the tents in a canyon.

The following afternoon we arrived into the village of Confital late after climbing over a massive pass. We were nearly out of water, had no more bread, and we were all hungry.

I raced around town buying provisions while the sun sank lower by the minute. By the time we got ready to leave, it was late and there was no sense in pushing on. We headed to the school in the hopes of camping there. As we pulled in the school gate with our heavy bikes, the gatekeeper came over.

"Is it possible to camp here tonight?" I asked.

We enjoyed staying with an indigenous family in the highlands of Bolivia.
We got a kick out of trying on their traditional clothes, while they enjoyed
wearing our bike helmets.

"Mmmmmm," she mumbled.

"We were looking for an *alojamiento*, but there aren't any in town and it's too late to push on. Can we set up our tents here?"

Eventually she agreed as long as we promised to leave early in the morning.

Surrounded by a throng of curious kids, we set up our tents. We got out our mats and sleeping bags to organize ourselves.

And then the gatekeeper came up again. "You will have to pay to stay here."

"How much?" I asked. We fully intended to give her some money before we left.

"You need to leave something for the school."

"How much?" I repeated.

"100 *Bolivianos*."

100 *Bolivianos*? That was more than she would make in a month!

We packed up.

The problem was that, by now, it was dark. We frantically threw our gear together and lashed it to the bikes.

As we pulled out of the school in the growing dusk, a man flagged us over and invited us to stay on the cement floor of his store/restaurant. We spent the evening laughing and playing with Zacarias and his entire family in a big room with people coming and going and talking and eating and watching TV. They dressed us in their indigenous clothing; we put our bike helmets on their heads.

I sat back watching everyone laugh and play together and was more thankful than ever that my sons had the opportunity to be there.

Just as we crested the top of our final pass, I heard the **POP** of a broken spoke. We pulled into a small restaurant to eat lunch and fix my bike. This time, it was an actual spoke that broke, not just the nipple. A spoke on my brand new wheel that I brought back from the USA.

"You're screwed," John told me. "Once one goes, the others will follow. There's no way you'll make it to Argentina."

John pulled out one of my few spare spokes and threaded it in. "You realize how serious this is, don't you? I can fix this, but your spokes will be popping one after another."

All four of us were somber as we dropped down off the pass pondering the idea that my bike might not make it. Even so, after being above 11,000 feet for over two months, it was bizarre to drop down. I had forgotten how easy it was to breathe and had gotten to the point where I took the cold for granted. Two thousand feet lower made a world of difference.

We set up camp on the side of a mountain overlooking the massive descent that would take us into Cochabamba. A stunningly gorgeous view spread out before us, and we could see the road snaking down amongst the hills. The broad expanse of the Andes was nothing short of breathtaking as a bright orange sunset made the whole area glow as if on fire.

DAY 799 It was an awesome twenty-mile downhill run to drop down off the mountain, then another twenty-five miles of rollers into Cochabamba, where we immediately sought out the Verhage family. They were staying in Cochabamba for a while and the boys couldn't wait to meet up with Jesse and Sammy once again.

The fifteen months since the four boys had played together in Honduras melted away as they quickly got reacquainted. They were thrilled to be together again. The four boys dashed off to an internet café to play games, while John and I chatted with Michael and Ciska.

"Sometimes you reach a crossroads in your life," Michael said as we sat around the dinner table that evening, "and you have to choose which way to turn."

236

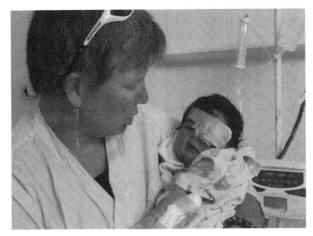

We spent many hours at the children's cancer ward at Hospital Materno Infantil in Cochabamba. Here I attempt to comfort an infant with a massive tumor behind her eye.

For Michael and his family, that crossroads had appeared a couple months earlier. That day the family of four visited a Bolivian hospital and met a thirteen-year-old cancer patient named Mariela.

"We had a choice that day," he said. "We could choose to turn our backs and continue our travels, or we could choose to step in. We made the choice to help a fellow human being."

Since that day the Verhage family had managed to arrange for Mariela's medical treatment and raise over $8000 to rebuild the family home so that, when Mariela was able to return home to her village, she would have a relatively sanitary place to live.

Our family reached that same crossroads that evening. The funds the Verhages raised were gone, yet Mariela still needed further medical treatment. Her cancerous leg had been amputated and she needed a prosthesis. There were also school expenses for a girl with dreams.

Could we turn our backs and pedal away? Or would we make the same choice Michael and his family made? In many ways, it would have been so simple to ride away and let someone else deal with Mariela and her cancer. But who? Were we placed in this situation of coming to Cochabamba for this purpose?

As I lay in bed that night, I thought about Mariela and about my responsibility in the world. "If it was Davy or Daryl lying in that Bolivian hospital bed, I would want people to reach out and help him."

And so we made the choice to help. We did what we could to assure a positive future for Mariela.

The next few weeks were a whirlwind of activity. We spent time at the pediatric cancer ward at the local hospital. We wrote letters. We set up an

We met up with the Verhage family in Cochabamba and planned to ride with them several hundred miles. On our way out of town we stopped to say goodbye to Mariela, a cancer patient we had gotten to know.

official charity in Bolivia to receive funds. We sought out an attorney to lay it all out so the doctor could use her discretion for where the money would go.

The whole time the four boys were inseparable. They watched movies and played video games. They ate all their meals together and thoroughly enjoyed their time with each other.

"I hate to take the boys away," I mentioned to John one day. "It's so magical to have Jesse and Sammy to play with."

"I know," he replied. "It's so good for them to have other kids to hang out with. I wish we didn't have to leave."

The very next morning we were eating breakfast with Michael and Ciska. "We're thinking about riding with you guys to Santa Cruz," Ciska said. "The boys really want to cycle with you guys."

That was great news! Santa Cruz was nearly three hundred miles away and it would be wonderful to have companions on the road.

Early in the morning our caravan hit the road. We were three tandems and two single bikes just as when we cycled together in Honduras. Leaving Cochabamba, we had a long climb before we would drop down into the Amazon basin. Unfortunately, our weeks off the bikes had affected all eight of us.

"Whaddaya think? Should we call it a day?"

We had planned to make it to the top of the climb so we'd be poised for the massive drop down in the morning, but it was a tougher climb than we expected and we were all tuckered out. When we pulled into a small town with a school, we figured we would ask. More accurately, I should say, Michael decided to ask. After our experiences with Bolivian schools so far, we would have passed on by.

"Of course!" the guard said when approached. He was more than willing to open the assembly room, a large room more than capable of accommodating eight cyclists. Rather than a cold night camping by the side of the road, we ended up with a roof over our heads, chairs to sit on, a table to use, and we even had access to a warm shower!

As we organized our gear, we had asked the cleaning lady if there was a restaurant in town. There wasn't, but we figured we would be fine with the PB & J, nuts, and raisins we carried in our panniers. We certainly wouldn't starve.

A few hours later the *señora* walked in with an enormous bowl of food — fried chicken, sliced tomatoes, rice, and potatoes. An enormous bowl — enough for an army of cyclists.

We never, ever expected her to fix us an enormous dinner, but were ever so grateful. All eight of us ate till we were stuffed.

"Times like these make such great memories," Sammy said. I wholeheartedly agreed.

We topped out at 3707 meters (12,160 feet) around noon and started our massive descent into the jungle. As soon as we crested the top and arrived onto the Amazon side of the Andes, dense fog swirled around, encompassing us in a blanket of clouds. We plummeted down through a tight canyon as dense vegetation magically appeared. I was startled at how different the Amazon side of the Andes was from what we had been cycling in for so long.

It was a quick six-thousand-foot drop to where we found a sleepy little village with dozens of roadside stalls selling local flowers and snacks for motorists. Seeing as how there were absolutely no places to pitch the tents along the road snaking around the mountain side, we figured the village could very well be our only chance at a place to sleep.

Michael managed to sweet talk the commander at the military base into offering us their recreation room for the night. With comfortable couches, a massive big screen TV, ping pong table, and Foosball, we enjoyed the evening tremendously.

We spent the night in a classroom at a school. Everyone from the cleaners to the administration were overly kind to us and they all showed up in the morning to see us off.

The following day we dropped down to 290 meters (950 feet) in the Amazon basin. It was hot. It was humid. It was buggy. Even so, the four boys had more fun than a barrel of monkeys. We opted to take a day off to hang out, and the boys spent a couple hours playing in the pool, then they rounded up old, broken chair seats as shields and sticks as swords and created a whole magical world.

"*En garde!*" Daryl shouted as he brandished his sword and shield. "Who goes there?"

"It's only I!" responded Sammy. "I am friend."

We chatted and played until well into the night, then collapsed into our hotel beds under rattling ceiling fans.

"Nancy!" John shouted way too soon, waking me from a deep sleep. "It's raining! The bikes!"

We jumped out of bed and dashed to the courtyard where our bikes were stashed under a tree. Rain fell by the bucketload as we quickly grabbed the bikes and wheeled them to the covered veranda.

"The laundry!"

Rain pelted my head as I quickly grabbed our nearly-dry, but now wet again, clothes hanging on the line. By the time I made it back to the hotel room, I looked like a drowned rat.

The possibility of rain wasn't even on our radar — the last time we saw rain was up in Ecuador. Now, we lay in bed listening to wave after wave of a torrential downpour blasting the area. We could only hope that wouldn't be a regular occurrence.

DAY 813 Our plan of an early departure was dashed by the rain and we got on the road just before ten, knowing the next town was miles away. Davy stayed right beside Jesse and Sammy on a tandem and chatted the entire day. He was thrilled to have other kids to talk with as he pedaled.

After so many months spent battling constant headwinds along the Peruvian coast and then climbing the Andes, I had completely forgotten how easy cycling could be. It was the perfect way to spend one's birthday.

It was my fiftieth birthday. Half century. The big five-oh and I couldn't have asked for more, other than a place to stay that night.

The problem with that particular stretch of road was a lack of accommodations. When we set out in the morning, we knew the next hotel was many miles away, and we figured we wouldn't make it. When we passed a military base after thirty-three miles, we decided to ask if we could stay. Maybe, just maybe, they would allow it.

Once the commander appeared at the gate, magic happened. He escorted us to a big beautiful room with four beds and plenty of floor space for the other four, then took us over to the canteen where egg sandwiches and Coke magically materialized.

We four adults spent the afternoon and evening talking with Commander Juan and his wife Gabi, learning about the government's efforts to eliminate illegal coca fields and lots of other interesting tidbits. The boys spent the afternoon climbing every tree on the military base, playing soccer on the massive field, and otherwise exploring the jungle environment with the commander's son.

Celebrating my birthday on a Bolivian military base was a wonderful way to celebrate, but mostly I was just excited that I *could* spend my fiftieth birthday there. I knew I was fortunate to be physically able to handle the stresses and demands of traveling by bicycle when so many others my age had health problems that prohibited them from doing what we were doing. To be able to manage the journey financially was a gift beyond words. And to have children who shared our passion for traveling on bikes was the best blessing I could imagine.

We followed the front range of the Andes down into Argentina. The best part of that part of the journey was paralleling the mountains and knowing we wouldn't have to climb up into them.

It was an easy cycling day under the intense sun, and we were ready to call it a day when we pulled into Yapacani. Unfortunately, all the hotels were either outrageously expensive or dumps. We pushed on.

A few miles later, we passed some *cabañas*, which had always meant "cabins" in the past. In Bolivia, it apparently meant outdoor restaurant. "You are welcome to camp here," they offered, pointing to one shelter that wasn't being used.

All eight of us piled in and the four boys immediately ran down to the Ichilo River. "This is way too Amazon-ish for me!" Jesse exclaimed as he happily ditched his shoes and headed into the mud with the others. Indeed, it was Amazon-ish. It was exactly what I thought of when I thought "Amazon jungle."

Rather than sleeping in some hot, stuffy hotel room with no windows, the night was pure bliss. A cold front came through bringing the soft, lulling sound of raindrops on the thatched roof above us. The temperature dropped sharply making the night pleasantly cool. The best part was falling asleep to the sounds of the jungle: monkeys and frogs, along with a large network of birds singing and cawing and insects chirping away.

The cold front that moved in overnight stayed with us into daytime. It was cold and windy, and we battled a strong headwind all day. As I pedaled along the jungle road, I was amused that we were bundled up in our winter woolies; that was not what we expected from the Amazon basin.

Our final day of cycling with the Verhage family brought us to Santa Cruz. Our week there was filled with numerous celebrations of John's 56th birthday with many new friends from Santa Cruz. We continued to enjoy our time with the Verhages, and met up once again with Anna and Alister. We had met them in Utah, Ecuador, Peru, and now Bolivia. South America was getting smaller every day.

We were 330 miles from Argentina, our fourteenth and final country. We would travel through the *chaco,* the area sandwiched between the Andes Mountains to the west and the Amazon basin to the east. It was a dry forest area with many thorny trees and bushes. And tailwinds, we were told.

That was music to my ears. The winds blew consistently from north to south and we flew, racing down the road with barely an effort. We enjoyed barreling along at fifteen miles per hour effortlessly. It was our payback for all those hours along the Peruvian coast.

We were thinking that maybe, just maybe, we would make it out of Bolivia without a visit to the local hospital. We had gotten an intimate view of hospitals in every country since Panama and I was hopeful we would give it a miss in Bolivia. Unfortunately, we weren't so lucky.

"I… I… I…," Davy stammered through his sobs. "I hit a rock or something and fell." He held out his hand and I noticed his baby finger was a bloody mess. I also noticed the fingernail hanging at a very awkward angle. "It hurts so bad!"

John and I scuttled about gathering up his bike and making sure Davy wasn't hurt anywhere else; he ended up with a few bruises and scrapes, but that fingernail dangling by a thread was the worst.

"Here are the options," I told Davy as he cradled his hand by the side of the road. "We can camp right here and you and I can hitch into town to the hospital, or we can see if we can flag down a truck that has space for our bikes and hitch into town that way, or Daryl can take your bike while you ride these last twenty miles on the tandem with Daddy. What do you think?"

In the end, Davy opted to hop on the tandem, so I bandaged his finger with gauze and antibiotic ointment, and we hit the road again.

As soon as we pulled into town, Davy and I ditched our bikes at the hotel and headed for the local hospital. The doctor deadened his finger and pulled the nail out completely. Davy happily reported that it didn't hurt nearly as bad as when they did his toes.

Total cost? $4.50 Add another $4.50 for painkillers and a roll of gauze and the total bill came to $9.00. If you count the $1.50 for a taxi to the hospital and back, it was up to $10.50. I didn't even want to think about what the bill would have been back home.

I had to laugh at how differently my sons perceived things. For me, such a traumatic experience as losing a fingernail in an accident would at least warrant a mention in a journal entry, but apparently not for Daryl. That night he wrote, "Today we woke up in a hotel that supposedly included a buffet breakfast. When we went up to the breakfast area to get our breakfast, a lady gave us a plate that had bread, butter, jam, and juice. We ate that and went to get more but, because they had given us a discount, we didn't get a full buffet. So we snuck over and got stuff while she wasn't looking. She caught me once and got pretty mad. I was tempted to see what would happen if she caught me again."

"Hey Dad!" Daryl shouted as he brandished a stick with some brightly colored something dangling off the end of it. "Want some underpants?"

I wondered about the people who drove down the road throwing underpants out their windows. It seemed to be a common practice in that part of the world; at least it appeared that way from the sheer number of them we found scattered along the side of the road.

"Why don't you burn them?" John responded. "Let's do our part to clean up the environment a little bit."

Daryl's eyes widened in surprise. "Burn them?" he asked. "Can we?"

"Might as well; we'll be here for a while."

John sat on the side of the road surrounded by various bits and pieces from my bicycle — the trailer had been disconnected and sat by the side of the road. My wheel was taken apart and John was busy fixing a flat tire caused by one of the nasty thorns we had recently encountered.

"Cool!" the kids shouted as they pulled out the lighter.

A few seconds later, Daryl proudly waved the burning underpants on a stick as one would a sparkler on the Fourth of July.

"Let's make a big bonfire!" Davy urged. "Quick — we can use the underpants as kindling!"

The boys scampered around collecting bits of dry grasses and cow dung to feed their fire while John and I got my bike put back together.

It was late afternoon when we pulled off into the woods to camp. It was peaceful and tranquil. The tents were set up beneath the trees, Davy and Daryl read quietly; John organized the bikes. I sat on a fallen log, writing. I looked around me at the beautiful forest and realized that times like these were what I loved about bike touring.

Easy riding through gently rolling hills. Long, relaxing lunch in a nice restaurant. Breaks by the side of the road with no bugs. And camping in the forest as the sun slowly made its way toward the horizon. It just didn't get any better than this.

As I studied the map to figure out what was coming, I noticed we were approaching the Tropic of Capricorn, which meant we were nearly out of the tropics. The spring equinox was right around the corner so days would be getting longer and longer as we made our way south.

Winter was behind us, spring was coming. I was happy.

Chapter 19

A Different World

Northern Argentina

Argentina! It had taken us well over two years to reach our final country, but our legs finally delivered us to her borders. Spirits were high as we passed through the border formalities. When we met the head honcho of the border post and he formally presented the boys with an Argentine flag for their bikes, we were flying even higher.

One more country. So close to our goal. We could see it in our minds' eye. We were so close we could taste it. The smell of victory was all around and nothing — absolutely nothing — could stop us now. We were strong. We were invincible. One more measly country to pass through and we could say we had reached that unreachable star!

"How do you think Argentina will be different from Bolivia?" I had asked the boys as we sat around the dinner table the evening before.

"Well, it's a richer country," Daryl responded.

"How will that affect our lives?" I prodded.

"I think our lives will be easier there — things will be more expensive, but I think the roads will be better."

He was right on half of that. Things were a bit more expensive, but the roads didn't even come close. Throughout Bolivia, we had cycled along  roads with nice shoulders and the surfaces were great. In Argentina, the surface was quite broken up and there was no shoulder at all. We pedaled on, battling truck drivers for a tiny spot on the side of the road, hoping things would change farther south.

It didn't take long to discover that we had entered a different world. As Daryl had realized so many months earlier, border crossings rarely changed anything. We needed to figure out a new currency, but that was about all that changed from country to country. Generally speaking, the culture and food on one side of a border were similar to what we would find on the other.

As we made our way through countries, we noticed things changing over time. We passed from one cultural area to the next, from one indigenous group to another. The changes happened slowly; many times we weren't even aware that it had changed until we compared pictures from a couple hundred miles earlier with what we saw now.

Typical foods of the regions gradually morphed from one to another with little regard to the political boundaries we call borders. For the most part we had plenty of time to get used to the new ways, therefore we weren't really even aware they were new ways.

But entering Argentina changed all that. In the blink of an eye, everything changed. *BAM!* Life was radically different than it was in Bolivia. Argentine life revolved around a six-hour siesta, but our daily routine simply couldn't. Stores and other businesses opened in the morning, but closed around noon. Everyone went home for a large family lunch, then napped or relaxed all afternoon before heading back to work around six in the evening.

That created a massive logistical challenge for us to deal with. We needed to arrive in town before noon in order to find food, but if we were delayed for any reason — if we encountered winds or big hills — then we were out of luck until at least six in the afternoon. In the middle of the day, everything was closed. Everything. They opened again until two or three in the morning, which didn't help us much as we weren't prepared to ride in the dark.

The siesta schedule went against every routine we had ever established as cyclists. We tended to get up early in order to arrive into town around two or three in the afternoon. In Argentina, we were quickly discovering, if we followed what we had always done we would be sitting under a tree for three or four hours before we could even think about finding food or looking for a hotel when we got into town. And even then food was hard to find as most restaurants didn't open until nine, when we were typically climbing into bed.

The other interesting trend we noticed in northern Argentina was a reverse of vegetation. I guess that was to be expected, but I never really thought about it until it started to happen. All of a sudden, I was reminded of Texas and Baja — complete with armadillos and cardon cacti. Seeing as how we were the same distance from the equator as southern Texas, it all made sense. We were just reversed. We figured we would pass through the same zones going south as we would going north.

It wasn't only what was around us that was changing; I started noticing major changes within us as well. Davy — my avowed vegan — had never eaten meat. Even when he was a baby he devoured mashed carrots and brown rice, but any kind of meat I attempted to put in his mouth came right back out — with force, I might add.

We were walking along the street in Santa Cruz a couple weeks earlier and I stopped to buy some meat-on-a-stick. "Can I have the potato skewered on the end?" Davy asked. That part came as no surprise. But when he asked for a taste of the meat, I was flabbergasted. And when he asked if he could buy a stick for his very own, I was bowled over. I figured he was hungry — very hungry.

Then came the day when our meals arrived in a small restaurant in some nameless Argentine town. I figured John and Davy would do their normal swap — Davy would give his meat to John in exchange for rice and potatoes, just like they had done for years. When Davy picked up his fork and knife and started to eat his *milanesa* (an Argentine version of chicken-fried steak), I was pretty much dumbstruck. I doubted my eyes would ever return to their original position after bugging out so far when he asked for more.

DAY 857 We were now 300 miles into Argentina. It was slow going, but we made steady progress. We were slowly figuring out how to deal with Argentina and had come up with a plan that seemed to be working. Rather than attempting to reach towns daily, as we had since southern Mexico, we accepted the distances, carried more food, and planned to camp in the woods. We enjoyed being back in our tents.

After a long day on the road, we set up our nylon homes in a lovely clearing in the woods, cooked a quick rice dinner, and climbed into bed. It didn't take long before I felt my temperature start to climb. Daryl slept peacefully beside me covered with only a thin, cotton sheet, but I lay curled up in both my fleece sheet and sleeping bag, shivering.

I had been sick a few times on the road, but nothing like this. I had no idea what was happening within my body, but this one felt serious somehow. Like there was something *wrong*.

248

I knew I was sick, but didn't realize yet just how sick. I was very determined to make it into town, but finally accepted that it wasn't going to happen.

By morning my fever was down. We stuffed our sleeping bags, rolled up our tents, lashed everything on our bikes, and hit the road. Twelve miles later we pulled into the tiny town of La Viña looking for food. My temperature was back up, and I felt like my lungs simply weren't functioning.

I slumped over the table of the small café, picking at my *milanesa*. Holding my head up was a chore that took tremendous amounts of energy.

"You must go to the clinic," the woman who ran the café insisted. "It's not far from here and the doctor will help you."

A few minutes later the doctor told me she thought I had bronchitis and handed me an inhaler. "Give this a try, but stay here in town tonight just in case it's something more serious."

Ibuprofen brought my fever down and the inhaler opened my lungs, so we took off, disregarding the doctor's advice to stay in town.

I felt great when we pulled into the woods to camp. Working together, we cleared two little spots of ground for our tents and got everything set up. Daryl climbed in one tent to get the sleeping bags organized while Davy did the same to the other. I cooked dinner and we sat on logs to eat. We were camped in a gorgeous spot and I was grateful for simply being there.

A few hours later, however, I was miserable. As I lay on my thin sleeping mat, curled up under my sleeping bag, my lungs didn't want to cooperate. Every time I turned over it felt like liquid in my lungs shifted and sent me into a massive coughing spasm. The fever returned and I started wondering how I would get to town forty-one miles away.

We knew something was seriously wrong. This was not just your typical, run-of-the-mill sickness. "We need to get you to town," John said as he helped me pack my bike in the morning. "Which direction should we go?"

It was twenty-four miles back or forty-one miles ahead to food and water. Staying put wasn't an option since we had only planned a few days between stores. I drugged myself up with Ibuprofen, took a deep breath from the inhaler and climbed into the saddle to keep moving south.

As I pedaled through the stunning scenery reminding me of a cross between Baja and Zion National Park, I was gasping for air, but any kind of deep breath sent me into spasms of coughing. I was determined to make it into Cafayate under my own power.

Pedaling on flat ground was hard enough, but getting up any kind of incline was impossible. I climbed off my bike and started pushing. "Mommy," Daryl advised as he pedaled past me on the tandem while I pushed up a tiny hill. "You need to hitch into town and see a doctor,"

He was right. I could go no farther. My body had betrayed me.

I realize now, with the benefit of hindsight, that I needed to take care of myself and allow John and the boys to take care of themselves, but that whole teamwork part of me wouldn't let go. My responsibility on our entire journey had been to arrange for food and water for our team and now, because of the time I had wasted, they didn't have enough of either to make it into town.

"I'll hitch into town, buy food and water, then hitch back out," I told them. "I'll camp with you tonight and hitch in to the hospital tomorrow morning." That was, very possibly, one of the dumbest decisions I've ever made.

"We'll find a campsite and leave a bike by the side of the road so you know where we are," John said. "We'll make sure we're easy to find."

I stood on the side of the road and watched as my three boys rode off without me. Davy, who had grown enough to be able to fit my bike, handled it like a pro. Daryl defected off the tandem and onto Davy's bike. John rode solo. Tears streamed down my face as I watched them pedal away and my heart broke at the thought that maybe, just maybe, the journey was over for me.

What would I do if something was seriously wrong? If I couldn't continue on, would they go without me? We were so close to the end I couldn't imagine them not finishing the journey; I couldn't imagine them doing it without me either.

One of the hardest parts of our journey was standing on the side of the road, watching Davy ride off on my bike. I didn't know yet what was wrong with me, but knowing that my three boys could head out without me meant I was no longer necessary.

My fever was raging by the time I reached town. Miraculously, I managed to find a small shop open during siesta time, bought food and a few gallons of water, then headed to the bus stop to wait. By the time I found my boys by the road, I knew I couldn't wait — I needed to get to a doctor. Now.

I stood on the side of the road yet again, silently pleading with each driver who passed to take me to the doctor, yet they zoomed by without stopping. I was desperate, but helpless at the same time. Davy stayed by my side the whole time, tirelessly flagging down cars and begging people to stop. John and Daryl intentionally stayed off the road to increase my chances that someone would stop. Ninety minutes later, a tour bus ground to a stop in front of me.

I climbed on board and waved goodbye to my son. "You're leaving him here?" the driver asked, astounded. Driver and tourists alike had a hard time leaving my baby boy, who wasn't so much of a baby any more, on the road while we drove away.

After I left my family, John sat down with pen and paper and wrote one of his few journal entries. "Today was what I would call a bittersweet day," he wrote. "It was sweet because the scenery was just simply awesome. Magnificent desert mountains towered above us on both sides as we rode the twisting, curving road through this spectacular valley. It rivals that of Canyonlands or the Grand Canyon with the benefit of it being uninhabited and wild.

"Late in the afternoon, we pulled off the road, walked down a path and set up in what was an ideal campsite — certainly one of the top ten sites of the trip. As the sun set the entire mountain side lit up in thousands of brilliant colors. The spires, canyons, and mesas highlighted by shadows added to the grandeur of sunset.

"And the bittersweet part? Nancy got sick, real sick. More sick than any one of us so far on the trip."

"Mommy was sick," Daryl wrote in their ideal campsite. "She was so sick she couldn't ride her bike, so Davy had to ride it while she hitched into town. Davy was riding Mommy's bike, Daddy was riding the tandem, Mommy was in a small town up ahead. That left only me to ride Davy's bike. So I was hungry, hot, and riding Davy's bike. Today is not a day I'd like to repeat."

"You have pneumonia," the doctor told me. "Both lungs are badly infected. You'll have to spend the night in the hospital."

There were no available rooms in the hospital, so I stayed in the ER, watching people coming and going all night. My mind raced from one thought the next. At least it was only pneumonia — I should be able to recuperate from that. How long would it take? Winter was coming; we needed to keep going. We couldn't afford the time, but had no choice to take the time. Maybe John and the boys could continue on and I could catch up at a later date?

But then I came back to how grateful I was to be laying on that gurney in the middle of the ER with an IV pumping drugs into my veins. More grateful than I had ever been. The rest of our decisions could come later. For now, I had made it to medical help.

John and the boys poured into the ER the following afternoon. They had ridden through towering red sandstone formations to get to town, and then all over town searching for me. We were back together, although in circumstances we had never considered. John and I talked about future plans while Davy and Daryl quietly read books on their Kindles as they lay on my bed with me.

Once siesta was over and hotels would be starting to open up again, they headed out to find a place to stay. We had no idea if we were looking at a week or a month or three months.

Three weeks later I felt ready to risk heading out. More antibiotics had coursed through my veins in that time than had in my entire fifty years

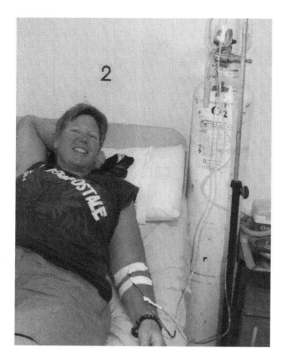

I was so happy when my family arrived at the hospital! As it turned out, I had pneumonia and would spend a whole week in the hospital.

to date, but they had done their job and cleared my lungs. I had steadily gained strength and endurance and felt ready to tackle the road once again.

We were nervous as we pulled out of Cafayate, afraid of pushing too hard too soon and causing a relapse. We set a self-imposed limit of thirty miles per day, vowing to stop at that point rather than pushing on. That approach worked great for three days and, when we reached our thirty miles, we found a nice spot on the side of the road to set up camp.

Our fourth day post-pneumonia, however, didn't go quite so smoothly. We pulled out of town and reached the open road to find tailwinds. Blessed, glorious tailwinds! We flew through the narrow valley with small mountains rising 3500 feet on our right side and massive snow-capped peaks hidden behind the clouds on our left. It was lovely. Sheer delight.

But then, the wind shifted into a cross wind and massive dust devils appeared ahead, moving slowly over the grasslands. Sometimes they stayed harmlessly off the road; other times we were suddenly engulfed in massive clouds of swirling sand blowing hard against our legs and arms. I didn't even want to think about what I was doing to my weakened lungs.

At one point Davy was a mere fifty feet ahead of me when an enormous dust devil barged across the road. Within seconds, he totally disappeared from view, then slowly reemerged from the void. "That was awesome!" he exclaimed as soon as I caught up to him. His face was black and his smile revealed teeth caked with mud.

Suddenly the wind changed and started kicking up massive dust devils. One minute, Davy was riding ahead of me, then he disappeared into the dust, then slowly reappeared. "That was cool," he exclaimed once I caught up to him.

We pedaled on as sand piled up on our bodies. My teeth crunched every time I bit down and sand accumulated under my sunglasses and ground into my nose and cheeks. My ears filled with tiny particles.

Finally, we reached our self-imposed thirty-mile limit. The wind was still howling and sand was blowing everywhere. Visibility was hovering right around fifteen feet. As much as we would have liked to get to a place a bit less sandy, it looked like conditions weren't going to change any time soon.

We managed to find a couple spots for the tents surrounded by tall grasses to shelter us from the worst of the wind and closed up the tents completely to prevent some of the sand from getting in through the mesh. Fortunately, it was a cool night so we slept comfortably in the sealed tents.

DAY 879 Early the next morning, we hit the road determined to get our miles in before the wind bowled us over. Had I known then that it would turn into one of those rubberband days — days that kept stretching longer and longer until I thought I might snap — I would have crawled back into my tent.

All went according to plan until 3:30. We had cycled twenty-five miles on a fairly good paved road, but then hit a dirt section for ten miles. Every time we hit a sandy patch, we ground to an immediate halt and tried to extricate ourselves by exerting every ounce of force we could on our pedals. That worked if the sand wasn't too deep. For the deep sand, however, no amount of pedaling would move our heavily loaded bikes. We were forced to climb off and, leaning our whole body into the handlebars, push the bikes until we cleared the patch. Fortunately, none of the sandy patches were more than a hundred feet long, but we quickly tired of dealing with them over and over again.

By the time we arrived into Los Nacimientos, we had cycled five miles longer than my self-imposed limit, and we asked for directions to the municipal campground. One of the great things about Argentina was the municipal campgrounds that most all towns had. They were clean, cheap, and very nice and we figured we would head there for the night.

"We have one," said the old, toothless woman who sold us soda, "but there is a better campground in Hualfin six miles away."

Hmmm... An extra six miles wasn't all that much. And Hualfin was a bigger town where we could find food. We had planned to camp in Los Nacimientos for the night, then ride to Hualfin in a nice, short ride the day after. But if we did those six miles today, we wouldn't have to pack up tomorrow. What's an extra six miles?

We piled back on our bikes.

Seven miles later, after bumping along a rocky road through the middle of nowhere, we still weren't in Hualfin. I flagged down a passing car.

"It's just right up there," the driver said. "You're there."

We pedaled another mile. And another. And yet another.

Six miles had stretched to ten.

We finally pulled into town. "Where is the campground?" I asked a woman standing on the side of the road with her baby perched upon her hip.

"It's a mile out of town," she replied. "Just keep going straight. You'll climb up a hill, and the campground is near the hot springs."

Did she just say hot springs? That part sounded good, but I wasn't thrilled about one more mile part at all.

We stopped at the grocery store and loaded up on food, then climbed back on the bikes. Nearly two miles later we reached the edge of town and the base of a colossal climb. By that point, I was exhausted and in absolutely no mood for a one-mile steep climb on dirt road, but what choice did I have? I shifted down and started up.

The dirt was loose and sandy. Our wheels spun out, so we got off and pushed the bikes up. "Let's just camp here," John said. "I have no idea where this campground is."

Just then an old battered pickup lumbered up the hill. I flagged it down.

"The campground is back there," the man told me as he gestured off the road to the right. "Turn here and go back about a mile."

By that point, the sun had already descended behind the red rock cliffs surrounding us. We took off slipping and sliding on the loose scree on the road, getting bogged down in frequent sandy patches. Nearly two miles later, we arrived into the thermal complex in near darkness.

All four of us jumped off our bikes and shifted into high gear to set up the tents in record time. We ate our pasta with pizza sauce dinner in complete darkness.

As far as we could tell, the setting was nothing short of breath-taking, nestled in a corner with what we thought were red sandstone cliffs on three sides. We took quick showers in the warm water and dove into our tents. We would find out in the morning.

That night I lay curled up in my sleeping bag reflecting upon the day. When all was said and done, we had cycled just shy of fifty miles, many of them on rough sandy roads. I was exhausted but no more than I would have been pre-pneumonia. Provided I didn't wake up to find the exertion had set my recovery back, I figured I was good to go.

The following morning all four of us stayed in bed. The sun rose, but we didn't. We couldn't think of a better place for a day off. All day we rested and relaxed. The boys climbed on the sandstone cliffs and we soaked in hot water for hours on end. In the evening, as the sun sank with a spectacular display of fireworks over the red sandstone, we built a campfire.

Davy and Daryl transformed ordinary sticks into magical pyro swords and daggers and had jousts and swordfights. They danced around the riverbed creating fantastical kingdoms and realms. It was wonderful to watch them play and create with that childlike innocence John and I adored so much.

I couldn't help but believe there was something about being outside in Mother Nature's handiwork that fostered that creativity. When we stayed in hotels, Davy and Daryl were plugged in like typical American boys — they watched TV, played Nintendo, or surfed the internet. But get them outside and there was no limit to their creativity.

I wondered if that might be the solution to many of America's problems — get kids outside. I saw it so clearly in my own boys, it made me wonder about all those kids who lived in an urban jungle and never experienced the joy of swordfights around a campfire under a crescent moon.

We were on a mission to get to Mendoza five hundred miles away. Through our website we had connected with a reader there who planned to organize a full week of wonderful activities for us and we were excited to get there. We made a pact to ride hard until we got to Mendoza, taking off only the minimum number of days to refresh and recharge our batteries. If we could do fifty-mile days, we reasoned, we would be there in ten riding days. Two weeks sounded very doable.

Whenever we talked with cyclists, we heard stories about the Patagonian winds down south. We were prepared to deal with high winds blowing us over as we approached the tip of the continent, but nobody had mentioned winds up north. In fact, nobody had mentioned anything about the north. In our minds we figured we would breeze through the north, and face the enemy down under.

But day after day when I climbed out of my tent and saw the sun hanging in the dirty sky looking like a large dusty pastel yellow ball, I knew the wind was kicking up more sand. Day in and day out we battled fierce winds that churned up massive amounts of sand into the air. We pedaled through the haze, barely making out the vague outline of mountains off in the distance.

Ascents were agonizing as we battled the dry desert winds. Descents were, more often than not, sheer torture. If they were open, winds blasted across the open plains blowing us back up the hills. Many times we descended through narrow canyons — a river on one side and the steep canyon wall on the other — pedaling furiously to maintain any forward motion at all.

My body was perpetually covered with a thick layer of sand and my lips were gritty from all the sand that stuck to my lip balm. When we smiled, our teeth were black. We were quickly learning that northern Argentina was no walk in the woods.

For the first time on our journey, we started carrying more water than our bikes were set up for. For 14,000 miles we had managed to find a water source every day, but now that didn't happen. Each time we reached a town we quizzed local people to find out exactly where the next water source would be. At times we needed to carry water for two or three whole days, which could translate to thirty liters or more. Two-liter Coke bottles were filled with water, then stashed in panniers or strapped to trailers. As we rolled out of villages, our bikes were loaded down like tanks, rolling heavily over potholes.

We pushed hard, taking only enough days off to keep us going. When we had a rest day, it wasn't all that restful due to the regular maintenance we needed to do. I hauled all our clothes into the shower with me and beat and stomped on them before hanging them to dry. John cleaned and oiled our chains to keep the bikes in working order. We needed to sort photos and upload them to the blog and type in journal entries. Guinness World Records required daily entries, so we made sure we kept our blog current with all the info they wanted.

Our thoughts were turning more and more toward getting back to the USA. Davy and I, riding side by side on the deserted country roads, planned our Welcome Home party in detail, including what kinds of cake we would make — Davy wanted chocolate with lots of frosting; Daryl wanted lemon. The boys talked for hours about what toys they wanted when they no longer had to consider carrying them on the bikes.

Just like on the Peruvian coast, we put blinders on and focused on making the miles with single-minded determination. Wake up, throw on dirty clothes, pedal, eat, drink, sleep. Rinse. Repeat. Days blended together into a blur. Miles fell behind. Many more miles lay ahead.

It was a long, hard slog but a few weeks after leaving Cafayate we pulled into Mendoza. Sean, as promised, had arranged for a police escort to get us into the city. We went straight to his house to stash our bikes for a while, then we were transported to a lovely hotel that had offered to host us. We were psyched — we made it to Mendoza. We knew we still had a long, hard ride ahead of us, but we put those thoughts out of our minds and determined to enjoy a week of luxury.

Chapter 20

2500 miles? But It's Only Two Inches on the Map!

MIDDLE ARGENTINA

We had been wined and dined for eleven days in Mendoza. We had enjoyed staying in luxury hotels with fluffy pillows and hot tubs. We went white water rafting, ziplining, and horseback riding. The local community hosted an *asado* in our honor with piles of luscious steaks and more bottles of wine than we could drink. Davy and Daryl had enjoyed playing with other American kids.

"The horseback riding was my favorite," Daryl wrote. "Davy, Daddy. and I had our horses go really fast. Mine was the fastest. Daddy thinks his was the fastest but mine was a little faster. One time when my horse was going fast I realized that my reins were too loose. While I was getting them back to the tightness they should be I hit a tree and fell off. Luckily my foot was still in the stirrup and I held onto one rein so I didn't get too cut. It still hurt though."

We had loved our break, but were itching to get back on the road. Winter was right around the corner and we knew we needed to get a move on. As reluctant as we were to leave the wonderful people we had met in Mendoza, we knew it was time. Our bikes were calling once again.

Together with our police escorts, we headed back to the house where our precious bikes had been stored, piled all our gear back on, and headed out. I had no idea I would be so happy to be reunited with my iron mis-

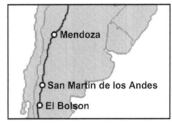

259

tress once again.

"Don't you miss home?" a small girl had asked me at the *asado* a few days earlier. "I think I would miss home if I did what you are doing."

That had made me think. What is home, anyway? Is home a physical place where you go after a long day? Or is it a concept — something more abstract than a physical locality?

My response to her was something I wasn't quite sure I truly believed at the time. "Home is wherever the four of us are together. It can be our tent or a hotel room or the floor of an abandoned hut."

But when we retrieved our bikes after being apart for eleven days, I felt like I was home. The moment I was back on the bike and knew we wouldn't be separated from them again for a while, I was home. I was comfortable. I had been reunited with my system of organization. I realized that was the key to home.

When I was with my bike, I had everything I needed and knew exactly where it all was. If I needed sunscreen or a nail clipper or my novel, I knew exactly which pannier to open. Every item had its place and I knew where that place was. It was comforting.

While visiting Mendoza, we had traveled with plastic bags and cardboard boxes. When we packed up to move to a different hotel, we crammed everything in and it was chaos. It was unsettling to live like that, but when I climbed back on my bike, everything was suddenly right with the world. It was comfortable. It was cozy. It was routine. It was normal. I couldn't help but think that was what home is. Our home, as a traveling family, looked a bit different from most homes, but it served the same purpose.

DAY 917 Not a cloud hung in the sky as we moved slowly southward, giving us perfect views of the entire snow-capped Andes range. The mountains ranged from 15,000 to 21,000 feet and were so clear I felt like I could reach out and grab a handful of snow off the tops of them.

If we had learned anything from Argentina, it was to seize the moment. *Carpe diem* and all that jazz. On those rare occasions when we had tailwinds, we knew to take full advantage of them and ride hard as it would most likely change into a headwind all too soon.

"C'mon, Nancy!" John exhorted. "Let's take advantage of this wind. Tomorrow we may have a headwind and we need to get the miles in." I, no matter how hard I pedaled, crept along at a snail's pace.

There were times when the difference between the tandem (with two people pedaling) and a single bike were huge, and these were exactly those conditions. Flat road, slight tailwind, good road surface. John was flying, and was growing increasingly frustrated that I was not. Davy and

I poked along.

After about fifteen miles I was getting equally as frustrated. I looked ahead at the road and knew I was putting in way more effort than I should be for that speed in those conditions. I stopped and spun my wheel. It didn't move. Not one, but two, spokes were busted.

"We don't have time for this!" John screamed as he yanked the wheel off my bike. "We've got a tailwind! We need to move!"

The second he had the wheel fixed, and while I was still putting my bike back together, he was off. Davy and I watched him ride off as we strapped the tent back on and hitched my trailer to my bike.

And that was the last we saw of John and Daryl.

Davy and I took off, riding after the rest of our family. Because of the different pace of the tandem, we didn't think anything of it. John frequently rode way ahead, then stopped and waited for us to catch up, but he never left the road.

Davy and I pedaled, and pedaled. Then we pedaled some more. We passed through the last town before seventy miles of desert, filled our water bottles, and kept going. Each time we crested a rise we scanned the road ahead looking for John's bright yellow drybag. Nothing.

Eventually, we stopped for lunch and ate salami, cheese, and tomato sandwiches that should have fed all four of us. We started to wonder just when we might catch up.

"This is strange, Mom," Davy said as we munched on sandwiches. "Dad always waits for us at least every five miles or so. He might go ten, but this is odd. He's never gone this far before waiting."

"I don't know," I replied. "He was so antsy to go and take advantage of the tailwind — maybe he just took off and forgot to wait."

We chased after him.

A few hours later we stopped for water at the only house in that seventy-mile stretch. "Are you guys with the cyclists that passed this morning?" the man asked. "They were on a double bike." John and Daryl had apparently passed hours earlier.

Davy and I pedaled furiously, taking very few breaks and those we did take were short. I was growing more and more concerned about Daryl; Davy and I carried our food and the poor little guy was most likely in tears due to hunger. Why didn't John stop?

Evening came and we were determined to catch up. The tail wind picked up and we crested the high point on the road and started down. Thirty miles had passed since we had last seen John and Daryl. How much farther could they have gone?

We raced down the hill, eyes peeled for that telltale yellow bag. Three miles passed under our wheels, then six. Still nothing. The sun was quickly making its final approach to the horizon. John and Daryl hadn't eaten since ten in the morning when we had all stopped for a quick snack.

This was very definitely not normal. This was not the way John acted. Could something have happened? Could there have been a medical emergency and they hitched into town? But why didn't they send a message back with a car?

At 8:30 I stopped when I saw a place to camp. Davy ran back and checked it out. "It's okay, and we could camp there, but I'm really worried about Daryl. He must be starving. Let's keep going."

We raced on through the Argentine pampas, determined to find his brother.

By 8:45 it was too dark to be on the road. We had no lights and were difficult to see. "Davy," I said, "We have no choice. We have to camp here." I had come to the conclusion the others were in San Rafael — most likely they had cycled fast and furious to take advantage of the wind and were sitting pretty in a hotel. Either that, or they were in the hospital.

Davy and I ate the last of our sandwiches and thought about John and Daryl, who were surely famished. All night I lay in our tent not knowing if I should be mad as hell at my husband for leaving me in the dust or worried about whatever medical emergency had befallen them.

The following morning Davy and I stuffed our sleeping bags and packed our tent, then headed out. We had thirty easy miles to go and we raced along the road hoping to reach San Rafael by noon, check email to figure out where John and Daryl were, and then either be outrageously furious or extremely concerned.

And then a car flagged us over.

"Are you with the cyclists back there?" the driver asked. "The father and son on a big bike."

What?!

"They asked me if I had seen two cyclists behind them, and I told them that there were two about fifteen miles behind. But now I see you and I realize you are the ones they were asking about."

I immediately flagged down the next vehicle heading back and sent a message that we were up ahead, then we found a drainage tunnel under the road to wait.

By now, I figured, it had been twenty-four hours since they had eaten. I could see the tears streaming down Daryl's cheeks. I flagged down another car. "Would you give this food to the cyclists that you will see down the road?" I asked. "I'm carrying all the food and they must be very hungry."

We waited. An hour passed. Then another hour.

4000 kilometers to Ushuaia?! I didn't know if we should be scared or thrilled!

Finally, I saw them crest the hill off in the distance. Just a tiny little speck, but a speck in the right shape. They had made it!

But I was still confused as all get-out. How had we ended up in front? When did we go by them?

"We stopped to wait for you six miles after I fixed your wheel," John explained. "We pulled into a park and Daryl was off playing while I watched for you, but I fell asleep and you must have passed then. I rode all the way back to where I fixed your wheel to look for you, then all the way back. By then, we knew you had passed us, so we bought some food and took off chasing you."

So all afternoon and evening Davy and I had been pedaling furiously chasing after John and Daryl who were behind chasing us. We rode until dark; they rode until dark. Our paths didn't cross.

We had all been reminded why we had the rule about never, ever leaving the road unless we were all together. We just needed to remember it.

Our route took us southward along the base of the Andes. We paralleled the massive chain riding through the foothills. One day, in the middle of absolutely nowhere, we passed a sign. It was a simple, unassuming sign in inauspicious surroundings. I pedaled past it at first — until I turned around for another look. It said: **USHUAIA 4000**.

It took someone who had spent thirty months pedaling 15,000 miles from Alaska to appreciate the significance of that sign. It meant we only had to cycle the distance of Idaho to Washington, DC, to reach our goal.

In many ways, that simple sign was cause for celebration: only 4000 kilometers (2500 miles) to go! Only one seventh of our journey left — which meant we were 6/7 of the way done. If sixty miles took us eight hours to pedal, we only had 320 hours left to cycle.

And yet, those very same reasons were cause for concern. We still had 2500 miles to cycle, which is, truth be told, a very long way. We still had four months on the road — 120 days of having to find enough food to eat, water to drink, and a place to sleep at night. We still had a whole lot of hours with our feet going around in little circles beneath us.

As I look back upon our journey now with the clarity of hindsight, I realize that the northern half of Argentina was probably the hardest stretch of the entire journey. Our minds were telling us we were nearly there — we were in our last country! We had cycled many miles with "only" 2500 left. Surely we could pedal those miles with our eyes shut.

"How much farther do we have?" John asked me as we ground up yet another interminable hill a few days later. "About 2200 miles?

"Yeah, something like that."

"Wow. Every 300 miles really makes a difference now."

All along, three hundred miles was barely a drop in the bucket, but now that very same distance put us a whole lot closer to Ushuaia.

Three hundred miles was about all we could deal with mentally; to think about 17,000 miles was just too vast, too much to focus on. Since the beginning of the trip, we had broken the journey into smaller, more manageable chunks — getting to Fairbanks, then to Tok, the Canadian border, Haines Junction. We never looked beyond that distance because our brains couldn't handle it. We slowly made our way across a country or state and rarely thought about how it fit into the bigger picture.

But suddenly we were seeing the big picture. We were reminded every kilometer how many more we had to pedal. We were forced to think beyond our normal three hundred miles by those kilometer markers on the side of the road. We were forced to think 3500 kilometers now. That was a stretch.

But that morning, when John mentioned about how each 300 miles made a difference, I started thinking, "How many *300 miles* do we have left?"

About seven. And that I could handle. Mendoza to Bariloche was about two *300 mile* stretches. Bariloche to Ushuaia about five.

Our journey had been terribly exciting and we had had some of the best times of our lives on the road. In retrospect, we enjoyed each and every day, including the hard times. I knew that all four of us would one day look back upon those years on the road with fond memories, and the lessons we learned would be with us forever.

And yet, I was ready for it to come to an end. When those seven 300-mile stretches were behind us and we had accomplished our goal of cycling from one end of the earth to the other, I knew I would be ready to head back home — for a little while anyway. I would be ready to have a stove I didn't have to haul out of my pannier and hook to the gas canister before I could use it. I would be ready to have a refrigerator. A toilet to sit on... A washing machine for my clothes....

It was the simple things I found that I missed — things most people took for granted. Things like being able to buy granola bars at the supermarket. Heck — things like *finding* a supermarket in the first place!

When it was all said and done, I knew I would miss our life on the road. I would miss the quiet peacefulness of climbing into my tent at the end of a long day. I would miss the excitement of not knowing what was beyond the next bend in the road. I would miss the sun on my face and being surrounded by Mother Nature's handiwork.

I made a pact with myself to treasure our last few months on the road. As I pedaled through the Argentine pampas and the wilds of Patagonia, I vowed to burn the sights and sounds and feelings of each day into my memory knowing it would come to an end all too soon. Or not soon enough, depending on which way my mood was swinging at that moment.

We found a lovely spot to camp in a sandy gully and pulled in with three hours of daylight left, looking forward to a relaxing evening.

That's when the wind picked up.

As I cut up zucchini, sand whipped up and covered my cutting board. Stones fell from the cliff I sat in front of. I built a shelter for the stove out of stones, but it only halfway worked.

While I battled to get dinner made, John attempted to put up one of the tents. He quickly concluded the only way to prevent the tent from blowing down the gully like a tumbleweed across the Idahoan desert was to have a body in it. Davy climbed in as a human stake.

An hour or so later, after we all ate a sand-laced dinner, I came back to our campsite after washing dishes at a small nearby creek and couldn't help but laugh. My tent looked remarkably similar to a bucking bronc doing its level best to throw its rider.

Daryl sat in the tent to hold it in place (Davy was holding down the other one) while John wrestled with it to stake it in place. As soon as he got a stake into the soft sand, the wind yanked it out as the tent bucked and kicked. His efforts held about as much as they would have held one of those steers at the Snake River Stampede.

We had no choice but to move the tent, which was no small feat in those winds. It took three of us, but we managed to get the tent moved to a spot where we could hold it in place long enough to get the stakes in semi-solidly. Daryl climbed in to help the stakes do their job and we crossed our fingers that they would kinda, sorta hold until morning.

DAY 926 *SWAT* I slapped at another white-ish fly on my leg as I pedaled along the rough dirt road under the blazing sun. I had quickly learned those flies, *tabanos* as they were called in Spanish, were not to be taken lightly. Each time one bit me, I walked away with a welt four inches in diameter on my leg. The area would be hot to the touch for three days before finally fading away into oblivion. Thankfully, the flies had only occasionally haunted us.

That came to a screeching halt the day we cycled away from Malargüe. We crawled up the fifteen-mile climb into the foothills of the Andes on a bad dirt road, all the while dealing with *tabanos* swarming around our legs. I quickly learned to glance down at my legs every third rotation of the pedals and to peel my hand away from the handlebar for a split second to brush them away. If I didn't risk losing control of my bike that way, I would soon regret it when my legs ballooned up.

"I'm tired, Mom," Davy said we bumped along the road. "Let's stop for a break."

"I wish we could," came my reply. "If you want to stop and deal with *tabanos*, go ahead, but it's not worth it to me."

Davy stopped his bike just long enough to take a sip of water before jumping back on his pedals.

Tabanos hovered around us, darting in when we stopped pedaling for a second. They chased us, tormenting us with the knowledge that the slightest lapse in concentration on our part would lead to massive itchy welts.

At last we reached a river, which would make a good camping spot. As soon as we ground to a halt, *tabanos* attacked, covering our legs and arms.

"Quick!" John shouted. "Get the tents!"

I ran to Davy's bike to unbuckle the straps holding one tent in place while John bolted to the rear of the tandem to get the other. "Daryl! Go help Mommy!" John ordered. "Davy, I need you here!"

All four of us scrambled to get the tents set up, all the while dancing as we scraped our legs against one another in order to brush the biting flies away. As frantic as I was to get in my tent and away from the flies, I cracked up when I looked over at John and Davy. "You're doing the *tabano* dance!" I called out.

266

Unfortunately, I couldn't dance as I peed behind a bush and ended up with five massive itchy welts on my bum.

As soon as the tents were set up, we climbed inside and quickly zipped them up. We sat, licking our wounds, listening to the buzz outside. I came to the conclusion that the mosquitoes we dealt with in Alaska were benign little fellas compared to what we had now; never again would I complain about something as trivial as a mosquito.

Fortunately, the *tabanos* went to sleep with the sun so we were able to crawl back outside late in the evening to get organized and cook dinner.

Our campsite was quiet and peaceful once the *tabanos* went to sleep, but that all changed at some point in the night. I heard it long before I felt it; the wind roaring through the trees above us and slowly making its way lower as the roar intensified. Then finally, the tent was hit by a mighty blast of wind and trembled and shook like Elvis' hips.

Over time, I came to the point where I knew the exact timing of the gusts — the dull, faraway roar rapidly increasing to an earsplitting shriek, then — BAM! We were rockin' and rollin'. Every few minutes another gust moved through and all I could think was, "I hope it's a tailwind."

Early in the morning, daylight was just beginning to shine on the many small rivulets of water across the valley. A few clouds hung above us like purple cotton candy in an otherwise white sky of early dawn. And the wind howled.

I climbed from my tent and studied the road ahead. "John," I said, "it looks like the road is doubling back — see how we'll cross the bridge, then come back along the other side of the river?"

"I've been looking at that," he replied. "I hate to think positively in case I'm disappointed, but I'm thinking we might have a tailwind after all."

Sure enough, once we doubled back after the bridge, the wind was our friend. We flew.

And kept flying even though we wanted to take a break.

The *tabanos* were out in force, and they swarmed us mightily every time we even thought about stopping. We grabbed a quick snack and kept pedaling.

The first thirty-five miles went fine. Great, in fact. We flew along the mirror-flat road and were having a blast if you didn't factor in the *tabanos*.

Then came the dirt road. For some inexplicable reason, Ruta 40 had dirt stretches periodically; I wondered if they kept them just to remind us that the whole 5000 kilometers of the road used to be dirt. For the most part, the dirt parts weren't too bad, but this segment didn't fit that category.

The whole twenty miles was loose, deep gravel dotted with small sections of fine, slippery sand. Our wheels didn't roll well in deep gravel or sand.

Our speed dropped to a crawl as we wrestled our bikes through the dirt. Each time a truck passed, massive clouds of dust spewed into the air. It was hot, we were covered with sweat, and all the dust quickly caked onto our bodies.

Fortunately, the road crossed the river one last time before we headed into a very remote section, so we camped along the banks of the mighty Rio Grande and all four of us went for a swim. The cold water felt delightful on my *tabano*-ravaged and sun-parched skin. Unfortunately, we no longer had our filter to refill our water bottles, so would have to stretch what we had.

We had thought things were tough already, but they were about to go to hell in a handbasket. Christmas Day began much like any other — trying to get the bikes back out to the road. We had camped in a sandy ravine and it had been a challenge to get the bikes down to the camping spot; it was nearly impossible to get them back up.

Kids and adults worked together to push the bikes through the deep sand unloaded — knowing full well there would be no way to get them up with all the weight. We trudged through the deep sand back and forth a bunch of times carrying armloads of gear. By the time we started pedaling, I was already tired.

We headed up on the loose sand and gravel road. I do mean up. The sun was intense and there was absolutely no way to escape it. Not a tree in sight, not a single big rock that might provide a bit of shade. Nothing but low scrub brush for miles and miles — that, and the interminable wind and *tabanos*.

To make matters worse, we were running low on water. Even though we had opted to forego a cooked dinner the previous evening in favor of dried fruits and nuts in an attempt to save water, we were still running low. It had been over sixty miles since the last village and we had no idea where our next water source was.

I was pretty much fried after ten miles of climbing on the rough gravel road; my energy level was down to about negative ten. Daryl hopped off the tandem to help me push my bike up the hill.

The dirt road ended and pavement began, but the hill continued. By now, we were out of water and my mouth resembled sand paper. I was becoming more dehydrated by the minute and could think of one thing and one thing only: get to water.

We camped by the river and all four of us jumped in for a cold bath - it felt wonderful on our fly-bitten and sun-parched skin!

We crested what we thought was the top and screamed down — for less than a mile. We dropped into an exquisite little valley with two bright blue lagoons surrounded by lovely mountain peaks, but I didn't care about any of that. There were also houses. I dropped my bike, grabbed my water bottle and took off running.

The woman gladly offered to fill my bottle, picked up a stick with an empty coffee can attached to the end of it and dipped water out of her well for my bottle. I smiled and said thank you, dropped a few chlorine tablets in just to make sure, then started the interminable wait for my water — precious water — to be safe to drink.

The other thing I had noticed as we dropped into that small valley was the massive climb to get out of it. While John and I slowly crept up the climb, the kids had a race — Davy pedaling up the wide sweeping curve and Daryl running straight across the desert. I'm not sure who won, as by then my water was ready and I sat on the gravel shoulder of the road and drank and drank and drank.

Although the water helped, it was one of those "too little, too late" things. I was already dehydrated and nothing but lots of water — and oodles of time — would reverse the effects.

"I think this might be the top," John said as we took yet another break near the top of that climb. "It really does look like the top." Wishful thinking does amazing things to one's perception.

A few miles, and what seemed like 35,000 feet higher, we took another break. By that point, I was in bad shape. We sat under the blazing sun snacking on dried fruit and nuts and I was shaking and feeling faint. "I gotta go," I mumbled. "I need to find some shade."

Normally, getting on my bike was a simple affair and I didn't even think about the effort involved, but that time, it took three tries to get my leg up and over the saddle. Three tries and a whole lot of energy I didn't have.

Amazingly, we really were at the top that time (after a twenty-mile climb), and we raced down around huge sweeping curves into the tiny village of Ranquil Norte — and arrived smack dab in the middle of siesta. Everything was closed. Everything. The clinic, the police station, and the one kiosk in town.

The one thing that could have helped my dehydration more than anything else was soda — loads of sugar and lots of liquid. As much as I didn't like soda, I had hoped for a great big bottle of Sprite. Unfortunately, it wasn't available since the kiosk was closed. We collapsed into chairs on the veranda of the kiosk and sat there, not quite sure what our next move would be.

"The map says the next town is eight miles away," I mumbled in my semi-comatose state. "It should be downhill."

We filled a couple of water bottles — just in case — and set off.

Sure enough, it was downhill. Until we got out of sight of the village anyway. Then it started climbing again.

I ground to a halt and started walking. Daryl jumped off the tandem and helped me push. Davy raced on ahead and I could only wonder where that kid got his energy.

"I have a feeling we have more climbing," John said as I approached him, nearing the top of the climb. "See that ridge there? It goes behind this little hill, but I have a feeling we'll have to climb over it."

He was right. Daryl and I practiced pushing some more.

Amazingly, once we cleared the ridge, we really did start down. We raced down through a narrow canyon and thought maybe, just maybe, we would make it after all.

That's when the wind picked up. It had been a bit windy all day, but now it was a howling gale. As we descended through the canyon, part of the time we pedaled furiously against a headwind, another part we flew like

After a day that seemed to go on forever, we thought we had finally reached the village. Then we discovered it was still three more kilometers - up a steep hill and against the howling wind. I was exhausted beyond belief at this point and could barely even push my bike even with Daryl's help.

eagles with the wind at our backs, and the last part we held on tight to try and control our bucking broncs.

We made it through the canyon and onto a wide open plain. We flew toward Barranca with the wind at our backs, but I could see the climb coming at the end of the open plain. We attacked it with gusto, knowing we were close.

"How much farther, Mom?" Even Davy was getting tired.

"One more mile, sweetie," I assured him. "I bet we'll see it once we crest this hill."

But we crested that hill and... nothing. We started down, screaming through yet another canyon. No sign of the village. I could see a small settlement up on the hillside, but that couldn't be it as it was way too far. I was wrong.

We reached the bottom of the canyon, crossed the bridge into the province of Neoquen and into the grove of trees that always indicated some kind of settlement, but this time there were only trees.

"Where is the town?" I asked the driver of a car I flagged down.

"It's up there two miles."

"UP there?" I asked, dread growing in my voice.

"Yes. It's a climb the whole way."

I very nearly sat down right then and there and burst into tears, but I couldn't summon the energy to get off my bike. Even if I had gotten off, I would have been swarmed by *tabanos*. We started up.

"This is a fitting way to end the day," John mentioned as we took a short break about a mile into the climb. "A massively steep climb against a killer headwind. It just somehow fits. I think God is trying to tell us something."

271

Maybe He was telling us not to be so bloody stupid and to turn around and fly home.

Daryl and I pushed my bike ever higher, and I was growing more weary with each step. My walk was no longer a walk, but a slow shuffle. I stumbled higher, stopping for a breather every twenty-five feet. The town was so close, yet way too far away.

At some point, Davy took my place pushing my heavy bike with Daryl, leaving his smaller, lighter bike for me. John rode on ahead, while the kids and I stumbled up the hill toward town. I would like to say my heart was full of pride at watching my boys rise to the challenge and manhandle my heavy bike up that hill against the raging wind, but truth be told, I was too exhausted to feel much of anything.

We somehow managed to make our way to a small hotel where we could finally, truthfully, say we had made it. Forty measly miles in ten grueling hours.

I wished my day was over at that point, but I still had three hungry boys to feed. I dropped my bike off at the hotel and headed to the small store. Our Christmas dinner was pasta and garbanzo beans with pesto. Then I climbed into the shower and collapsed into bed.

I hoped I would never celebrate Christmas like that again.

The following day we took the day off, knowing how exhausted our bodies were. Even the kids, normally little bundles of energy no matter how taxing the journey, hung around in bed watching TV, working on their math, and writing in their journals.

"Yesterday was one of those days that just never ended," Davy journaled. "We thought it was going to be fifteen kilometers to the first town; it ended up being 35. Then we thought it was going to be all downhill for fourteen kilometers to the town after that and it ended up being 28 and half uphill. Most of the downhill parts had such a strong headwind that we had to pedal.

"The day was hard, even though it was Christmas Eve. We had some M&M-type things on the road, even if the road was almost all dirt.

"When night came we all went to sleep and then this morning woke up with a bunch of candies from Santa. Mom says she'll take us out for ice cream to celebrate Christmas once the store opens after siesta."

I had started another nosedive into despair, although I didn't recognize it at the time. It had been an extraordinarily difficult six hundred miles from Mendoza. Long distances with no water, high heat, long climbs, bad roads, and biting flies had taken their toll. Although I kept going, I was emotionally fried. My body functioned on auto-pilot.

Each morning we arose early, packed our bikes, and headed out into the unknown. Some days were surprisingly easy, others were grueling. Rarely did a day go by without another gear failure. So far it had been nothing major — a Kindle, the strap holding my cooking pot to my rack, a hole in our waterproof bag — but we knew it was only a matter of time. Spokes kept popping on my bike, causing untold amounts of worry. John replaced our worn-out tires and brake pads with our final set of spares.

The four of us were more like robots than human beings. Devoid of feeling, emotionally wiped out, bodies pedaling without thinking. We were falling apart — both physically and mentally.

The physical part was fairly easy to take care of, but the mental half of the equation was harder. We were finding it harder and harder to remain focused and motivated to keep going. We could patch together our gear, but would *we* hold together long enough to reach Ushuaia?

It would have been so easy to hole up and vegetate for weeks, but we knew we couldn't. We were racing Old Man Winter and none of us wanted to be pushing our bikes through two feet of snow. If we were going to make it to Ushuaia, we needed to push on. Time was a luxury we no longer had.

There was a part of me who felt we should climb on a plane and head north. Why bother with the last 1700 miles? It would be mile after mile of barren pampa with blasts of wind so strong they would knock us off our bikes. Did I really want to deal with that?

That was the question of the day: did I really want this? Was getting to Ushuaia that important?

As I had learned up in Peru, bike touring was 90% mental and 10% physical and I now agreed more than ever. Yes, I *could* physically push on. I *could* keep my legs going in circles for hours and hours, but did I *want* to push on? Did I have the mental fortitude to deal with another two or three months through Patagonia?

The hardest part was that all four of us had to make the decision together. All four of us had to agree on what we would do. If I wanted to head home, did all four of us call it quits? Or did I agree to push on in order to support them? How does a team balance all those questions?

 We pulled into the small town of Zapala as high winds whipped sand into our faces. Tears streamed down my cheeks as my body attempted to wash sand out of my eyes. Communication between

my husband and I was unnecessary; he somehow knew I was at my breaking point and another night in the tents would have broken me. We pedaled
from hotel to hotel looking for something even remotely within our price
range.

After finding a cheap hostel, we dragged our bikes to a spot sheltered
from the wind, unlashed all our bags to haul them upstairs, then locked our
bikes together before heading up to the dorm room. John and the boys got
out the laptop to play video games while I headed to the shower.

Warm water coursed over my body as tears fell from my eyes. I was beyond exhausted. It took everything I had to remain standing in the shower.
I thought about what still lay ahead: about all the stories I had heard about
the Patagonian winds. Nobody even mentioned northern Argentina, yet
this had been the most difficult thing I had ever done.

I dried my body, put on my one set of clean clothes, then went and sat
on my bunk. I made no effort to stop the flow of tears as I pulled out my
journal.

"I want to reach Ushuaia," I wrote, "but I want to get there tomorrow. I
don't feel like spending another fifty or sixty nights camped by the side of
the road. I don't feel like battling winds straight from the depths of hell for
another couple months. I don't feel like being bitten by *tabanos* and having to forage and gather food from poorly stocked stores in order to keep
my children fed and healthy. I don't want to stuff my sleeping bag and roll
up the tent every morning. I don't feel like pedaling my heavy bike up
twenty-mile climbs."

Was reaching Ushuaia on two wheels important enough to me to continue on? Was accomplishing this goal that I had dedicated so many years
of my life to worth the inconveniences and pain it would take to get there?
Did I really want to do this?

I told myself I was tired and my spirits were low. I reminded myself of
what Daryl said back in northern Peru when I hit bottom: "All you can do
is continue on and things will get better." But still, there was a huge part of
me saying quit now. There was also another side saying it would be worth
it in the end.

As much as I would have liked to quit, I wasn't quite ready. We took a
couple days off before hitting the road again. I wanted to reach Ushuaia
with every pore in my skin and I wasn't ready to call it off, even though I
was convinced I would hate every pedal stroke from Zapala to Ushuaia. I
would make it if it killed me.

Chapter 21

Are We Having Fun Yet?

PATAGONIA

I was Skyping with some kids in Birmingham, Alabama, a few days later. A little girl with a cute button nose positioned herself in front of the camera and said, "My name is Drew and I want to know if it's fun, what you're doing?"

For a moment I wasn't quite sure how to respond. Is it fun? Is it *fun* grinding up hills at two miles per hour? Is it *fun* when the winds are so strong we feel like we're riding bucking broncs in a rodeo? Is it *fun* when the air is so cold our fingers feel like they'll freeze and fall off our hands like icicles crashing to the ground or when it's so hot we could fill buckets with our sweat? Is it fun when a cold rain is falling and we're pedaling furiously to try and outride it?

Is it fun?

Then I looked into the camera and smiled at Drew and said, "Most of the time it's fun. Most of the time we're like little kids riding our bikes around the neighborhood. We've got the sun on our faces and the wind in our hair and we're seeing the world in the best way possible. We get to cycle through tiny little villages and see life as it really is rather than seeing it through a glass filter. We're not encased in a metal cage — we're out in the real deal. Most of the time, it's great fun.

"There are other times when it's not fun. There are times when it's hard — really, really hard. There are times when it's so hard I feel like I can't take another step and feel like I'll collapse to the ground right here, but I know that if I don't push on I could quite

275

A major storm moved in with lots of wind and rain - we took refuge for the night in a gaucho's shed, complete with sheep skins drying on the rafters.

literally die. There are times when our journey is the hardest thing I've ever done in my life and it's not fun at all.

"But even those hard times are wonderful," I said, even though I wasn't sure I believed it. "When I look back on those hard times I can see how much I grew or the lessons that I learned. Those are the times wonderful memories are made — the times when the four of us all jumped in with every strength we had and worked together to get our entire family through.

"Living your dream won't always be easy or fun," I told the kids, "but it will always be wonderful. When you truly make the decision to live your dream and do your *big thing*, you'll forge ahead even in the hard times.

"But you know, Drew — that's how life is. Life is mostly fun. Most of the days, we wake up in the morning and look forward to the day that's coming. Most of the days we'll slide through whatever we have to do that day and all will be well and life will be fun. But there are other days that are most definitely not fun. There are days that are tougher than a bed of nails. There are days when anything that *can* go wrong *does* go wrong and there are days when we think we can't handle one more day of this.

"But we can't quit. We can't just throw up our hands and say, 'I'm done with life! This isn't fun!' We don't say that because we know — deep down inside of us we know things will be get better. We know that, if we just press forward, things will turn around and the sun will come out again.

276

We'll reach the end of that hill or the wind will stop howling. Life will be fun again — someday."

We had 1500 miles to go and I was trying to convince myself that I had spoken the truth. Was this really worth it? I preached the idea of living your dream and never giving up to the school kids who followed our journey, but did I believe it? Was it worth it to push through the hard times? Were the rewards worth it?

We had pushed through hard times before and I could say, with the benefit of hindsight, that it had been worth it, but now I wasn't so convinced. I was tired. Bone tired. Exhausted beyond anything I ever dreamed of before.

As I look back upon that time now, I can see how our utter exhaustion was the key to finding the turning point. We got up early to get packed and hit the road, but nobody was looking forward to climbing on the bikes. John and the boys started a game of kick the bottle, which killed an hour or two.

We forced ourselves on our bikes and managed to ride seven miles before stopping for a break. We talked, we ate boiled eggs, we threw rocks at ants, at signs, and at each other. Ninety minutes later we finally climbed back on our bikes.

And then six miles later we stopped again. John took a nap in a drainage tunnel under the road, Daryl gathered sand in a discarded Coke bottle, Davy read his Kindle, and I wrote in my journal.

We had a wicked headwind and didn't feel like battling it, so we didn't. We killed time instead. When we arrived at a river and could see the massive climb on the other side, we called it a day.

The boys spent a few hours playing in the river; amazingly it was fairly warm rather than the frigid snow-melt rivers we had encountered earlier. I took a bath and cooked rice for dinner. John set up the tents.

We hadn't made much progress, but had managed to enjoy the day in spite of headwinds. We were well on our way to bringing the magic back.

The following evening we managed to find a river to camp by as well. It was a brutal day spent battling headwinds and fixing a total of three flat tires, but somehow, a river to bathe in at the end of the day made all the difference in the world.

We were arriving into the famous Argentine Lake District, where lakes and rivers were plentiful year round. Although that didn't solve our headwind or broken spoke problems, it solved a whole host of other problems. Somehow, nothing seemed so bad when we had water.

By now I was breaking at least one spoke every day and we feared the worst. Our blog readers came to the rescue by referring us to a Canadian

The Lake District of Argentina

family who was headed our way in a few weeks. If we could only limp along a couple hundred miles to Bariloche where they would hand over not only a whole box of brand new spokes, but also a new Kindle, we would be set.

DAY 947 Davy and Daryl were turning thirteen and I was determined to create a special birthday for them. We were staying in an outrageously crowded campground in the very touristy San Martin de los Andes, but that didn't diminish their excitement at all. As soon as the stores were open we set out for a trek around town to figure out the very best birthday party we could make.

The boys looked at every bakery they found until stumbling upon what they felt was the perfect birthday treat — a luscious chocolate cake for Davy and a lemon meringue pie for Daryl. Clutching their boxes, we headed for a supermarket for ice cream and a can of whipped cream. On the way, I happened to see a small bike shop, so walked in to see if, by some odd chance, they happened to have spokes to fit my bike. They did! And they agreed to rebuild my wheel.

All four of us sat around the campground more content than we'd been for ages. Our boys were thrilled with their birthday celebration and I'd gotten the best birthday present I could imagine in a new wheel that, with any luck, I wouldn't have to worry about. And if it didn't hold, I had a whole box of spokes arriving soon.

"We turned thirteen today," Daryl wrote that night. "Mommy thinks that is a big thing but I don't. It's like going from eleven to twelve but one number higher. If twelve was secteen then that would be becoming a teenager, but it's not so thirteen is a big milestone. It doesn't make any sense."

The following morning I looked up at the trees above my tent and could see them swaying in the wind. It wasn't just your normal, everyday gentle swaying in a breeze; it was a violent, bent-over-nearly-to-breaking-point swaying going on above me.

"It's not worth it," I told John. We could have packed up and gone anyway, but we had learned the hard way that battling headwinds meant expending tons of energy getting twenty miles and burning ourselves out. I rolled over and went back to sleep.

A few hours later, the rain moved in, and we huddled in our tents listening to the ping of water bouncing on the fly. We might be riding into Ushuaia through snow when we eventually got there, but at least we weren't riding in rain today.

We slowly moved through the Argentine lake district, enjoying the abundant water in the region. The scenery was radically different from the Argentina we had seen so far and having water readily available for drinking, cooking, and cleaning made our lives much easier. Although we didn't enjoy riding in cold rain, even that didn't seem as bad as the harsh dry winds from farther north. My spirits, although tenuous at best, were starting to climb after hitting bottom not too long ago. While I couldn't yet say I was enjoying the ride, I was, at least, not hating it.

"Oh crap," I thought as I looked at the toothpaste covered blob lying in the palm of my hand. "Crap, crap, crap."

I walked over to where John stood at the edge of the river brushing his teeth and grinned broadly showing him my brand new smile. "Look," I said as I held out my hand.

"What the hell?"

"My crown fell out," I told him, emotionless. "My brand new crown that I got in La Paz. I was just brushing my teeth when I felt something weird — that's the crown right there in my hand."

John just stared at me blankly. Our immediate thoughts were of the delay this would mean. Ushuaia was still a long way away and it was now the end of January. Summer was quickly coming to an end; fall was on its way. We couldn't afford any more delays.

As soon as we arrived into El Bolson, I asked for a campground and a dentist. After getting John and the boys situated in the campground, I jumped on my bike and made a beeline for the dentist. We could only hope it was an easy fix.

As it turned out, my tooth broke off. The skeletal remains of my original tooth were what had been holding the crown in place, and it succumbed to the passage of time and broke off, which meant there was nothing to glue to the crown to.

"You have basically three options," Carlos the dentist told me. "I can glue it on and you can treat it very carefully; it'll last a couple weeks, if you're lucky. Or I can make a temporary tooth out of acrylic; that will last six to eight months. Or I could do the job right and insert a screw into the root canal so we can attach the crown to that; that'll last for at least ten years. The bad news is that it'll take at least four days even if we rush it."

We were stuck. I slowly pedaled back to the campground to break the bad news to John and the boys. We were antsy to move. We were only 1200 miles from the end of the road — four *300 mile* segments. We were so close we could taste it, yet now we couldn't move forward. We were stuck in a crowded Argentine campground.

All evening, we moped around, going through the motions. Conversation was minimal as we all thought about wasting a week in Bolson. I cooked pasta on autopilot. We sat at the picnic table eating in silence. I had partway rebounded from hitting bottom, but now could see myself headed there again.

Nighttime came with a threat of rain in the sky. I flung our tarp over the bikes as they leaned on a tree next to John's tent, and climbed into mine. My thoughts were too preoccupied with my tooth to pay much attention to detail. I drifted off to dreamland hoping the dentist would be able to work quickly.

DAY 962 "Nancy!" John screamed a few hours later. "Davy's bike is gone!" I scrambled out of my tent and looked bleary-eyed at where the bikes had been stacked together and covered with the tarp before I had gone to sleep. Now, my bike lay on the ground about ten feet away, and Davy's was gone. Vanished. Disappeared into the night.

"The gate!" I said. "Check if the gate is open!" John took off running to the gate at the other side of the crowded campground as other campers climbed out of their tents rubbing sleep from their eyes.

"It's locked!" John panted as he ran back a few seconds later. "That means the bike has to be inside the compound."

We called for the boys — they quickly put on shoes and came out to help. "The bike has to be here. Quick! Search the campground!"

We all took off at a run — it couldn't have gotten far.

As I ran, the security guard for the campground came running. "Our bike!" I shouted in Spanish. "It's gone!"

He grabbed his cell phone and alerted the rest of the crew. While he talked with the others, I looked around, wondering how they could have gotten the bike. Then I saw Davy's tire tracks running across the dirt road of the campground leading to the fence.

"They took it over the fence!" I called out. It would have been a challenge — the fence was easily six feet high with three layers of barbed wire on top — but certainly not impossible for a strong young man.

We all dashed out the gate, running to where they had lifted the bike over the fence, hoping to find the tracks leading us to its whereabouts. As John and I scanned the ground for tracks, the guards continued on, then came back and waved us on.

The bike was there, hidden in the weeds just beyond the fence. Our swimsuits and rain pants had been hurriedly taken from one pannier and strewn about the ground. The others were still zipped shut.

As John and I walked the bike back to our campsite, the guards kept going. We saw them out on the road talking to others. Talking… talking… and then two of the people took off running into the woods on the other side of the road.

"That was them," Jorge the guard told us when he came back. "They were hiding in the bushes and we found them, but when we tried to get them back here, they pulled knives on us. We let them go."

We were feeling extraordinarily blessed that we got the bike back, but more than a bit frustrated at ourselves. We had been so preoccupied and in a pity party about my tooth that we hadn't locked the bikes. Fortunately, I had covered them against the rain, and that was what saved us. I was more grateful than ever that John was a light sleeper and woke up when he heard the tarp rattling.

Chapter 22

Reaching the End of the World

TIERRA DEL FUEGO

"How much longer do you think it'll take you to reach the end of the world?" asked a truck driver at a gas station a week later as we filled up our stove fuel bottle.

"About six to eight weeks," I replied. It came out naturally; I didn't even think about it. Not at the time anyway.

But later, as we continued down the long lonely road, I realized the significance of those words. I said, "six to eight WEEKS!" As in, I could finally measure our remaining time on the road in a matter of weeks. Not years. Not months. Weeks. We were getting close.

We had left the western side of Argentina to cross over to the east coast. Very few cyclists traveled that route, so we knew next to nothing. We did, however, know the road was paved and that was good enough for us. We figured we could deal with whatever else nature threw at us.

And Mother Nature threw just about everything possible our way. We shivered in record low temperatures, then less than a week later she gave us record highs. As Davy wrote in his journal: "We rode for a while and then it got hot. I don't mean just like normal hot, I mean hot like you can fry eggs on the road hot. I mean REALLY hot."

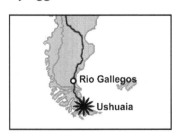

The Patagonian steppe is something that has to be seen to be believed. For miles on end, grasslands stretched in all directions. Guanacos, relatives of the more common alpaca and llama, grazed on the grasses. As we approached, they gracefully leaped over the fence lining the road and ran off into the

The endless pampas in the Patagonia region of Argentina

distance. Rheas, a small ostrich-type bird that stood roughly three feet tall, ran alongside us, at times for a mile or two. Armadillos scurried across the road.

Every long-distance cyclist who had ever cycled Patagonia talked about the wicked crosswinds in the area. Unrelenting winds blowing from the west caused cyclists to pedal leaning at a 45° angle against the onslaught. Every cyclist except us, that is.

For some reason, Mother Nature took pity upon us and served us tail-winds. Blessed, glorious tailwinds. We raced through Patagonia at record speeds, frequently covering eighty or ninety miles in relatively easy days. Rather than needing to camp out on the wide open pampas as we expected, we were able to reach towns where we could take shelter at night.

We watched as the kilometer markers on the side of the road ticked ever downward. We were close. Oh, so close. Every morning we climbed back on our bikes, hoping beyond hope that our good luck would continue and each night we thanked our lucky stars for the tailwinds we had enjoyed.

We were on a roll and nothing could stop us now. Even when John and Daryl caught their wheel on the edge of the pavement and crashed to the ground, tearing up John's arm and smashing their brake handle to smither-eens, John rigged up a work-around and we continued on.

But when his pedals refused to engage, we figured we had hit our limit.

There were lots of guanacos grazing in the pampas of Patagonia. They gracefully leapt over the fence as we approached.

With 350 miles to go, the tandem was busted. John and Daryl tried to take off after a break, but the pedals just spun without engaging. After about six or seven revolutions, it finally "caught" and he was able to move forward, but the next sixty miles into town were a constant battle. Every time John stopped pedaling for even a few seconds, he didn't know if it would engage again or not.

"It's over, Nancy," John told me as we cycled side by side on the empty road. "This bike won't make it."

"But we're almost there, Daddy," Daryl said from the back of the tandem. "We have to make it."

Discussions were somber as we cycled toward town. Could John and Daryl borrow a tandem for the last few days? From whom? What about single bikes? Maybe we could find single bikes for them?

"I'd rather ride a single than quit now," Daryl told us.

A few days earlier we had run into a group of local cyclists and had the phone number of one of them in Rio Gallegos. It was a long shot, but we could only hope he would know someone who could help. "Hello Hugo? We're here, in Rio Gallegos, and I have a huge favor to ask...."

Within a few hours, Hugo had a mechanic over to check out the tandem. The mechanic took the wheel back to his shop as we brainstormed how we would get to Ushuaia without the tandem.

A few hours later, the mechanic was back with a functioning wheel. It had been merely gunked up with grease and dirt and needed a good cleaning. Within four hours of arriving into town, John's wheel was good to go.

DAY 1002 After crossing the border into Chile, Tierra del Fuego loomed large ahead of us. It was a large island off the tip of the continent of South America, just on the other side of the Straits of Magellan. The sun shone brightly and we had an awesome tailwind taking us directly to the ferry that would transport us to the final leg of our journey. I could barely believe we were actually there.

We stowed our bikes, then climbed to the upper deck of the ferry to get a better view of Tierra del Fuego. Named "Land of Fire" by Magellan due to the fires of local people his crew saw as they passed through the narrow straits, Tierra del Fuego had captivated my imagination for many years. Now, I was there.

Rolling off the ferry, we parked our bikes beneath the "Welcome to Tierra del Fuego" sign for photos, then pedaled onto the island. Amazingly, it was no different from the flat pampas we had cycled for thousands of miles. I'm not sure what I expected, but my mind had somehow conjured up images of fantastical landscapes that, sadly, were nonexistent.

Evening came and we pulled into a field to set up camp.

"What's that?" Daryl asked as he pointed into the pampas a short distance away. "See that animal?"

"It's a fox!" Davy exclaimed.

"No way," I said. "There's no way a fox would be that close to us."

"It is," John assured me. "See it? It's a fox for sure."

As we watched the fox romp and play, another came out to join it. Then another. Before the evening was over, we watched as five

We camped in a farmer's field right next to a whole group of foxes. It was so much fun to watch them play!

285

foxes ran and jumped and tumbled like little puppies, all within a few feet of where we were camped.

The following morning I stumbled out of my tent and headed behind a tree for my morning pee. As I squatted in the woods, I looked out and saw a fox playing about fifteen feet away. I stayed there, crouching in the woods, and watched as another fox came up. And then an armadillo scurried into the picture. And then another fox!

My legs burned from squatting, but I didn't want to break the magic as the foxes batted the armadillo around playfully. Maybe Tierra del Fuego was as magical as I had imagined, just magical in a different way.

That afternoon, I cycled along the perfectly flat road marveling at the unique situation we were in. To my left — east — the sky was bright blue with white, puffy, cotton candy clouds. To my right — west — the sky was black with clouds churning in a nasty roiling mess. I wanted to stop for a picture, but knew we were counting the seconds before it hit.

"How much farther?" John called as I pedaled behind him. "It looks like rain's coming!"

"Eleven miles!" I called back.

"Let's go!" he said. "Let's try to make it to town before it hits!" We pounded the pedals, our legs pumping like pistons.

We didn't make it.

We watched as the storm raced closer and, six miles from town, the wind moved in with a passion. We stood on the side of the road trying, mostly in vain, to hold our bikes up against the assault. As I struggled with my rain jacket — sleeves flapping wildly while I tried to maneuver my arms into them — my bike bucked like a wild colt. At one point, the wind picked up my trailer and deposited it about a foot or so from where it had been a moment earlier. John lost control of the tandem and his bike crashed to the ground. Davy was actually sitting on his bike to hold it down.

"We just passed a bus stop!" I shouted to be heard over the roar of the wind. "Let's go take shelter back there!"

Davy and I turned around to walk our bikes back. "There's no way I can get my bike up," John yelled. "Come back and help!"

Davy managed to get his bike a hundred feet to the shelter without problem, but I lost control and my bike tumbled down. Against the tremendous force of the wind, there was no way I could get it up. John ran across the street to help. Working together, and with raindrops pelting our legs and faces like BBs from a high-power gun, we pushed against the wind to get my bike to the shelter.

This was the last bit of flat grasslands before we entered into the wooded areas of southern Tierra del Fuego.

With two bikes safely out of the wind, it was time to get the tandem to the bus stop. All four of us grabbed hold of the bike and held it up against the wind. By now it was hailing and bits of ice bombarded us with an astronomical force. We struggled toward the shelter.

Finally, we reached the tiny bus shelter, propped the tandem next to the other two bikes, and crowded inside, listening to the wind howl and shriek outside. "The wind actually picked me up and moved me over a couple of feet," Davy grinned. "That was amazing!"

"It was amazing all right," Daryl quipped. "Amazingly painful."

Fortunately, the storm was fairly short-lived and, once the worst of it had passed, we headed into town. We figured we deserved a bit of luxury after that so checked into a hostel and called it a day.

Sailors have a saying that south of 40° it's lawless; below 50° it's godless. We were in godless territory now and, even though we weren't on the ocean, I couldn't help but think that was a very apt description.

The wind on the island of Tierra del Fuego was relentless and there was absolutely nowhere to go to escape it. Every thirty or forty miles, if we were lucky, we passed a small bus stop about the size of a typical outhouse in the USA and we welcomed the chance to get out of the frigid wind.

"We've got nearly everything against us," John pointed out as we strug-

For our last night on the road we found a lovely spot deep in the forest to camp.

gled toward a tiny bus shelter. "Wind, rain, and cold. The only thing in our favor is hills — at least it's fairly flat." He had summed up our day perfectly.

Daryl stumbled toward the shelter with tears streaming down his frozen cheeks. "My feet hurt," he sobbed.

I went back to our earlier practice of layering wool socks and plastic bags in his shoes. Under his tights I covered his legs from ankles to knees with heavy wool leg warmers. He still complained about being cold, but at least he wasn't in enough pain for tears any more.

"I've come to the conclusion that I don't like dirt roads," I mused as we bounced over the rough dirt Chilean road.

"Didn't you already know that?" Daryl asked.

"I don't like them either," Davy added. "Unless they're a BMX track."

The road surface through the Chilean part of Tierra del Fuego was dismal and my top speed was a measly seven miles per hour. John, on the tandem, couldn't even come close to that. Patches of loose gravel threatened to send us tumbling to the ground, gusts of wind threw us all over the road, and the cold ate into our cheeks, fingers, and toes.

There was a time, back when I was young and foolish, that I enjoyed the rough and tumble challenge of dirt roads, but now I had decided I preferred asphalt. I didn't like the intense concentration needed to maintain control on dirt roads; having to concentrate on that patch of road six feet ahead of me watching for an errant rock or patch of loose gravel that would send me sprawling. I didn't like how my whole body stiffened when I hit loose stuff and how my bike wobbled and my wheels slipped and slid. I didn't like how sore my arms and shoulders got after a few days on dirt roads or the *whump-whump-whump-whump* of washboard.

By three in the afternoon, seventeen miles short of the border with Argentina, we saw dark rain clouds amassing ahead. We accepted defeat, surrendered to Mother Nature and her warriors, and headed off the road to camp.

As we set up camp, the promised rain came and we scrambled as the ground grew muddier and muddier. Cakes of mud built up on our shoes turning our feet into leaden weights and everything that touched the ground was immediately covered with a thick layer of goo.

Mother Nature wasn't making our final approach easy.

The flat grasslands of the pampas faded into the background as we entered the woods of the southern region of Tierra del Fuego. It felt strange to see trees ablaze in fall colors after spending so much time cycling through barren grasslands.

We had hoped for a special camping spot for our last night on the road and we couldn't have found a better one. We pulled off the road into an old forest with an amazing density of trees. The ground was littered with fallen trees and the whole lot was covered with craggy strands of greenish moss hanging down like an old man's beard. "It's almost magical," John said as we pushed our way in with our bikes. I agreed.

John and I sat quietly on fallen logs as the boys ran and explored. They climbed trees and discovered hidden forts and played with Ninja swords. Our months in the barren grasslands of Argentina had been hard on them and they were happy to be back in the forest.

Communication between my husband and I was all but unnecessary after spending 24/7 together for nearly three years. We somehow knew what each other was thinking and feeling with a simple glance. Facial expressions and body language were all we needed. During breaks, we now sat quietly rather than chatting like we had done for the first year or two of our journey. I couldn't help but wonder what would happen when our journey was over and we went back to real life. Would we continue to share that special bond? Had we forgotten how to communicate? Only time would tell.

DAY 1018 We awoke to a cold, dreary rain. For months I had fantasized about our final day on the road and I wanted more than anything for that final day to be special. I wanted crystal clear skies and magic. So when we awoke to rain, I wanted to curl up and go back to sleep — I wasn't about to ride my final miles in rain. But people were waiting for us, so I crawled out of my sleeping bag and packed up anyway.

I slunk out of my tent into the dreary surroundings and, for the last time, packed my gear. Tears fell slowly as I packed my sleeping bag and rolled up my pad. Our adventure was over. Forty miles away lay Ushuaia, my impossible dream and unreachable star. Ours had been a fantastical experience, other-worldly in many ways. And now, just a few miles away, lay the end of the road.

It was almost as though the good Lord above knew how badly I wanted good weather. By the time we got on the road, the rain had passed; a short while later the sun came out. Under the glorious rays of a brightly shining sun, we cranked to the top of our final pass while the sun sparkled off the lake below and illuminated the trees around us, bringing out an enchanted array of blues and greens.

Mabel and Roberto, our hosts in Ushuaia, met us at the top of the pass and together, we plunged down the other side. I could see my goal in my mind's eye — the wooden sign in front of the Beagle Channel at the very southern edge of *Tierra del Fuego* way down at the pointy tip of South America. *USHUAIA El Fin del Mundo* it would say. I knew, because I had seen pictures. Lots of pictures. That sign was engraved in my mind — a permanent fixture, it seemed.

We pedaled through the most majestic valley I had ever seen, with craggy snow-capped mountains surrounding us, encapsulating us in magic. My thoughts roamed, and I realized I had no idea what it would be like to finally reach that sign after nearly three years of trying to get there.

We had spent 1018 days cycling 17,285 miles through fifteen countries. Together as a family we had cycled over passes higher than the highest peaks in Colorado and battled headwinds stronger than I had thought possible. Our legs had endured the painful onslaught of grains of sand blasted by ferocious winds, and our skin the effects of way too many hours in the blazing sun. And through it all, it was visions of that sign that had kept me going.

I had spent many hours pondering what my thoughts would be when we finally reached the end of the world. As my legs cranked, I thought about that sign and what it would mean and how it would change my life. How would I feel to actually get there? To pedal that final mile and know that we had accomplished what we set out to do so long ago? To know that

The weather turned out not to be so bad on our last day of riding.

we — our ragtag family — had met our goal, our *meta*, as they say in Spanish?

Would I be excited beyond comprehension? Would I race toward the sign and throw my arms in the air and scream and shout and whoop to the gods?

Or would I be too exhausted to even care? Would I pull up to the sign and wearily lean my bike beside it as I had leant it against so many other signs. Would it be just another day among 1018 of them?

Honestly, I had no idea.

We raced on — determined to reach that sign I knew was up there. The sign! It was so close! Adrenaline coursed through my veins as we drew nearer to Ushuaia.

We rounded a corner... and there it was — the first sign! The one on the outskirts of Ushuaia. *Bienvenidos a Ushuaia.* We didn't even stop: just raced past at high speed.

And then around another bend and the entire city of Ushuaia lay before us — a sprawling city lining the banks of the Beagle Channel. We were

At the end of the road in Ushuaia!

there — Ushuaia! But still, we hadn't reached the sign.

Guided by Mabel and Roberto, we made our way through town, pumping wildly to reach our final destination. My thoughts were all over the map, but every one of them focused on that sign. We followed the main road paralleling the channel for a few miles, then turned left and started down. I could see tourists wandering about, but my eyes didn't stray from the road ahead; we couldn't risk an accident after all we had been through.

Weaving through traffic, we made our way to the port and suddenly our guides stopped. "There it is," Roberto said as he pointed toward the water.

The Sign! *USHUAIA El Fin del Mundo!* The only thing separating us from the sign was one lane of traffic and a few curbs. Daryl hopped off the back of the tandem and started running. The rest of us pushed our bikes those last few meters.

I wearily leaned my bike against the sign, then stood back to look at it. We were *there*. We had made it. We — my little family and I — were at the southern tip of the world. We had dreamed the impossible dream and reached the unreachable star. We were there, and it felt oh-so-sweet.

I felt elated, deflated, and everything in between. I was ecstatic and euphoric and walking on clouds. I was sad and gloomy and down in the dumps at the thought that our adventure was over. I was prouder than I had ever been in my life and more humbled than I thought possible. And it was all jumbled together into one big emotion-fest that no words can describe.

We had done it. We — the Vogel family from Boise, Idaho — had done it. We had done the impossible.

Epilogue

From the End of the World to the Real World

BACK IN BOISE

It's now eighteen months since the day we reached Ushuaia. Eighteen months of reflection upon the lessons learned from an amazing journey.

We hung around Ushuaia for ten days before boarding a plane bound for the USA. What had taken us nearly three years to cover on our bikes took only ten hours flying, and suddenly, we were in a new world.

I expected our reentry to be hectic. I expected us to be running around like chickens with our heads cut off as we frantically tried to line up a place to stay, get stuff out of storage, arrange for the kids to go back to school, and do all those other things I knew would pop up. But I did not expect to feel like I had taken my head and crammed it into a blender turned on high.

Our plan had been so reasonable. Because we didn't know what our long-term plans were, we planned to rent a house with a six-month lease while we figured things out, but once we got to Boise, reality struck. Finding a six-month lease on a house was impossible and we weren't willing to sign for a year. Our house, the one we had rented out, was now too big for us and we knew we didn't want to move back into it. All of a sudden, our world had turned upside down and sideways all at once.

In addition to the unexpected housing challenges, we were surprised to realize we weren't really American anymore. In many ways, my sons were more like ESL (English as a Second Language) kids than native English speakers. When a friend asked Daryl to put a book in her living

294

room, Daryl asked, "Which room is the living room?" The idea of "PE clothes" was a foreign concept and my sons simply couldn't figure out what their teacher was referring to. Life in the US was confusing, but our brains were telling us it shouldn't be — we were, after all, native-born Americans.

I felt like we were American, but not American. We had lived and traveled in other countries way more than we had lived in our own. We were flexible and adaptable and willing to learn, but that was hard when we were expected to know our way around. Many times, we didn't even know the right questions to ask.

But more than that, I fought an internal battle: a battle I didn't expect and couldn't explain. I wanted to stay in Boise, Idaho, and put down roots. I wanted to move into a small house and get my beads out of storage and have my own kitchen with running water. I wanted to be able to take warm showers and have a toilet to sit on rather than squatting behind a tree. In short, I wanted to settle down.

Settling down, however, was somehow wrong. It didn't fit with who I was. I was a traveler; that's how I had defined myself for many years. If I settled down, I would somehow betray who I was: the person I had worked so hard to create.

Was I still a traveler? My panniers were packed away. My tent and sleeping bag were rolled up and stashed. We planned to stay in Boise for the foreseeable future. Did that change my status? Did it change who I was?

We had been in the USA for two months when I had a revelation. That day, I realized my story had never been about the cycling. It was never about the travel.

My story was about pursuing your passion and following your dreams. It was about chasing rainbows, finding your pot of gold at the end, and shaking hands with the leprechaun. It was about the idea that it's okay to leap out of the box and grab life by the horns and live it on your own terms. You don't have to live the way anybody expects you to live — you can live the way you want to live!

And that meant me too.

I didn't have to explain my desire to settle down in Boise. I didn't have to justify my choices to anybody. If Boise was calling me, I was free to listen. I could jump back in the box if I wanted to.

A short while later, we purchased a small house and fixed it up. We're in that house now and the novelty of hot running water, my own toilet, and a stove that magically gets hot with just the turn of a knob has not worn off yet. We are enjoying putting down roots in Boise, and I can't think of any place I'd rather live.

Four months after we finished our journey, we received notice from Guinness World Records that Davy and Daryl had been denied the record. We had followed the guidelines to a T and they commended the boys for their efforts, but while we were on the road, Guinness had made the decision to no longer recognize records in the "youngest" category.

It was while we were fighting headwinds in Peru that Abby Sunderland had attempted to become the youngest person to circumnavigate the world in a sailboat, and her boat was damaged in a massive storm. Alone and terrified, she waited in the middle of the ocean for a French freighter to rescue her. And Guinness World Records then decided they wanted nothing to do with "youngest to do anything."

"It's not fair!" Davy said when I told him about the letter.

"We did everything they asked for!" Daryl added.

And they were right. It wasn't fair. It wasn't fair that a gigantic, trusted corporation like Guinness World Records would tell a couple of boys, "If you do X, Y, and Z, then we'll award you the record," and then not do it.

The outpouring of support from the blogging community was nothing short of phenomenal. Dozens of posts went up in support of Davy and Daryl's accomplishments, and we hoped Guinness World Records would realize how wrong they were.

In the end, we accepted that sometimes life isn't fair and we moved on. "We still have the world record," Daryl tells people. "It's just not recognized by Guinness."

And that's just fine. We know what we've done. Davy and Daryl know exactly how many miles they rode on those bikes. They don't need a certificate to remind them.

We knew all along that our journey was not about a world record; it was about time together as a family, exploring our world, and learning about ourselves and others. An official certificate hanging on the wall would be icing on the cake.

Davy and Daryl are proud of what they've accomplished, yet rarely talk about it with their friends. Every once in a while, they'll take the Ripley's Believe It or Not book or Boys' Life Magazine to school to show others the stories about their journey, but mostly they live in the moment like teens all over the world.

Both boys chose to go back to school half time, and are taking advanced math and science classes in addition to PE. We're homeschooling the rest. They are also involved in a robotics club and Boy Scouts. Davy has taken up running and enjoys cross country and track. Daryl joined the swim team.

I look forward to watching my sons grow into young men and I often wonder what the future holds for them. In many ways, they are typical teenage boys who like to play video games, but in other ways they are extraordinary. They have a confidence that I'm sure will serve them well throughout life.

John is keeping busy chopping wood to get us through the winter, maintaining our rental units, and creating a documentary film about our journey. He is also teaching the boys computer programming.

I couldn't wait to dig my beads out of storage and have enjoyed getting reacquainted with them. I've started working at craft fairs to sell my work, which encourages me to continue playing with my beads. I also realized that one of the best parts of having a blog was inspiring others, so I morphed our blog into a site to inspire and encourage others to pursue their own passion and to reach for their own unreachable stars.

How did our journey change us? I think the biggest thing is that we know — all four of us — that we can do anything. If we can ride bikes from Alaska to Argentina, then we can do anything. That idea has permeated everything we've done since we've gotten home. We know the world is our oyster and, if we put our mind to it, we can accomplish anything.

The trick, we've discovered, is making the decision. I've been asked repeatedly what the hardest part of our journey was, and my response every time is, "Making the decision." Committing yourself to a big goal — whatever that goal is — is difficult. It will consume every moment of your life for years but, if your "why" is big enough, you'll make it happen.

My "why" was big enough. My desire to spend time with my family exploring our world, supporting my sons in their quest for the end of the world was enough to get me to Ushuaia. And that same "why" drives me now.

I'm so very grateful I took that leap.